WHAT IS A "GOOD" TEACHER?

David Booth | Richard Coles

Pembroke Publishers Limited

© 2017 Pembroke Publishers
538 Hood Road
Markham, Ontario, Canada L3R 3K9
www.pembrokepublishers.com

Distributed in the U.S. by Stenhouse Publishers
PO Box 11020
Portland, ME 04104-7020
www.stenhouse.com

All rights reserved.

No part of this publication may be reproduced in any form or by any means electronic or mechanical, including photocopy, scanning, recording, or any information, storage or retrieval system, without permission in writing from the publisher. Excerpts from this publication may be reproduced under licence from Access Copyright, or with the express written permission of Pembroke Publishers Limited, or as permitted by law.

Every effort has been made to contact copyright holders for permission to reproduce borrowed material. The publishers apologize for any such omissions and will be pleased to rectify them in subsequent reprints of the book.

Library and Archives Canada Cataloguing in Publication

Booth, David W. (David Wallace), author
    What is a "good" teacher? / David Booth & Richard Coles.

Issued in print and electronic formats.
ISBN 978-1-55138-327-9 (softcover).--ISBN 978-1-55138-928-8 (PDF)

    1. Effective teaching. I. Coles, Richard (Richard E.), author II. Title.

LB1025.3.B66 2017   371.102   C2017-903703-X
                                  C2017-903704-8

Editor: David Kilgour
Cover Design: John Zehethofer
Typesetting: Jay Tee Graphics Ltd.

Printed and bound in Canada
9 8 7 6 5 4 3 2 1

Contents

Preface *5*

Introduction *7*

    Defining the "good" teacher *7*
    Professional beginnings *7*
    Moving on but not forgetting *9*
    Starting out *11*
    Frameworks for examining excellence in teaching *12*
    Challenges affecting teacher development *18*

1. Develop a "Teacherly" Identity *22*

    1. Enjoy and appreciate being among students *23*
    2. Be a model and mentor for your students *25*
    3. Establish, value, and nurture student-teacher relationships *27*
    4. Be caring, compassionate, and mindful *31*
    5. Be aware of ego, self-efficacy, and confidence *37*
    6. Build a classroom community *39*
    7. Be willing to innovate, adapt, experiment, change, and grow *43*
    8. Support critical and creative meaning making *48*
    9. Strive to be engaging with students *52*
    10. Set high expectations for every student *55*
    11. Reflect often *57*

2. Know Your Students *61*

    12. Know, respect, and advocate for each child *61*
    13. Maintain a sociocultural responsiveness to students *64*
    14. Support a learning pathway for every student *68*
    15. Recognize ages and stages *72*
    16. Create strategies for supporting differentiated instruction *77*

3. Develop Your Teaching Strategies and Techniques *81*

    17. Establish clear learning objectives, outcomes, and standards *82*
    18. Recognize the dynamics of the classroom *87*
    19. Invite and support student voice *91*
    20. Incorporate inquiry groups into the curriculum *94*
    21. Demonstrate effective classroom management *98*
    22. Employ technology effectively *100*
    23. Ask open-ended questions and welcome student questions *104*

4. Understand How Effective Schools Work *108*

    24. Recognize the school as a strong professional community *108*
    25. Join and participate in planning and teaching teams *112*

26. Learn how assessment procedures can increase learning *114*
27. Value a range of literacies and numeracies throughout the curriculum *119*
28. Recognize the significance of the arts in education *122*
29. Include the community in your frame for teaching and learning *131*
30. Develop a reflective action plan *139*

Conclusion *141*

Final thoughts on becoming a "good" teacher *141*

References *143*

Index *153*

Preface

Imagine the complexity of attempting to answer the question, "What is a 'good' teacher?" I can think of no educators more uniquely equipped to respond than David Booth and Richard Coles, colleagues and friends. David and Rich have been teachers, teacher educators, researchers, authors, supporters of teachers, and champions of teachers for more than fifty years. Over those years, they have worked around the world, in classrooms with students and their teachers, in faculties and schools with beginning and experienced teachers, in universities with graduate students and faculty members, and in large auditoriums and lecture halls, with educators, policymakers, and community members, exploring and reflecting on how to better serve learners by becoming better teachers. It is this network of co-learners who contribute to exploring the central question of this book.

As is demonstrated by the multiplicity of perspectives that the two authors and thirty other teachers share, there is no one particular pathway for becoming a "good" teacher. Instead, the contributors underscore that teaching is a relational act, which centres on the learner and requires individual teachers to draw upon their strengths and their new areas of learning in order to support the growth and development of all learners in a particular context each and every day. The authors draw from their research thirty characteristics of the "good" teacher, gathered under four categories: the teacher, the taught, the teaching, and the community. However, they stress that becoming the best teacher you can be requires that all teachers understand their own personal resources so that they are agents of their own professional development. Engaged teachers continue to take courses, read professional books and journals, engage in classroom research, collaborate with colleagues, engage in mentoring relationships, attend conferences, and continually adapt and learn about and from and with their students. In every aspect of education, we want the best for our students, and we try to work together to utilize the contributions of all of us in moving toward professional excellence.

This book emphasizes that teaching is not about a single position or role but rather about an approach to the work of being among learners and learning.

It is an open, questioning, thoughtful, reflective learning stance that promotes sharing and development for all. Classroom teachers, instructional and school leaders, university instructors, students, parents, policymakers, and community members all teach and learn and mentor and share their ideas and insights in this book. As I read the experiences of the different voices representing each of the characteristics of good teachers in the authors' model, I remember and rethink my own queries, mistakes, mentors, and discoveries throughout my own career.

Most importantly, as this collection shows, the authors do not just support and facilitate the growth of teachers; they embody it. They live the experience of continuing to strive to understand the issues of teaching every day. They read voraciously about all aspects of teaching and incorporate new thinking in their practice. They seek colleagues and connections who continue to extend and deepen their growth. And it is these co-learners who provide many of the insights into good teaching in this book. Teaching is about being in community.

Teaching is a brave and demanding profession. It requires provocation and risk and change. As the stories of the contributors here indicate, it's important to embrace the new, such as the possibilities of technology; it's important both to question and to maintain orthodoxies; and it's important to dialogue and listen and observe. Embracing uncertainty and the learning that comes from mistakes, seeking collaboration and looking to the learner and to your colleagues for support, are among the lessons outlined by the "good" teachers in this book.

David Booth and Richard Coles synthesize decades of learning from, with, and on behalf of teachers, so that we all can consider and reconsider how to continue to grow in our profession. They illustrate that the work inherent in teaching is not so much being a good teacher as it is continually *becoming* one. "Good" teaching is the pursuit of a lifetime.

> Dr. Kathy Broad,
> Teaching/learning coordinator,
> OISE/University of Toronto

Introduction

Defining the "good" teacher

> "Great teachers grow in similar ways. They experiment, they extend themselves, and they find new ways to nourish themselves; realizing that not all ideas are viable, but with many new ideas percolating, teachers can continue to develop themselves and their students in a dance of continuous learning."
>
> Robert E. Quinn et al, *The Best Teacher in You*

Research indicates that the single most important influence on student success is the "good" teacher—experienced, knowledgeable, caring, and dedicated. The most effective means for supporting these teachers is to offer them means of learning from teachers of excellence. But there is no single model of excellence, no one style that all must adhere to, no teaching method that every teacher should follow. We need to build on the strengths of our own personalities to discover how we can progress professionally. We can begin to and continue to develop our "teacherly identity", adding to our construct of how we can best serve our students.

But there are distinctive characteristics of excellent teachers that we can examine and then explore and integrate into our own teaching personas. Most of all, we need to understand and care for our students in meaningful and significant ways. This doesn't mean we have to create a new personality, or model ourselves after celebrated teachers in films and novels; it does mean that we can learn and grow as we engage in a self-discovery process, supported by the different modes that we meet every day in our practice, and in our professional growth events, locating biases and exaggerated fears and discovering whole new strengths hiding in the shadows of everyday duties. We become better incrementally, each new piece of learning opening up other areas we can explore. The most important aspect of teaching success is to accept that, as in all important endeavours, we need to practice to improve.

Professional beginnings

David Booth

Challenging our own assumptions is the first step in professional development. Teaching the way we remember we were taught, following scripted teaching plans, demanding excessive self-discipline from students, teaching for the test, blaming previous teachers, complaining that administration wouldn't discipline unruly students all of these failings were part of my classroom beginnings. What were the forces of change in my teaching life? It was a combination of factors: I taught in a very conventional school during my first two years. The principal and I were the only males on staff, and all the other teachers were much older, much wiser than I, and very committed to their profession. There were very few students who caused trouble, and each teacher seemed to have a specialty that brightened her classroom life — puppetry, visual arts, writing, mapmaking. (Today, I am ashamed to say that I saw these women not so much as mentors but as competitors.) New teachers were assigned to a series of workshops (art, music, drama, reading), and I attended every one of them faithfully. However, when my English supervisor came to demonstrate a lesson for me, my life changed.

William H. Moore brought such an air of integrity and cooperation to my students, engaged them in such fascinating poems and stories, listened so intently to their contributions, and honoured their presence so clearly, that I began to glimpse what teaching could be. He was British with an accent, six feet four inches tall to my five feet seven inches, and had a history as an air force commander. Given the differences between us, I would have to find my own way of being a true *teacher*, and I began the journey, strengthened and mentored by Bill for forty years.

As I remember those days, I realize that I was always partnering with other teachers, that I needed someone skilled to bounce ideas off, to argue towards understanding, to take risks in the knowledge I had a safety net, to discover new techniques, to attend courses, change schools, and grow up. My list of mentors is long — Bill Moore, Bob Barton, Barbara Howard, Chris Leibold, Bill Manson, Frank McTeague, Chuck Lundy, Ian Hundey, Howard Reynolds, Larry Swartz, Tony Goode — and it continues with Rich Coles. I can't teach alone, and if I could I'd add the thousands of names of students who created learning with me. As for your list: have you begun it yet? Better write the names down so they are in your memory bank forever. There are traces of each one of these teachers in everything I do as an educator. And so many names are missing.

I now videotape and transcribe the work of the students when I am a guest teacher in their classrooms, and I learn from their reflections and thoughts about their experiences in letters I receive from them after they have returned to their classrooms and their own school programs. These letters often reveal a teaching moment I had missed or misjudged, or demonstrate further insight by the children from the cool distance of "after the events." I treasure them, and each time I read through a bundle that a teacher has been kind enough to send along, I am struck again by the clarifying that occurs for all of us when we take time to consider the implications of the events in which we have participated.

When I was at a conference in New York a few years ago, a teacher approached me after my talk with tears running down her cheeks. She asked me the question that became the soul of this book: "How do you get to be good?" In the heat of battle, all I could think of was: "You have to hang around good people." But the important part of that question lay in the asking of it. Until we recognize our need to alter or rethink our teaching selves, how will we know where to look for help, or what kind of support we need? For each of us as teachers, this has to be a personal journey, over time, with others, self-assessing, wondering, observing, and exploring the myriad of resources devoted to teacher development, as we will outline later. Fortunately, I have recently had extensive time and opportunity to read about teacher growth, thanks to the amazing library at my faculty, online resources, academic articles, teacher blogs, book reviews and commentary, and now I want to apologize to that questioning teacher and share what I have discovered about becoming "good." If that teacher contacts me, I will send her a copy of this humble book, and hope and trust that she will find better and deeper questions to ask about her own journey, with suggestions for creating an action plan that may lead to a more fulfilling and more confident career.

Stacey Wagler, an Ontario teacher, reminds us in a letter after attending a conference of our dreams of becoming a teacher:

> I spent many evenings in my early teaching years sipping tea with my grandfather and re-thinking my career choice. My grandfather was a teacher in the late 1920s and early '30s. He quit teaching because he simply could not afford to raise his family of 9 children on a teacher salary. But he was always a teacher! He would often come and help me in my classroom when I was having difficulty with particular students. He always came to school in a 3-piece suit, freshly shaven and a smile on his face. He had the heart of a teacher and love of learning—… I lost Grandpa 3 years ago at the age of 98. So, really, I had my fair share of time with him. It has been so long since I heard that "love" spoken about teaching. The staffroom nowadays can sometimes be negative, but we need to find someone who shares the Joy and Passion of teaching.

Moving on but not forgetting
Rich Coles

"Though the road's been rocky it sure feels good to me."

Bob Marley

> "Five teachers remain in my heart forever.
> "Each made me feel that I was an honoured part of the whole:
> "Al Downs: His wit and charm helped me to stretch my creativity and to laugh at life!
> "Robbie Charlsworth: She surrounded herself with exciting people and ideas and when she included me I grew much taller.
> "David Booth: His mesmerizing strength of character taught me to stay true to my beliefs.
> "Bob Barton: His magical demonstration lessons using drama revealed a model for teaching that I have kept all my life.
> "Mr. O'Rourke: My high-school English teacher demonstrated that every student must feel respected."
>
> Lynda Pogue, artist/educator

The summer before my first year of teaching s was a time of mixed emotions. I was grateful and happy to be hired but somewhat overwhelmed by the reality. Year one, my assignment was a grade four/five class in an urban school. My location was a portable classroom in a far corner of the playground. The diverse students' life experiences and circumstances were in stark contrast to my own. Would I survive? Would the kids thrive? A colleague in an adjacent portable left after Thanksgiving. Lots to learn! Teaching reminded me of driving. After you obtain your license is the time when you really learn to drive.

At my first school there were many good models and mentors. Careful observations and discussions revealed many reasons for my colleagues' success. Students flourished in classrooms where the teachers cared about them and the students knew that they cared. Caring is necessary in the first years of schooling right through to graduate school study. Caring teachers challenge their students and have certain expectations for their learning and membership in the class and school. They demonstrate their caring by knowing their students, listening to them, and providing a safe place to learn. For many young people being in class is the best time of their day. Caring teachers provide opportunities for young people to develop their interests. Clubs, sports activities, drama, and music productions before, during, and after school are valuable experiences for learning and often the reason for being at school.

Good teachers, I discovered, are also wonderful colleagues. In my early years I shared a large extended classroom with Val Kuhn, a cheerful, creative teacher. She knew how to make learning relevant and enjoyable. Jim Eddison, who we poached from the UK, was always willing to help with numerous activities that were so enjoyable for the young people. Many professionally rewarding years were spent teaching with a team of middle-school teachers following the recommendations of the Association for Middle Level Education. Mariana Wenisch, an accomplished interior designer and our design and technology teacher, always kept us organized and appreciated our humour. Gina McMichael, who was fluent in several languages, was a role model for our students and invaluable in making connections with the community. Sheldon Griesdorf mentored and inspired many young adolescents as they navigated the daily flow of middle-school life. He debunked many "urban negative legends" about middle-school learners. Students in his class experienced success, joy in learning, and self-confidence, often for the first time. Many years after being in his class, numerous students would visit him to reminisce and talk about their current life stories.

There was also a desire for me to develop my expertise as an educator. Working as a language arts teacher ignited an interest in literacy and reading. At the Ontario Institute for Studies in Education (OISE) of the University of Toronto, classes with Frank Smith and John McInnes introduced me to the research and writings of many literacy scholars. The numerous scholarly writings of Ken and Yetta Goodman resonated with my experiences working with multicultural urban youth. John McInnes was a thoughtful mentor who encouraged me to pursue doctoral studies with Ken and Yetta Goodman at the University of Arizona. This was a life-changing decision. At the University of Arizona, many grad students and professors shared their knowledge, research, and questions about literacy and deep learning. Visiting scholars enhanced the stimulating environment. Ken and Yetta have always been incredibly caring and generous in sharing their knowledge and thinking. Many memorable social gatherings took place at their home. After a meal of delicious southwest cuisine Ken and Yetta would recall many stories of their experiences travelling the world. We have continued our friendship and my time with Ken and Yetta at conferences or during my visits to Arizona enhances my professional growth and remains special to me. There were also many occasions to enjoy the beauty of the Sonoran Desert. With Fred and Inta Gollasch, the "Australian Connection," we enthusiastically cheered for many Wildcat sports teams.

International or regional conferences provide opportunities to network and interact with researchers and practitioners who are engaged in many aspects of education. Many years ago at a conference, I first met Frank Serafini, a true Renaissance man. He is a scholar, guitar player, photographer, humorist, wine connoisseur, and gracious host. Our "grand conversations" and sharing of ideas and resources have greatly refined my thinking about literacy, learning, and life. David Booth's notions about teaching and learning are visible in classrooms around the world. We talked at a conference and have met for the last few years to discuss many facets of education. His writings and master presentations have inspired many teachers to focus on the important aspects of learning in their classrooms.

There are still many questions about literacy, learning, and teaching I want to investigate in the coming years. These are very exciting times in education. There is a solid foundation of research and classroom practices from multiple perspectives to electrify learning. There are also numerous knowledgeable teachers who ensure the best learning experience for each child or youth.

Carol Dweck's book *Mindset: The New Psychology of Success* represents her significant work on teaching a growth mindset for building success in your life's work.

Starting out

In this book, we have chosen to start with the positive energy that surrounds good teaching, with examples of teachers recognizing other teachers for their contributions. It is surprising how one new and different approach can affect other aspects of teaching and promote new ways of thinking about change. We can move forward when we recognize effective teaching, when we discover insights about effective teaching from our own observations — as students, as coworkers, as classroom visitors, as in-service colleagues, as members of a professional book club, as parents, as administrators. We recognize good teaching, we learn from it, and we absorb it into our own ways of working.

This book is not a teaching manual; our profession is too complex and significant to think that everything we need is in one text. We hope you will consider the thoughts in this book as an invitation towards examining your own life's goals as a teacher. In reading the experiences of other teachers, in reflecting on the prompts we offer as starting points, in thinking about the characteristics we have gathered from stories and research, you can recognize your own gifts and talents as an educator, and then enrich those qualities and extend your reach while you teach, thinking deeply and relinquishing the fear of change, and, over the years of teaching, morph into the best you can be for the students in your care.

Like the moon, we pass through distinct phases, sometimes unnoticed because of the clouds, but still happening. We take courses, we volunteer, we work with special classes, and sometimes we wear out, temporarily we hope. Then we need to regroup, step back, lie on the couch, bake muffins, breathe again. And in time, the newly-hired teacher in the room next door begins a new project, a different way of being among school children, and we jump back into the whirlwind called school, holding her hand, mentor and mentee all at once, and the moon is suddenly full. Allow these phases and stages, and don't hold on to guilt or despair; look for the clues when you need to change again.

We hone our professional skills through practice and supported reflection, remembering to strengthen our inner qualities through mindfulness and processes that focus our senses, as well as living "outside the game" in a full life. It certainly helps to have expert equipment in the classroom and school, and an environment that adds to our "game". But when we were working with teachers in Mexico City, who teach children in the rural, mountainous regions of their country, without the usual classroom resources, their passion and excitement for their work removed from my mind the barriers of needing fine buildings to bring about a literacy mandate. We need dedicated, committed teachers to help children grow.

We hope this book will act as a framework for your own journey as a developing professional, so that you can become fully engaged in exploring your capacities, talents, skills and relationships, building satisfaction and commitment for being the best you can be in the context of your classroom and school. By reading about teachers like yourself, you may find inspiration and support from how they construct their teaching personalities, seeing what works for them and which aspects you can adapt and adopt for your own teaching success. Sharing the ideas of others can help us all to maintain and sustain our teaching strengths. But most of all, we hope to support your passion for teaching, for being among schoolchildren. We have also included poems and excerpts from children's literature about us teachers; sometimes the insights of poets and authors can strike a special chord.

We hope this book will be helpful for:
- future teachers who want to know the teaching goals that matter;
- inquiring teachers who have questions about their own work lives;
- teachers who want validation that their practice is theoretically sound;
- principals who have a vision for their schools and want support to help their teachers to revise their teaching;
- curriculum specialists in school districts with questions about teacher goals, concerned whether today's educational strategies will meet the needs of the students;
- teachers who are in mixed grades or changing divisions, or with an unusual grade sampling;
- teachers who want to hear voices of other teachers in the field;
- teachers who are distressed or overwhelmed, who want to find comfort and reassurance in knowing they are part of a teaching/learning community;
- teachers who want to be revitalized, pumped up, excited again about working with young people;
- teachers returning from school leaves, nervous about their understanding of new methods and strategies; and
- teachers who come into teaching mid-career and want to know how to continue to work towards professionalism.

"If we teach today as we taught yesterday, we rob our children of tomorrow."
John Dewey

> My role as a teacher is complex and changing:
> I need to lead but I need to respond.
> I need to inform but I need to listen.
> I need to instruct but I need to collaborate.
> I need to evaluate but I need to teach.
> I need to demonstrate but I need to participate.
> I need to organize but I need to become involved.
> I need to manage but I need to support.
> I need to model but I need to assist.
> I need to confer but I need to observe.
> I need to criticize but I need to appreciate.

Frameworks for examining excellence in teaching

In our quest for excellence in teaching, we must construct some evaluative procedures. This has proved to be a complex process. School districts have come under scrutiny as the accountability of teachers and administrators has expanded. The move toward standardized testing, the comparison of test scores for different schools, principals, and teachers, the observation by assessment teams of teachers as they are conducting a lesson — along with the hiring of professional companies outside the school system to evaluate teacher performance, submitting a final score of success — have all made evaluation a more elaborate and difficult process We consider a teaching portfolio that includes a variety of assessment modes to be a more useful tool for exploring a teacher's professional effectiveness. But we want the teacher's own understanding of progress and success to be the most significant component of our measurement of worth, and this adds value to the characteristics we are sharing in our model as touchstones for understanding professional growth and building teaching capacity.

Today, provinces, states, and school districts offer guidelines for assessing teachers' competencies. The following schemas for determining teacher excellence lead to our present variation of these frameworks, based on the characteristics of excellence in teaching as drawn from the research found in relevant books and journal articles, supported by the voices of teachers and educators and parents who describe teachers they have observed doing superb teaching in a variety of contexts.

1. THE ONTARIO COLLEGE OF TEACHERS OFFERS ETHICAL STANDARDS FOR THE TEACHING PROFESSION, AND THE PROFESSIONAL LEARNING FRAMEWORK FOR THE TEACHING PROFESSION

A. Ethical Standards for the Teaching Profession
- Care (compassion, acceptance, empathy, interest, and insight for developing students' potential and well-being and learning through positive influence, professional judgment, and empathic practice),
- Trust (professional relationships based on fairness, openness, and honesty),
- Respect (honour human dignity, emotional wellness, and cognitive development, modelling respect for spiritual and cultural values, social justice, confidentiality, freedom, democracy, and the environment).

B. Professional Learning Framework for the Teaching Profession
- Ongoing professional learning
- Commitment to students and student learning
- Professional knowledge
- Professional practice
- Leadership in learning communities

2. EDUCATOR DR. HELEN ZHAOYUN YANG OUTLINES TEACHER KNOWLEDGE

Over the last few decades, scholars have reached the consensus that teachers play a central role in enhancing students' achievement. Since Lee Shulman's (1986, 1987) seminal work on teacher knowledge, scholars in various fields have refined his model to meet the needs in their specific fields.

Subject matter knowledge (SMK) goes beyond knowledge of a set of facts. It requires an understanding of the substantive and syntactic structures of the subject matter. Substantive structures are ways in which the concepts and principles of a discipline are organized to incorporate facts; and syntactic structures are the bases on which truth or falsehood, validity or invalidity are established.

Curriculum knowledge. "The curriculum is represented by the full range of programs designed for the teaching of particular subjects and topics at a given level, the variety of instructional materials available in relation to those programs…"

Pedagogical content knowledge (PCK) refers to the "special amalgam of content and pedagogy that is uniquely the province of teachers." PCK includes two subcategories: knowledge of students' understanding, and topic-specific strategies of instruction.

Each kind of knowledge has its subcategories and sometimes overlapping properties… Research findings also indicate that teachers' knowledge is not static but dynamic. It is altered by changes in school curriculum and teachers' choices of approaches and learning directions for their professional development. Subject matter knowledge may be changed by the requirements of an official curriculum, as well as the expectations of schools, students, and parents. Pedagogical content knowledge is developed over many years of teaching. It depends on the approaches and directions of teachers' professional development, what they teach, and who they teach.

On Excellence in Teaching, a compilation of writing by fifteen contributors edited by Robert J. Marzano, focuses on three different areas of teaching excellence: theory, systems, and classroom.

3. OUR REFLECTIVE MODEL: TOWARDS PERSONAL AND PROFESSIONAL TEACHER DEVELOPMENT

In our development of a model that can assist you in becoming the best teacher you can be for your students, we have examined the research, alongside our experiences as teachers and teacher educators, and have opted for a series of the characteristics that appear to represent teaching at its best. Knowing that, as authors, we are still discovering insights, techniques, and truths about effective teaching, and struggling to apply them to our own understanding and practice, we are hoping that readers will recognize the generalized nature of our model, and perhaps discover that the journey towards professional excellence continues for life, just as it does for other professionals — doctors, lawyers, nurses, social workers, community leaders.

Most of us begin as teacher candidates at a teachers' college and then move too quickly into the responsibilities of the classroom, with all the challenges of today's educational climate and settings. Rather than becoming overwhelmed with our sense of inadequacy, we need to be supported by the mentoring of strong colleagues and the professional development opportunities available in school, in our district, in books and journals, and in online communities. The professional journey continues throughout our careers, in phases and stages, depending on all of the factors that can influence us — families, health, changing locales, school values, leadership issues, curriculum development, and so on. But there are constant characteristics that are significant to student well-being and success, and we can all check our own attitudes and dispositions and make changes, small ones at first, as we come to recognize how, as individuals, we deepen and extend our professional selves.

To aid in each teacher's personal professional checklist, we have included different voices — stories of teaching from the world of children's books, voices of teachers and administrators who share their observations of real classroom examples of honest teaching, and voices of writers and researchers who have considered the role of significant teachers in their lives, so that as you read about the teaching lives of others, you can find similar stories and events, discover new thoughts and directions about your own teaching, and add to your repertoire of classroom strategies and techniques. We have found thirty characteristics that contribute to achieving excellence in teaching, and we understand that they all flow throughout a teaching career, often in waves, sometimes with undercurrents, and usually in the midst of reflecting about the complexities and conundrums of school life.

A teacher's first years can feel isolating. From Isolation to Conversation, *by Dwight L. Rogers and Leslie M. Babinski, details a professional development strategy called New Teacher Groups that enables teachers to open up about the problems they face.*
Teaching gets easier with experience, and The New Teacher Book, *edited by Terry Burant, Linda Christensen, Kelley Dawson Salas, and Stephanie Walters, is specifically for new teachers entering the field, with excerpts from teachers who have taught from K to 12.*

ORGANIZING THE CHARACTERISTICS OF "GOOD" TEACHING

Since we all follow our own different paths for growth, we trust you the reader to see where these characteristics fit into your own teacherly identity, and how different aspects of them can signal for you as a growth-oriented educator those changes you might make in how you construct your teaching life. You will also find suggestions of books, websites, and journal articles that may add to your teacher knowledge, or offer a road map for finding supportive information as you reflect on your journey towards becoming the best teacher you can be for your students.

We have organized our findings, our stories, our thoughts, our felt data, under four categories, creating our model or framework for examining the discrete characteristics of good teaching: **the teacher, the taught, the teaching,** and **the school community**. Of course, different characteristics flow through all four groupings, and that is at the heart of our model.

Our teacher characteristics can be revealed in a myriad of ways, depending on place, time, life events, the contexts of educational organizations. But to recognize that all characteristics matter in some way, that they morph into different clusters, that they take centre stage at times and stay in the shadows in others,, these are the foundations of what we hope will evolve as we read, discuss, reflect on, and reconsider how we can adapt as professionals, and work toward becoming the teachers we deserve to be.

How will we balance these characteristics in our own teaching? How will we finder deeper self-awareness without trying to become someone else? In truth, each teacher must become their own change agent, recognizing when to alter, learn new strategies, find colleagues who can support new ways of working, listen to the students' voices throughout the year, read, take courses, discover other modes of affecting student growth, and accept that we can continue to alter and pursue stronger methods and behaviours for being among youngsters. We grow over time; we change when we become aware of how change will help our students to become self-learners, and when we find greater satisfaction in our professional selves. We come to enjoy our work, often in spite of the challenges outside our control. The excitement that comes from discovering how each student functions in the whole of the class feeds us and drives us as creative beings, and we come to engage in the teaching puzzle simply because it fulfills us.

We continue to honour those teachers from our lives who have given us new paths to travel, better options for educating children, mentoring and wise counsel, who have sometimes become friends and colleagues, or we treasure distant memories of others to whom we are grateful. We have been among teachers almost all of our lives, thousands of hours sitting in classrooms in elementary and secondary schools and university auditoriums, and at professional development sessions. That is why we need to challenge our assumptions about the construct called teaching. What if we are not locked into our fading memories of how we were taught, but rather use our past experiences as research data to examine how we could transform those methods for each new generation of students?

TWO MEMORIES OF DON JESSE, A "GOOD" TEACHER

1. Nancy Steele

"Have you got any glue? I have to stick these corks to my neck." It was my first day as a middle-school art teacher at a private K-12 school in London, England, and this demand came from someone I imagined must be one of the many other teachers I had yet to meet. He was dressed fairly casually but his head was wrapped in bandages which were bulging in a spot over his left eye. I managed to find him glue that he felt would do.

"What happened to your head?" I asked.

"Oh, I'm going to give birth to my lesson plans for the year in my first period class. They are on computer tapes that are in that lump. I'll start with a headache. Just like Zeus giving birth to Athena. I'm teaching mythology first period." Who was this madman? I thought.

During my five years at the school I learned that performance was a major ingredient in the magical mix that was my friend, and mentor, Don Jesse. Students all knew his reputation for starting the year off with some literary stunt or other. He was a collector of antiques and luckily had understanding friends at Stratford. The next year on day one, to start his Shakespeare course he brought in an ornate wrought-iron double bed, which he had decorated with vines and covered with roses. When his students arrived, they found him "asleep" in the bed wearing a fabulous donkey headpiece borrowed from the prop shop of Midsummer Night's Dream. Sadly, I was teaching at that time and didn't get to watch as he woke, proclaiming, "What do you see? You see an ass head of your own, do you? I see their knavery: this is to make an ass of me..."

Don's classroom was a work of art: students' poetry and drawings covered the walls as did articles from newspapers with comments or questions from Don attached. The furniture was constantly rearranged to suit the needs of the day. The wilted daisy on his desk had a sign pinned to the vase begging someone to compose an ode to it. Don loved life and lived it to the full. He was not beyond embellishing a story and was sure I would believe him when he told me that the yogi meditator he had brought in to demonstrate the power of the mind had lifted himself off the floor and sailed across the room in front of his amazed students.

We were all a bit disappointed when he didn't seem to have done anything to celebrate day one of my last year with him. When questioned he replied that this was the year of the Queen's jubilee and then, smiling broadly, he revealed that he had painted his back teeth red, white and blue.

2. Wendy Lawless

My teacher, Don Jesse, at the American School in London, taught me seventh grade English in 1974. This wildly theatrical and mercurial man who wore jeans and turtlenecks (not suits like the other male teachers) and changed his facial hair every week demanded our attention. I was riveted. Mr. Jesse was always in motion, spouting poetry and Shakespeare while walking inside the circle our desks made. If you didn't know a word, he'd throw the dictionary at you and holler, "Look it up!" We read Edgar Allen Poe, the Scottish play (which he took us to see in the West End with a very young Helen Mirren as Lady M.), David Copperfield, Jane Eyre. We memorized 'Ozymandias" and soliloquies. And we wrote. He was the first person to encourage me to write. His praise of and attention to my writing meant the world to me. I ended up becoming an actress first before turning to writing but I still credit Mr. Jesse with giving me my love of words. He opened up a world for me and I will never forget him. He is retired now and lives on a farm in Cornwall.

WHAT STUDENTS WANT FROM TEACHERS

- **Relationships matter.** Students want to know their teachers better, and they want teachers to understand their passions..
- **Context and relevance matter.** Students, especially high school students, want authentic learning experiences. They want to solve problems, but they want them to be grounded in their world.
- **Students want agency and voice.** They want to be active drivers in their own learning. They want to have choices, various ways to learn, and opportunities to explore their passions within formal learning environments.

- **Students learn in many different ways.** Students and teachers emphasized that they each learn differently. Students want opportunities that address these learning differences...

Dr. Mary Ann Wolf,
Getting Smart.com

WHAT CAN WE LEARN FROM STUDENT VOICES?

Preparing Teachers for a Changing World, edited by Linda Darling-Hammond and John Bransford, is a comprehensive examination of the issues and concerns facing educators.

- I think you could teach us by doing things the same way but we should have out our Scribbler and take notes. If we take notes than we can look back on the notes and study them before a test.
- Maybe if you make the people who aren't paying attention answer all the questions and if they can't, you make them stay in, they'll remember to pay attention next time.
- Sometimes I get off track but I blank my mind and try as hard as I can to get on track. I think independent work on your own is good too.
- When Mrs. Windmarch came in you told her that we were dead. She told us to hold out a hand and put it up in the air. "You Can Do It!" she yelled and then she smiled. My point is to maybe make a joke once in a while to get us awake. Or pick up the pace a bit when you are teaching.
- You can:
    not let anyone talk;
    say things once and don't repeat them;
    give more seat work;
    not let us do as many fun activities.
- I personally like to go out of the classroom to do things. Maybe when Mr. Rosehill comes he could take half of the class into one room and teach. It could make learning fun.
- You could separate the girls from the other girls and put them next to a boy so they won't talk as much.
- Mrs. Stickney can give extra work for the people who don't pay attention in class or who have 3 warnings.
- Not to shout at someone if they forget something!
- Please try to just shake it up sometimes. Give us a variety of work and activities and don't just stick to the same type of lesson every day.
- Work can be made more interesting by giving more freedom to the students. If a student really enjoys the subject they can explore it farther and learn more, and become better students and better citizens.
- To engage all students in the lesson instead of just saying what we need to do that day in class.
- To relate assignments more to the students and make them less busywork and more in terms of variety. They should provide variety in class every week to keep things interesting
- Make projects more fun to do by giving us more options and more visuals in class because some people learn better that way.
- To help those even if they have advanced thinking, and teachers should put more energy in paying attention to children, and fix the situation where those who are good kids get yelled at more often than those who fool around on a daily basis.
- Make sure the students fully understand what's being taught before moving on to something new.

- Try to get to know students and talk to them before class or something to make everyone feel comfortable around you. So, you're not the "mean" teacher.
- Slow down and teach the subject more instead of assuming we know and understand the material.
- Just be more understanding and try to put themselves in the students' shoes.

Challenges affecting teacher development

While we will always face challenges as teachers, they need not be barriers to effective teaching. We notice how some teachers seem to thrive on working with and/or around a perceived problem and continue their effectiveness with their students; others of us need supportive colleagues to find ways to cope. If we don't panic or feel like a failure, or feel thwarted or depressed by these difficult factors, we can begin to consider how to handle them, perhaps through community discussions, a teacher neighbour, supportive personnel, online dialogues, parent conversations, or even changing grades or programs, and, if necessary, schools.

But every teacher will confront similar challenges at some time in their career, and how we cope will determine our effect on our students. Never be afraid to seek help, encouragement or guidance; choose your advisors carefully, and continue to find out the causes of the difficulties, ways of handling them, and then remember that the students are your first consideration. Working within the system is the first choice so that students are not put at risk or abandoned. And systems are always complex and multi-faceted. How you fit in will take time and work:

- Continue to grow in content knowledge and increase expertise in the use of instructional methods. See these competencies as a means of strengthening your teaching and adding to your self-efficacy.
- Classroom size can affect student success. Differentiation is more difficult with larger numbers, but you can work with your grade team to develop a plan for team teaching or for including volunteers. You may be able to integrate subjects to save time or to give a stronger context for the students.
- Classroom management may require some new strategies: workshops for teachers, new resources with helpful books or online suggestions can provide different ways of approaching difficult students. Many students have difficulty self-regulating or developing relationships with other students and the teacher. Of course, a supportive classroom community will allow students to work together and reduce confrontation or friction.
- Bullying is a problem that requires a school policy that everyone follows. There are excellent books for teachers outlining strategies for handling bullying in positive ways. Cyberbullying is a new form of bullying that teachers and students need to be aware of so together they can find ways of reducing opportunities for trouble.
- Curriculum guidelines can be seen as problems, limiting creative and student-driven opportunities, so this requires teachers to work with experienced mentors to find ways of delivering curriculum in different ways, so that students and teachers have voice and agency in how topics and skills are to be included in a healthy and interactive program. How we teach what we have to teach is the art of teaching.

Kathleen Cushman, in her book Fires in the Bathroom, *includes observations and remarkable insights by students about their teachers and their learning.*

- Common core standards and examinations cause difficulty if they control how children are to become engaged in learning. High-stakes testing puts a great deal of pressure on many students, but an effective teaching/learning program means students will be prepared for tests, and we will need to resist preparing for tests all year long. Sharing learning goals with students means they will be aware of what they need to work toward this year, and continual feedback will support their successes as learners.
- School leadership requires effective teams to make changes, with ownership on the part of all teachers. Effective leaders realize they need to work alongside teachers in building a learning community.
- Budget cuts cause us to rethink our priorities, and to work with the administration and the staff to make the best choices possible. It may be helpful to become advocates for school funding needs with parents, district leaders or unions.
- Technology can make learning engaging for students, but schools need to achieve budget parity across the district. Social media platforms can work well if monitored carefully, and if structured as part of the curriculum. In many aspects, technology can facilitate learning, but it can also cause distractions if students are not aware of how technology is to be used in a lesson.
- Parent involvement can lead to a stronger school community. Schools need to be aware of the cultural backgrounds of families and acquire strategies for building and maintaining relationships with parents. Family factors such as illness, divorce or poverty can cause students to lose focus or act out frustrations, so teachers need to attend to each student's life situation. A hungry child, for instance, will have difficulty learning.
- When parents are defensive or even angry, resist the urge to argue. Instead, move the discussion to the library, or offer to get the coffee, or show some of the student's artifacts that reveal progress, and then potential. If necessary, arrange another time when you can have supportive staff in the interview (the special education teacher, a literacy consultant, the principal.) Ask for their suggestions as to how all of us can help their child; that has to be the goal. Be sure to shake hands when the interview is over.
- Faculty or administration who may appear unsupportive and uncooperative may cause teachers to feel isolated or fearful. Teachers need to find a teaching buddy who can help bring about constructive feedback with coworkers, so their students do not live in a conflict, tension-filled environment. We can all be civil and respectful with each other. We need to continue to find ways of building connections with staff and administrators — volunteering on committees, coaching after-school groups, etc.
- Personal home situations can affect a teacher's disposition, energy, and relationships with students: health issues, stress, family difficulties, course projects, lack of colleagues' respect, are all factors that require support and tolerance from others.

You Have to Go to School — You're the Teacher! by Renee Rosenblum-Lowden offers a wide array of classroom management strategies that will empower teachers at all points in their career and provide them with resources to make their teaching more engaging and successful.

GOOD EVERYDAY TEACHING PRACTICES IDENTIFIED THROUGH A LONGITUDINAL STUDY

Dr. Clive Beck and Dr. Clare Kosmin, professors, OISE/University of Toronto

> We are conducting a longitudinal study of 40 teachers, of whom 20 (originally 22) began teaching in 2004 and 20 (originally 23) began in 2007.

Each year we and our team interview the teachers and, where possible, observe in their classrooms. Most are elementary (K-8) teachers working in relatively low SES schools. While the study is ongoing we report here on the period to 2016, their first 12 and 9 years of teaching respectively.

One finding of the study is that conditions for teachers over this period have become more challenging, partly because of larger class sizes and reduced special education support, but also because of increased and frequently changing school system initiatives. However, nearly all the teachers have remained in the profession, sustained their motivation, and continued to improve their practice. We have not seen the kind of "plateauing" or "burning out" sometimes associated with early- to mid-career teachers, although some wonder how long they can last if conditions stay as they are or deteriorate further.

Among the many good teaching practices identified among the participants in our study are the following:

Relevant and flexible programming
The teachers over the years have made their programming more relevant to their students by focusing on real-world and way of life learning. To this end, they have become quite flexible in their teaching, spending more time on the more relevant topics in the curriculum.

Student voice and choice
The teachers have grown in the extent to which they provide opportunities for students to say what *they* think, thus enabling them to "construct" their own ideas and share their many insights with others in the class (including the teacher). Related to this trend, the teachers are giving students more choice in how they fulfill course requirements and which aspects of topics they explore.

Helpful and feasible student assessment
Many of the teachers in our study have found ways to give immediate feedback to students and write quick notes on students' abilities and performance during class time, thus making assessment more individualized and helpful to students and more feasible for the teacher. With this approach, there is less after-school marking and a solid basis for completing report cards and responding to queries from parents.

Effective classroom organization
The teachers have learned how to establish classroom routines and a "flow" of learning activities so that disruptive behavior is kept to a minimum and learning is continuous. A range of learning activities are used repeatedly (e.g., literature circles, math discussions, debates, writing in a scrapbook, independent silent reading, brief class presentations) that students become familiar with and enjoy.

Strong teacher-student relationship and class community
The teachers have grown in their ability to develop a good relationship with their students and build a class community in which students feel safe and included. They are "friendly but firm" with their students, carefully

facilitating their learning but also interacting with them in a genuinely social manner.

DEVELOPING TEACHERS' PROFESSIONAL LEARNING

Carol Campbell, professor, OISE/University of Toronto

> Teachers at different stages of their career and life also require equitable access to quality professional learning, whether as a beginning teacher, an experienced teacher, or transitioning into formal leadership and beyond. Access to high-quality professional learning experiences and resources—for example, mentorship or research-informed professional learning materials—varied considerably within and across the research we conducted. This type of variation is not inevitable, not desirable, and highly negative. Connecting to the larger question of Canadian education in a world of educational improvement, we have much to be proud of, but we have persisting and emerging inequities to identify, understand, and address. Research has a vital role in holding up the mirror, whether through qualitative and/or quantitative methods, to provide evidence and understanding of inequities for students, educators, and communities, and in seeking to inform policy and practice solutions in Canada and in a world of educational improvement.
>
> *Canadian Journal of Education/Revue canadienne de l'éducation*, 40:2 (2017)

Sonia Nieto in *Why We Teach Now* reminds us that "there is no way to be anyone else's version of a great teacher; there's no formula; you can only be your best version. Resist pressures to blend into a homogenized teaching mold or lose the power of authenticity." In a competitive and evaluative culture that often envelops some schools and districts, it might help to remember James Fowler's suggestion that we frame our life in terms of "vocation" as opposed to "career." Rather than focusing on the achievements of others, we follow our own path, augmented and enriched by the talents and experiences of our colleagues, rather than competing with them, and strengthened by our own gifts, while understanding our own limits and opening new vistas, "freed from the sense of being all things to all people." We need to be valued, but that process begins with "self-recognition," and continuing to develop as professionals is the best way of building "self-worth."

TEACHER VOICES

- Each day will be different. Some days will feel unsuccessful, others wonderful. This is the way of the world. Start each day with a fresh outlook.
- Don't dwell on mistakes. Don't be afraid to explain why things went wrong.
- Apologize when necessary. Don't harbour grudges or play favourites.
- Never give up on your students. Lift their spirits when you can, and they will lift yours.
- Open classrooms can lead to open minds.

1

Develop a "Teacherly" Identity

MY JOURNAL

Wally Karr, student

October 1

Ninth grade isn't so bad, but so many teachers! You have to learn what each teacher is like, what they expect you to do, how they handle discipline, how hard they mark, if they return your essays, if they are preparing in class time for their night course, whether to answer in class, if they have a sense of humour, who are their favourites, who do they pick on, how much homework they give, when will they be away, if they had a fight with their spouse, if the guy cut himself while shaving, do they smoke or have coffee breath. Oh my god. Eight of them, never mind the 24 other kids in my class — 6 weird ones, 2 footballers, 3 cheerleaders and 2 nerds like me. I forgot about how everyone has to dress in the newest jeans: where are school uniforms when you need them?

And then there's the principal! We only saw him at the first assembly. Grey suit, grey hair, grey everything. But the vice-principals: two women — one old, one young. I always hope it will be the old one I have to talk to. The young one wears high heels that click down the halls, warning of an impending tornado, with her arms filled with folders and a huge designer bag falling off her shoulder. She is there to keep control of us, and she is determined to handle the task, come hell or high water, as my dad says. We are not an easy bunch of students. Just ask the guy in the washroom with the black eye.

Two thousand students in one school. There are three different lunch times so we can all take turns eating in the cafeteria. Yesterday I was hit on the head with an orange somebody threw at me. Where were the teachers? What if they took turns eating with us in the caf? I don't think the young VP eats; she is what I would call skinny, but the girls think she's cool. Welcome to high school! Funny thing is, I like being here. And, hey! maybe my moustache is beginning to grow.

1. Enjoy and appreciate being among students

If you can keep yourself in good spirits, your students will follow your example. If you set a positive tone in your classroom, by maintaining a positive attitude as often as you can, by knowing your students' names and information about who they are, and by greeting them with a smile each day, they will quickly recognize that you are where you want to be, spending valuable life time among your students.

Look for sources of inspiration: books and films about good teaching; children's and young adult books that illustrate, that with all the challenges, a life in teaching can be satisfying and rewarding; colleagues who are passionate about teaching, about learning; workshops and conferences where you have opportunities to mix with teachers from different places and schools; chat lines and blogs with educators from different countries; students on teams and in plays and tournaments who bring excitement to your teaching life.

Children and youth spend thousands of hours in classrooms during their elementary, middle, and secondary education. Good teachers design their classroom environments to enhance the cognitive, social, and emotional development of their students. Nurturing classrooms display the creative artifacts of students' investigations and knowledge building. These classrooms reveal cultures where learners are collaboratively engaged in developmentally appropriate, challenging intellectual pursuits and where all students are valued. The classrooms also cultivate a climate and spaces for learners to shape their thinking and ideas. Students discuss their work, take time to reflect about their learning, and have opportunities to develop positive relationships with their classmates and teachers.

Caring interpersonal relationships are characterized by patience, persistence, facilitation, validation, and empowerment for the participants, as outlined in Geneva Gay's book Culturally Responsive Teaching: Theory, Research and Practice.

Focus: Laughter belongs in the classroom
Rich Coles

Humour is a ubiquitous feature of our daily lives and often a way of expressing or enhancing our enjoyment and appreciation of others. Think about the past few weeks and your experiences with different humorous episodes. Various kinds of media, workplaces, social settings, and leisure activities are fertile sources for numerous forms of humour. In classrooms, humour can serve many positive and negative functions. Jokes, physical actions, funny examples, puns, humour related to the unit of study, riddles, funny stories or comments, creative language usage, cartoons, and "unintentional humour" (e.g., gaffes) are some positive examples.. However, sexual humour, ethnic humour, aggressive humour, targeting humour, sarcasm, and teasing have no place in the classroom.

From our personal experiences, we know that humour can be used appropriately and inappropriately in school and other settings. Humour and laughter occur in all cultures although there are differences in terms of the appropriate subjects of humour and when it is appropriate to laugh. According to an analysis of humour in people's daily lives, 11 percent were a result of jokes, 17 percent came from the media, and 72 percent took place spontaneously during social interactions with other people. Different theoretical explanations address the fundamental elements of humour. Effective use of it in the classroom calls for some understanding of its cognitive, emotional, and social aspects. Incongruity theory emphasizes that humour is processed by a heightened recognition of a stimulus such as an image, idea, passage, conversation or event that contains a surprise or perceived incongruity or inconsistency. But the incongruous stimulus must also be interpreted or resolved as such by the child or youth. Students who do not recognize the incongruity cannot make sense of the humour; they "just don't get it." This theory emphasizes the cognitive aspects of humour. When generating humour an individual plays with ideas, words, nonverbal actions or images in creative ways to elicit a humorous response. The cognitive processes of manipulating ideas students use to solve a joke are similar to those they employ in problem solving and the processing of creativity.

Superiority theory argues that laughter comes when people with a sense of superiority, disparage others they feel are inferior. In the classroom, for example, some students use humorous comments to target and make fun of and put down other learners who do not have the financial resources to wear the current trendy designer clothes. Superiority/disparagement theory emphasizes the emotional and social aspect of humour. This aggressive form of humour is inappropriate for the classroom.

Arousal theory posits that humour and laughter represent an interaction of cognition and emotion. The pleasurable emotion of humour is what psychologist Rod A. Martin calls mirth. The degree of mirth elicited by various experiences seems to be a combination of cognitive evaluation of the humorous stimulus and physiological arousal during the episode. Other adaptations of this theory suggest that stress and tension are released by humour and laughter.

Humour in the classroom has been associated with many benefits. Appropriate humour has been related to positive classroom environments that help to reduces stress, boredom, tension, and student anxiety, and increase students' enjoyment of learning, motivation, perceptions of their own knowledge development and more positive attitudes toward their learning. Positive, appropriate humour has been correlated with positive teacher evaluations. A sense of humour is rated as a quality of a successful, effective teacher. It may facilitate the development of a positive relationship between a teacher and a learner.

Evidence that humour enhances learning is mixed, with some scholars finding that humour improves learning while other studies find no relationship between the two. Several factors may account for these inconclusive findings. There have been concerns about some methodological flaws such as studies being short in duration, insufficient integration of humour into the lesson, and irrelevance of humour to the lesson. And did the students understand the humour and genuinely find it funny? However, there are some findings to consider when employing humour. There is support for using it to gain and maintain the attention of students as long as it is relevant to the content of the learning experience. And humour should be used in moderation to illuminate important concepts. Too much humour can reduce the credibility of a teacher. Educators also need to be sure that their humour is appropriate for the ages and diverse cultures of their students. If students cannot make sense of references or contexts then the humour becomes confusing.

Some teachers skillfully and thoughtfully use various appropriate humour strategies during interactions with students. However, some teachers feel that humour is not one of their positive personality traits. But these teachers can still use humour to make learning more enjoyable for their students. As the students enter the classroom, teachers can greet each student with a smile and a few encouraging words. There are useful resources containing numerous examples of integrating humour into every subject area. Some examples would include: reading and discussing funny picture books, or young adult novels, engaging with

---

Humour seems to be best viewed as a form of interpersonal communication that can be used for a variety of purposes in teaching, as evidenced in Rod A. Martin's The Psychology of Humor: An Integrated Approach, *and in his article with N. A. Kuiper, "Daily occurrences of laughter: Relationships with age, gender, and Type A personality."*

the students in a variety of word play activities (e.g., find numerous words for laughter with audible examples, develop text sets of amusing materials or collect jokes, riddles, and cartoons dealing with the current topics of study. When reading humorous picture books such as: *The Recess Queen, The Extinct Files: My Science Files, The Incredible Book Eating Boy,* or *The Secret Knowledge of Grown-ups* the class discussion can lead to thinking and ideas about what makes these books funny. And when investigating humour in the classroom students have opportunities to develop an understanding of both appropriate humour and the potential personal devastation of some forms of inappropriate humour such as taunting.

Positive emotions aroused by instructional humour may lead to more positive attitudes toward education, greater motivation to learn, and enhanced performance in the classroom. And who doesn't like a good out-of-control, loud, teary, rib-shaking bout of laughter?

2. Be a model and mentor for your students

Modeling learning

As teachers, we need to model our own learning with our students as often as possible:

- We can share portions of our reading lives with our students. We all remember teachers who read us a letter they had received or an editorial from a newspaper about an issue they cared deeply about, who showed us the novels they were reading or the information books they had found about their hobby.
- If we belong to a book club, we can share some of the proceedings with our students (How are the books selected? Who decides what we will talk about? When do you find time to read the books? How do make sense of the books you are reading? How do you notice your own use of the reading strategies?) If we are taking a course, we can show our students the texts and articles we are using, revealing our own modes of sorting, marking, or highlighting texts.
- We can share our own thinking strategies as we read aloud/think aloud in classroom discussions. Students can see how we construct meaning in a variety of ways with different types of texts, how we continue to grow as learners. We want our students to notice us as learners, to be aware of our own thinking and strategies, how we handle our own moments of confusion and breakdowns.
- A strong, motivated teacher models the behaviours that they want their students to demonstrate. Mentoring a student in difficulty leads towards building a supportive community for all.

CONNECTING OUR HEARTS WITH MENTORING WEBS

Jim Strachan, education officer, Ontario Ministry of Education

> Inside all of our students who come to school each day are their hearts, and inside every heart of every student are their hopes, dreams, and wishes for their lives and learning.
>
> We know creating a safe place for the hearts of our students is a critical precondition for learning but in order to do this I think it is essential that the hearts of the educators supporting our students are also safe, and secure, and

supported. I see this as a reciprocal process. In other words, our students can become part of our mentoring web and we can become part of theirs.

Looking in the mirror

Mentoring is an act of learning. One of the most powerful things a mentor can do is help their colleague hold up a mirror to their practice and in this mirror see all their strengths and attributes, not just the flaws and challenges of what isn't working. Through this de-privatization of practice, the quiet victories and moments of beauty that teaching provides can be surfaced, elevated and celebrated. This is authentic "inside out", learner driven collaborative professionalism.

As mentors one of our biggest challenges is to hold up this same mirror to ourselves and not just see our own flaws. Simply put as a profession we are incredibly hard on ourselves. Our day ends and we don't celebrate our 19 "quiet victories", we reflect upon the one (or two or three!) things that went wrong. In other words, we fail the "best edu-friend" test. If our colleague came to us with their challenges, concerns and worries we'd be so accepting and understanding but somehow, it's difficult to give this same level of acceptance to ourselves. We're reluctant to acknowledge celebrate and elevate our own strengths and attributes.

Building mentoring webs

Our learning from the New Teacher Induction Program (NTIP) is helpful here. Through our longitudinal research we found that high growth new teachers access 5–7 different mentor supports (i.e., they built a "mentoring web"). The more strands in each of our webs, the stronger and more resilient the webs are.

With these supportive webs, our hearts as educators are warmed and our well-being is supported. Our warm hearts create a space for continued personal and professional learning and growth for every educator and ultimately every student.

Supporting resources for mentors:
Mentoring for All eBook: http://tiny.cc/mentoringforall
Teacher Learning and Leadership Program: https://www.teachontario.ca/community/explore/tllppke
TeachOntario Talks: https://www.teachontario.ca/community/explore/teachontario-talks

3. Establish, value, and nurture student-teacher relationships

We need to find ways to build strong relationships with our students, to show interest in them as well as their learning, to build a rapport both with the class and with individual students, and when necessary to advocate for them. Students need to sense that we care for them, for their well-being inside and outside school. In surveys, students often rank "caring" as the most important characteristic of good teachers. And this includes the teacher demanding the best work from the students, as long as there is an awareness of when home difficulties sap their energy. It can be a constant struggle to help them to achieve in spite of challenges.

Participating in schoolwide activities — bake sales, sports events, art shows, music nights, graduation — allows students to see that you are a significant part of the school culture; you value being among them. And a true rapport with your students means their deeper participation in discussions, in interviews and conferences, in approaching solutions to problems and difficulties. Healthy and strong relationships are developed through small interactions and daily signs of caring.

High-quality teacher-student relationships are another critical factor in determining student engagement, especially in the case of difficult students and those from lower socioeconomic backgrounds. When students form close and caring relationships with their teachers, they are fulfilling their developmental need for a connection with others and a sense of belonging in society. Teacher-student relationships can be facilitated by:

- Caring about students' social and emotional needs
- Displaying positive attitudes and enthusiasm
- Increasing one-on-one time with students
- Treating students fairly
- Avoiding deception or promise-breaking

Nicolás Pino-James, PhD, educational researcher, *Edutopia*, 11/12/2015

Mirror Images, by Casey Reason and Clair Reason, examines what leadership means in the modern classroom, and how teachers can be more effective leaders and effect positive change in their classroom and profession.

Young people develop their thinking abilities and social dispositions by interacting with peers, other youngsters, adults, and their environment. The relationship between the teacher, each student, and the other learners becomes an integral part of the interplay in the classroom. This dynamic interaction helps students develop an awareness of other viewpoints as they examine their own beliefs, standards, and values, increasing their ability to reflect on their own attitudes and behaviours. Students construct understandings together that would not be possible alone and are able to learn about and respect the uniqueness of others.

Relationships with friends, classmates, and teachers help students to cope with the sometimes rigorous demands of a mainstream classroom. Through working with more peers who have different strengths and experiences, through a process of "scaffolding," learners can extend their learning. Learners with different skills and backgrounds collaborate in tasks and discussions and thereby arrive at a shared understanding. Through working with peers and building a sense of belonging, students are more likely to be able to bridge the distance between their developmental levels.

Learning needs to become an active process, where learners make discoveries, developing their skills at prediction and intuitive thinking; where they can select tasks that are challenging, initiate activities, exert intense concentration, and expend great effort.

Teacher development advocates encourage teachers to actively acknowledge student voice in decision-making power. Students can gain access to information and resources for making effective decisions, have a range of choices, develop an ability to exercise assertiveness in collective decision-making, increase positive thinking and the ability to make change, learn skills for improving personal or group power, change others' perceptions by democratic means and involvement in the growth process, increase their positive self-image, and begin to understand how to sort out right and wrong.

More and more researchers, institutions, and support organizations worldwide are advocating for the inclusion of students in educational reform efforts. They see the inclusion of student voices as a vital element, an essential component of effective reform efforts and organizational development in community organizations. It is not enough for young people to simply listen; we have an obligation to include students in meaningful, interactive practice.

When students feel the liberation that comes from having a say in what they read and write, what they interpret and construct, they have a stake in creating and maintaining a classroom that stimulates and supports deep learning. At the same time, the teacher is freed to concentrate on how to best guide, inform, and strengthen their abilities. Students can gain a sense of ownership and of the responsibility that accompanies it.

A grade nine student expresses his thoughts about learning:

> **The Most Important Thing I Have Learned about Learning**
> I have learned a lot over the past few years about what makes school a successful experience for students, especially those who struggle academically. I have learned that teachers need to be explicit in teaching students what works and what does not work for them. I have learned that giving students' choice in the ways in which they demonstrate their understanding is important. Integrating Ministry-provided technology into lessons and ensuring that students use it daily can be the difference between an engaged student and a disengaged one. In Grades 7 and 8, teachers expect us to be able to advocate for ourselves — this skill needs to be taught.
>
> But the most important thing that I have learned is that every student needs to feel part of the class. Education has and will continue to move forward, technology will advance, and expectations will change, but one thing will remain the same: students' engagement and success depend on a teacher's ability to see them for who they are.
>
> Matthew Cote

Relationships take time to build, but with consistency and role modeling, teachers can build an atmosphere of mutual respect, for if students feel respected, they will most often respect the teacher and the classroom. A fair yet flexible teacher applies the rules evenly and consistently, and this usually generates respect by the students. Follow the maxim: be fair, firm and funny.

Teachers Have It Easy: The Big Sacrifices and Small Salaries of America's Teachers, by Dave Eggers, Nínive Clements Calegari, Daniel Moulthrop

A teaching job is envied by many, with many thinking that teachers have it pretty easy with summer vacations and other perks. This book tests that theory, and uses teachers' voices to describe the actual working conditions faced by teachers.

TEACHING A TEACHER
Carlos Ossa, PhD, college instructor, Chile

Having graduated with a BEd degree, I was interviewed for the position of librarian by the principal of a boys' school in Santiago, Germán Aburto. When I entered in his office, I noticed that amid the mare magnum of students' hand-made souvenirs hanging from the walls, with a number of multicolour Scout's scarfs, there was an actual anvil crossed upside down by an actual sword with the school motto "Here we forge our arms", beside his desk. It impressed me. A man in his late fifties, wearing a T-shirt, with his eyeglasses lacking one of their lenses. He was just coming from the school patio after being a referee in a students' football match.

My job interview lasted more than 3 hours. It started by his stating that I was already in, so the interview became a sort of induction to that school's life. The first thing he told me was, "You have to trust your students, no matter what." To me it was a shock — how to trust students in a school library! Opening the shelves to them? That was my first reaction to the challenge (when I presented such a plan, it was immediately accepted). Trusting students was something I had never heard in my student life. I thought that maybe "trusting students" was something teachers had as a background strategy, something I had never noticed.

After I'd spent one year as a librarian there, Germán asked me to move from the library to become a Language and Literature teacher for grades 8 to 12. I had recently obtained my BA, becoming eligible for the position. Germán warned me that as learning is an ongoing experience, grades are not definitive judgments, that nobody should be treated only according to their grades, that what happens in one year can be a disastrous experience, but that might change during the next one to a glorious redemption. For him, testing weeks should look more like a spring fair, where every student would show off what they know well, not what he or she doesn't. He pushed me to do the same. That man was changing my way of understanding my new profession and my identity in ways I had never expected.

The first day of my first testing week (he called it "the learning fair"), he ambushed me at my classroom door. I had just given my students the sheets with the questions, and I was ready to invigilate them, as I learned to do throughout my life. He then knocked on my door and silently he called me out, with a hand gesture. He invited me to go for a cup of coffee, and I replied that my class was having a test. He said, "I know, that's why. Leave them alone. You have to make room for their character to grow. Trust me, they will not cheat. And if they do, there must be a pedagogical way to solve the situation."

After all, they did not cheat. At all.

Trusting students is a rare quality to find in schools. Germán showed me a way to be a teacher, by trusting not only in testing time, but in every stance during the school day. I learned to never doubt the word of a student. That if I were a reliable person, they would never cheat or fool me. Today Germán Aburto is retired. His Facebook page is constantly bombarded by people's greetings and daily thank-you notes; his former students still consider him their teacher, someone who taught them how to live their adult lives in loyalty and trustworthiness. As happened with me.

PERSONAL RELATIONSHIPS WITH STUDENTS
Justine Bruyère, PhD, primary teacher, Austin, Texas

During my research, in the summer of 2014, I sought to establish relationships with 15 kindergarten aged participants. Throughout the investigation, I engaged students in drama lessons, hoping to form personal bonds and a strong sense of community. The weekly lessons incorporated drama and literacy, often encouraging students and teacher to act in role, use puppets, and eventually write about those imaginative experiences. I believe that the creative arts — music, dance, and, in particular, drama — offer students many of the skills necessary to participate and play an active role in a literate society. The arts help to release feeling, encourage discovery, and bring about thoughtful responses. In our rapidly changing and technological world, students need to be able to form relationships, contribute ideas, and solve multifaceted problems that go beyond textbook teaching.

With all of this in mind, during the twelve weeks of data collection, I mentored and befriended the participants in this research. I earnestly followed a three-step process linking: *interest, praise, and follow-up*. During the *interest* period, I relentlessly queried and doted on the students in this research. I listened to them talking, involved myself in their conversations, and committed their interests to memory. In between our visits, I looked into specific areas in which the children had indicated an interest. When we reunited the following week, I spoke with more authority and excitement about video games, American Girl dolls, and Whiffer Sniffer Key Chains to name a few. This extra attention is a confirmation to the child that the adult deeply cares about him/her. For the *praise* portion of my relationship building process, I gave consistent, authentic, and specific feedback. Too often, teachers give out empty praise statements to students, such as "Good job", "Way to go" and "Awesome".

During our ten weeks together the students made a great deal of progress. It would have been easy to fall into the empty praise pattern. However, at its core, a more responsive pattern of praise compelled me to be present and thoughtful when interacting with my student participants. Therefore, when I gave the students meaningful praise they expressed a sincere desire to continue their efforts in writing, drama, and/or reading activities. Finally, the *follow-up* stage involved sharing specific stories of praise with the parents of students in my research. I did this either in person, when parents came to pick up their child, or through emails and/or text messages. Oftentimes, I was able to include a photo or a video. Without hesitation, parents would often hand down my compliments to their children. This had a trickle-down, positive effect on my relationship with each child, for the child's learning, and for this research.

The very nature of this literacy program, which ran from 5:30-7:30 p.m., might predict tired and cranky kindergarteners, too worn out to participate fully at the end of a long day. The opposite, however, turned out to be true. This research helped to add to a body of research, dating back over a hundred years, that asserts drama as having a positive effect on classroom dynamics and group cohesion, thus simplifying and accelerating the formation of relationships, friendships, and a community which learns together. Several weeks into the Monday Night program, students were making friends and showing more outward signs of comfort (smiling, laughing, talking, sitting close to a new friend, etc.) in our group. Student participation was positively informed by this comfort. By illustration, students who were barely moving during our song and dance warm-up activity in the first weeks of programming were confidently moving their bodies with giggles and grins by week four. Over the weeks our group had evolved, from 15 people converging one night each week, to a community of young learners who share common interests and experiences and were sincerely excited about our weekly learning.

This research has taught me, perhaps most of all, the importance of relationships in the classroom. The *interest, praise, and follow-up* process helped me to quickly move from my position as a new teacher to a fun and caring companion. The students in this small study were given a way to think about learning that was filled with positive affirmations, friendship, adventure and wonder. This approach allowed for the creation of imaginary and relevant scenarios while challenging students to their fullest capabilities.

TEACHER VOICES

- Inside school matters; outside school matters as well.
- Connect your students to the world of experts outside school: Ted talks, visitors, You Tube presentations, older students who return from secondary school or college, student teachers, parent volunteers.
- Help students research summer programs, inexpensive camps, volunteer tutors like Big Brothers/Sisters, peer mentors, business volunteers, web sites, Blogs, grandparents. Can you make these information-seeking occasions an inquiry project with your students?
- Support the learning that students do on our own: music lessons, sports, holidays, camps, clubs.
- Attend some of their sports games, their choir and drama presentations. Volunteer as support for excursions.

4. Be caring, compassionate, and mindful

Love your work, but be aware when you can do more to improve your techniques and express your passion for teaching. Many teachers find any discussion of their emotional health and working with an open heart difficult to handle. But this is part of our need for humility, rather than a fear of being seen as a failure. We are always impressed with anecdotes of teachers who recognize that their actions were not successful in handling challenges with a class, a student or a colleague. After spending a summer teaching in Canada, a British authority on educational drama wrote to each of the students in his course a letter apologizing for not being aware enough of their needs as beginning teachers. His course was well-evaluated by the students, but he knew in his heart that there could have been better ways of building a stronger community that summer.

We can learn to forgive ourselves, to practice self-compassion, and to move forward with new knowledge. But we don't over-indulge. For example, we had a colleague who discussed her divorce with her students for twenty minutes every morning; she should have sought professional counsel instead. We learn to accept criticism with an open mind, if we trust the person involved or if we recognize their knowledge about the challenge. Criticism can be tough to grapple with, but if it is fair and useful, we try to listen and understand. For some extremely severe challenges, it may benefit you to work with a teaching coach who has greater experience in offering techniques and strategies in a particular aspect of teaching that will strengthen your own potential.

Another aspect to grapple with is the concept of forgiveness. This may involve a difficult student, or a colleague who has crossed a boundary. In handling these complex situations, it is necessary to confront the problem, but not to fall into bitter grudges which sap energy and allow for no invitations for reconciliation. Rebuilding trust takes time and commitment, but it is most often worth the effort. An understanding teacher will encourage understanding in their students.

A sense of community increases cooperation among students and reduces disruptive behaviours; it becomes a normal way of thinking and acting if students are motivated to support each other in group activities and feed-back sessions, and the teacher needs to model this communal sense in interactions with students. We build connections, and we highlight how these are made and strengthened as we build an inclusive community of learners. It is hard to have meaningful conversations with our students if we don't feel we have an authentic self in their eyes, if we can't find our real voice and integrate how we feel into how we behave. This is sometimes called "the immediacy of the teacher," actually being present at the moment of dialogue creation, listening with honest intent.

What we must do, though, is remain completely in the present, and listen carefully to the spontaneous ideas that the work generates, and then help frame their thoughts so that we can find more meanings together.

CATALYST FOR BECOMING A HOLISTIC TEACHER

Merlin Charles, PhD, university instructor

The environment in which I grew up, particularly my first encounter with formal education, which began at age 5, was the catalyst for my interest in holistic education. On weekdays, my brothers and I walked from Papillotte to the Trafalgar Primary School — a one-room school house, with its four pillars conspicuously perched on an area of undulating land alongside the winding road...

The classrooms could be distinguished by the large, square blackboards, each facing in a different direction — north, south, east and west. I can still visualize my little "corner" filled with young learners — some keener than others. I think I fitted well into the latter category, and I could still hear my voice blending in unison with those of my fellow pupils, as we sang simple songs, recited nursery rhythms, together with the alphabet or the mathematical tables. I feel a deep sense of connectedness to this, and other forms of learning, much of which formed part and parcel of the environment, and the whole idea of bringing education into alignment with it. For instance, given the problem of space within the schoolroom, teachers would often take the children outside for long periods, if the weather permitted.

As I recall, there were only four teachers in the whole school including the Principal (or Head Teacher). Teacher Henry was my favorite teacher, and the first person outside of my family circle to ignite in me, a joy for learning and the desire to be the best that I could be. He was always full of encouragement and praise. I once overheard him saying that "Merlin is a very bright child" — an image of myself that was so positive that I did everything that I could,

Good relationships and coping strategies are key to our success in every area of human activity. See The EQ Edge: Emotional Intelligence and Your Success, *by S.J. Stein and H.E. Book.*

to keep it intact and shinning in my soul, like the bright Caribbean sun. As I write these words, I am reminded of the poem by Dorothy Law Nolte (1969), "Children live what they learn", particularly the line that reads, "If Children live with praise, they learn to appreciate".

I can certainly appreciate the fact that Teacher Henry was totally committed to nourishing the souls of his students, and therefore went beyond the prescribed English and Mathematics curriculum, after it's 2000-mile journey across the Atlantic. In addition to ensuring that we were well au courant with the biographies of our own local and regional heroes, he also ensured that we had a holistic education, in many ways. His most "highly recommended" text was a reference book entitled *The Students' Companion* — part almanac, part dictionary, an encyclopaedia of sorts, in one compact, portable volume. Teacher Henry loved the arts and took pleasure in highlighting our individual talents; he would organize numerous shows and concerts that the whole community could enjoy. A big fan of Shakespeare, he also enjoyed sharing with us several quotes from various philosophers or "men and women of wisdom", which he encouraged us not only to learn, but also to actively practice. I feel inspired to share three of his favorites as follows:

> *I pass through this world but once, and any service I could render to any human being or animal, let me do it now, for I may not pass this way again.*
>
> *Good name in man and woman, is the immediate jewels of their souls. Who steals my purse steals trash; 'twas something, 'tis nothing, 'twas mine, 'this his, and has been slaved through thousands. But he that steals from me, my good name, robs me of that which not enriches him, but makes me poor indeed.*
>
> *The heights that great men reached and kept, were not attained by sudden flight; but they, while their companions slept, were toiling upward in the night.*

I can still vividly recall the glimmer of enthusiasm in Teacher Henry's eyes as he uttered these words, and most of us eventually had them committed to memory. As for me, I took great pleasure in memorizing such beautiful lines and then repeating them to my parents, who were equally proud to hear me recite them. However, it was many years later that I really started to make connections to my early learning experience and to develop a deeper understanding and appreciation of what it means to have a holistic approach to curriculum, teaching and learning.

SOCIO-EMOTIONAL INTELLIGENCE IN TEACHING AND LEARNING
Dr. Bryan Wright, philosopher of education

Socio-emotional intelligence in teaching and learning receives little emphasis in the rush of covering the curriculum. Often students and teachers alike face the pressures of achieving standards measured by testing from the moment the school door opens to the echo of the closing bell, too often ignoring or repressing their social and emotional presence. As teacher leaders with our students, we will need to support the incorporation of skills that build social-emotional intelligence in our classrooms. We will need to help our students develop a capacity for compassion and empathy for others, to understand and manage their own feelings in social situations, and to recognize and understand the emotional responses of others.

Author and psychologist Daniel Goleman coined the term "emotional intelligence", and described it as "the capacity for recognizing our own feelings and those of others, for motivating ourselves, and for managing emotions well in ourselves and in our relationships."

Socio-emotional intelligence would then comprise:

1. refining our respective lenses of perception, and those of our students, to perceive a world marked by differences;
2. seeing the world through the eyes of the other;
3. modeling our awareness of our own responses to others for our students;
4. assisting our students to manage and respond appropriately without the threat of punishment or humiliation, to free themselves from aggressive behaviours;
5. valuing and respecting the lives and livelihoods of all others;
6. engaging in transformative change through meaningful interactions in collaborative groups;
7. seeking global social justice through generating discussions about deeply felt issues emerging in texts or classroom events;
8. exploring various solutions to classroom and school problems;
9. building relationships with students by communicating thoughtfully, empathizing when needed, and recognizing our own self-worth;
10. establishing a caring and nurturing learning environment..

Believing in empathy

Empathy on the teacher's part allows more learning to occur. If students sense the teacher is attempting to understand their position as learners, they will open their minds and try to establish connections, and a kind of circuit is established. As well, the teacher's own professional satisfaction deepens with the internal work of teaching, and both teacher and student are engaged in accelerated learning. Empathy isn't just about compassion; it also nourishes the connections between the students' minds and the new learning that is occurring. Empathetic teachers are able to understand the students' learning dynamic, and tune in to the flow of the thinking of the students. It is team building at its best, and it takes time to build trust on both sides.

Classroom management depends on the understanding that teachers and students have of each other, and tuning in to the feelings of others adds to the quality of the relationships in the classroom. But it mustn't be a co-dependent relationship; teachers must realize there are goals to be achieved, and high expectations are part of the process. However, if we are honest with our reasoning, open with our support, and require students to take action themselves, then we create a professional bond that clarifies the responsibility of teacher and student. There is no shame in asking for extra help for a student who has a particularly overwhelming problem. An effective school community will have procedures in place, and you and your students can benefit from this support.

FINDING VOICE THROUGH PHOTOGRAPHY
Lynda Marshall, secondary school literacy resource teacher, North Bay

The Photovoice project involved 14 boys with 14 digital cameras. The students were given the cameras and asked to photograph their lives outside of school. Handing them these cameras further developed the trust and mutual respect needed in a classroom. It also made the students active researchers, as well as participants. They were given a voice through photography. The boys were asked to document their photos through captions in either a writing journal or a video journal or both. These photographs were to include:

- physical environment — their homes, bedrooms, yards
- hobbies — Xbox, reading, television habits, skateboarding
- friends and get-togethers
- transportation — how they get to and from school, the mall, and movies
- extracurricular involvement
- out-of-school activities — sports, classes, and clubs
- people who are important in their lives
- what they are reading, wearing, and watching
- what they eat for breakfast, lunch, and dinner
- where they eat their meals
- family interactions

Documenting life journeys

Through picture and the written word, boys were given a voice. They were given permission to tell educators what they need in the classroom to be successful.

A few scenarios:

Tyler: Tyler announced he had nowhere to live. Of course, he could not take pictures like the other students. The other boys in the class were dumbfounded. They may all be from different backgrounds, beliefs, likes and dislikes, but they all had a home. Immediately, the class supported Tyler and echoed my own sentiment that I was so proud of him for being in his seat, in this class, period five, when he had no bed last night. Would he mind documenting his journey?

Tyler quickly agreed: he would call it his "couch-surfing adventure." True to his word, he shared daily, as he mowed lawns in exchange for a bed, bought broccoli for supper, and hung out with friends. Regardless of his lack of sleep, strange eating habits, and family problems, Tyler attended class every day, sharing and being supported by his peers, who were now his friends. At the end of the course, the boys were asked to respond to the most amazing, surprising, exciting, or unexpected outcome from this project: *Every* boy wrote about Tyler: Tyler with the droopy jeans, Tyler with the supposed attitude and the ear holes, Tyler with no home for three weeks. They wrote about how proud they were that he came to school and how much they respected him for his perseverance and resilience. They also wrote about appreciating their own homes and families even more after experiencing Tyler's journey.

Working with Multimodality by Jennifer Rowsell opens up the world of resources that schools can iprovide for interpreting and constructing meaning, from films to recordings to personal artifacts.

"Considering texts as sociocultural artifacts allows students to consider the artistic, structural, cultural, historical, political, and ideological ramifications of the production and reception of the texts students experience in and out of school contexts."

Frank Serafini, *Multimodal Literacy: From Theories to Practice*

Shane: Shane waited a few days before speaking out. He watched the photographs of his classmates' bedrooms, PlayStations, families, collections, and so on before raising his hand to say, "Ms. Marshall, I don't actually have a bedroom, so I do not know what to take pictures of for my project." The class went quiet as I asked, "Where do you sleep?" Shane explained that he slept in the living room at his house. He was afraid that when sharing began, the students might have made jokes or comments or ignored him.

Due to the sharing and the trust that had been building so quickly through Photovoice, the boys supported Shane immediately. They made comments like, "Cool! Do you get to kick everyone out of your room when you want to sleep?" and "I guess you get the TV all to yourself whenever you want? Must be great to watch the basketball games!" For Shane, a teenage boy, to share this information with a group like this is very telling. The instant support he received catapulted him into photographing every corner of his home, his yard, his family, and many other intimate parts of his world. He stood proud knowing he had nothing to hide.

REMEMBERING THE HOMELESS STUDENTS

David Goldberg, PhD, homeless youth scholar, student advocate, and teacher

In Canada, about 150,000 young people are homeless. In homelessness, these youth are dislocated and shunted aside—from a secure home, a stable community, a safe accommodation, and school itself. With a transient lifestyle, and uncertainty about where they will sleep and safely store their belongings, attending school on a daily basis presents difficult challenges. With scant social and political capital, these young peoples' voices are unheard—they are truly forgotten in schools and in larger society.

My doctoral research with 35 homeless male and female youth revealed a profound lack of connection between these young people and school. The youth explained that after class, teachers rush out to the next one, precluding a closer relationship. They said they had no connection with administrators, coaches, or other staff either. Tellingly, they shared that they could never divulge their home situation to *any* teachers or staff, for fear this information would "leak out." They dreaded the ridicule and stigmatization they said would result.

Schools are in a difficult bind with the topic of youth homelessness: what happens if a young person acts out, becomes stressed, or deeply depressed just by raising the topic? What happens if some parents complain that they keep their children safe and become angry that the school introduces other notions to their child? By avoiding the topic altogether, homeless youth are "erased" from the school curriculum, making it difficult for these young people to even recognize themselves in educational materials, never mind sharing their difficulties with teachers or staff.

I propose that schools broach youth homelessness in a gradual—and structured way. Accordingly, I suggest that a "Homeless Youth Day in Schools" transpire in a single day during the school year. High school students would research any aspect of youth homelessness that interests them including emergency crisis shelters, resiliency, depression, self-esteem, and, if appropriate, drugs. Some homeless youth could attend such a session, to answer questions, or to present artworks such as drama, visual art, or performance, about their experiences in homelessness. In my research, for instance, many youth generated outstanding artworks, in a variety of media, to represent their experiences—and struggles in homelessness.

Unlike the pervasive stereotypes about them, a "Homeless Youth Day in Schools" would reveal that homeless youth do have goals, intelligence, and much to offer their peers in an educational setting. Indeed, many of these young people survive homelessness because of their resilience, adaptability and intelligence. Just because they are thrust on the "margins of society" doesn't mean they stop learning; indeed, their learning is accelerated, especially given that their very lives are at stake. In closing, rather than passively "remembering" forgotten homeless students; we need to actively create safe spaces for *all* young people to partake in organized educational opportunities that are rightfully theirs.

5. Be aware of ego, self-efficacy, and confidence

Building a "teacherly" self

How can teachers begin the journey toward self-empowerment, professional self-worth or self-efficacy? With the challenges we have touched on, teachers need to build a "teacherly self" confident enough to move past mistakes or lack of knowledge, and recognize how we can change or adapt our experiences to present circumstances.

The term "adaptive confidence" is a good frame for determining how we can move past naivety, ignorance, stubbornness, ego, habit — all those characteristics we use to protect ourselves against perceived failures. What matters is that we can reflect and come to know how to change those actions, to transform them into stronger responses that will have greater effect on us and our colleagues and students. As the teacher becomes more confident, interactions with the students become more intrinsically engaging; we begin to understand the flow of teaching and learning, and "job satisfaction" moves teacher and students forward in the educational tasks at hand. It actually becomes easier to teach well than to not care.

THE IMPORTANCE OF A HEALTHY EGO

Mark Phillips, blogger, Edutopia, 17/07/2015

Teacher invisibility vs. being the centre of attention

Do you thrive on being the centre of attention? I did. I played out all of my ego needs to be the star lecturer, performer, comedian, actor, and conductor. I brought all of these sub-selves into my classroom. This wasn't bad for me, and I don't recall it being bad for my students. It met my ego needs and often seemed successful. But eventually I learned that there were many times when my class was better served by activities in which I more or less disappeared. When students worked successfully in small groups, I found myself feeling a void and struggled not to intervene or in some way be a strong, active presence. I knew that the minute I stepped into a group, I'd disturb its equilibrium and diminish its effectiveness in peer interaction. I had to struggle with my ego's need to be the star at centre stage.

Teacher ego and the connection to students

Here's a really tricky one. How do we maintain our own boundaries when we feel a deep connection with a student? Most often, this is a student who clearly feels close to us or would like to be. At one end of the spectrum is unprofessional behavior in forming an intimate emotional relationship (or more) with a student that we're attracted to. But this is the extreme. More often, the challenge is to avoid connecting with a student so closely that we lose our objectivity.

Balancing ego health with effective teaching

Our mission as teachers is transcending our own ego satisfaction, needs, and stories to focus on our students and what's good for them.
Doing something that we must do but that we know will cause a student to feel bad can challenge our need to be the nice guy.

Using our authority can feed our need to be in control and feel powerful. For me, something as subtle as creating an environment in which I became almost invisible while students helped each other was the best challenge that I overcame.

A core of healthy ego strength makes it much easier to focus more on what's best for our students and less on making ourselves feel important. And in terms of overall teacher well-being, the more that our daily life outside of the classroom meets our needs, the less likely that we'll need our teaching and our students to feed our ego.

"All human knowledge draws its sustenance from corporeal roots. Mind is inextricably biological and embodied: and what it can know is always grounded in the material and experiential world."

Wayne Bowman, (2004) "Cognition and the Body: Perspectives from Music Education".

BELIEVING IN HUMILITY

Jack Miller, professor of holistic education, OISE/University of Toronto

Humility is that place where we leave our ego needs aside and meet others in a place best described by Rumi: "Out beyond ideas of wrongdoing and right-doing, there is a field. I'll meet you there." This field is also a good place for teachers and students to meet. There is a mystery in teaching: we never fully know how we have made a difference in the lives of students. A sense of mystery is truly humbling and is often lacking in the talking heads on television and in the academy. Humility and awareness of the mystery bring an openness. Teachers need to have this openness to deal with the wonders and complexities of teaching. Of course, teachers need to develop knowledge of subject matter and have good lesson plans but more importantly they need to be able to work with what has been called the "teachable moment" that can arise at any time. This moment can be an incident on the playground that needs discussion or something that arises in the life of a student.

Teachers who have the qualities of humility and openness are able to create spaces where children flourish. In this environment students feel cared for. They realize that they are more important than any prescribed "outcome" set by the board or ministry of education.

I have been doing meditation practice for over 40 years and since the early 1990s I have been fortunate to have a teacher who has embodied humility and openness. Norman Feldman studied for years in Asia and his understanding of meditation practice has been helpful to so many students. His teaching is done in a manner that empowers each of his students. Once he was asked what characterizes a wise person and he responded that

Holistic Education and Embodied Learning, edited by John P. Miller and Kelli Nigh, is a collection of articles that add to our understanding of the holistic classroom and the holistic teacher:

wise people do not talk about themselves. This leaves a space for genuine conversation and dialogue.

Humility is closely linked with other important qualities such as compassion and wisdom that are also central to good teaching. Humility allows us to truly listen to our students; out of this listening compassion and wisdom can arise. It means not getting lost in dogmas or ideologies that prevent teachers from being truly present to their students. From this presence, deep learning can occur.

A BALANCED PROFESSIONAL AND PERSONAL LIFE

Maintaining your health (mental, physical, spiritual, social) means actively caring for yourself, building in time to renew, to distance yourself from school issues, to take a break or a holiday. Rich is a sports fan; David sees all the new plays. Of course at times we have fallen victim to our own weaknesses as overly committed and compulsive teachers. Since authentic learning and teaching are so overwhelming, we have had to struggle to add balance to our lives, and we have been fortunate to continue our work without "jobs," researching, visiting and working with students and teachers, running educational courses, speaking at conferences. Teachers who work in schools from 8 to 5, who participate in sports or the arts, who continue their professional growth, still need to find time to change venues at least one night a week or one day a weekend, to plan holidays, play tennis, grow flowers, paint pictures, make quilts, drive their own kids to sports games. We need to value breaks and rest and recreation. And often a summer course or conference in another country has provided welcome change and restored our energy. In his paper "Self-Efficacy Mechanism in Physiological Activation and Health-Promoting Behavior," psychologist Albert Bandura writes that

> Perceived self-efficacy is concerned with people's beliefs in their capabilities to exercise control over their own functioning and over events that affect their lives. Beliefs in personal efficacy affect life choices, level of motivation, quality of functioning, resilience to adversity and vulnerability to stress and depression. People's beliefs in their efficacy are developed by four main sources of influence. They include mastery experiences, seeing people similar to oneself manage task demands successfully, social persuasion that one has the capabilities to succeed in given activities, and inferences from somatic and emotional states indicative of personal strengths and vulnerabilities. Ordinary realities are strewn with impediments, adversities, setbacks, frustrations and inequities. People must, therefore, have a robust sense of efficacy to sustain the perseverant effort needed to succeed. Succeeding periods of life present new types of competency demands requiring further development of personal efficacy for successful functioning. The nature and scope of perceived self-efficacy undergo changes throughout the course of the lifespan.

6. Build a classroom community

Teachers who feel empowered want their students to think of themselves in similar ways. There are many aspects of their lives that students can control, and we can set parameters that encourage them to do so, to take responsibility for what they can control, and to examine with others the things that upset them so that they can explore ways of coping. To be a functioning member of a classroom community, students need a sense of ownership, a feeling that their voices will be heard. A classroom is not a democracy, but students should feel that they have a say in how members operate within a system for maximum effectiveness.

We can organize activities that help students to know each other and themselves better. Take time for class meetings, community circles, appreciation and gratitude comments, memory books, community service. If we feel there is no time for these types of community building, we are limiting the emotional and psychological and social well-being of our students, and as teachers we know we can increase learning in a safe and supportive, culturally respectful environment.

As good teachers, we try to create a safe and trusting classroom and school environment, considering the physical, social, and emotional well-being of all our students. Anti-bullying has become a crucial component of school values, and a class that has developed trust for each member and the teacher is most likely to handle issues of unfair treatment of students. There are different effective strategies for promoting responsible and equitable behaviours, including group dynamic exercises, morning meetings, and student councils. Discussion groups such a literature circles allow for student voices to be heard and for points of view to be argued and clarified.

Reflecting on classroom community

- Students in many classrooms come from a variety of linguistic, cultural, and social backgrounds. How can you and your school honour each family's way of life and at the same time develop a sense of school and classroom community?
- Are contributions from the students expected and welcomed in your classroom?
- Are there situations that require students to talk in pairs, in small groups, and as a class, so that the listening and speaking grow naturally from activities that the students regard as real and important?
- Do you keep dialogue journals with your students, on paper or online, where you share and model your own views and responses?
- Do you build your programs around content of real interest to the students, perhaps organized into thematic or genre units, rather than only around sets of skills?
- Do the students feel responsible for deciding at times what they will read and write and how they will interact with others during group activities?
- Does the way you organize your time allow for individual conferences and interviews, small-group mini-lessons on particular skills, and whole-class information and sharing sessions?
- Are the students helping one another become better readers and writers and problem-solvers, leaving you more time to work with individuals and groups?
- How can you include volunteers in the classroom to help you and the students?
- Consider in what ways parents, student-teachers, older student buddies, and invited guests can participate in your classroom.

- Consider occasions you can organize in your program for students to interact formally and informally with a variety of audiences: friends, younger or older buddies, and members of the broader community.
- What resource staff does your school provide for working with students with special needs in the regular classroom?
- How can you structure your program to make best use of their help in a classroom of students with different abilities and experiences?
- What changes might you make in your own personal attitudes and approaches to students branded with labels if you are to create a school environment that engages them in significant learning events?
- Some schools have used parents as researchers, involving them in drawing up questionnaires, holding interviews, and analyzing results and reactions. As a result, parents become informed about the school community and the programs being implemented. Can you organize a project for your area that would include parents in a significant way?

Educator Kathy Lundy's books offer ideas and examples of classrooms that present caring and safe places for students' school lives. See What Do I Do about the Kid Who…, Teaching Fairly in an Unfair World, *and* Creating Caring Classrooms, *co-authored with Larry Swartz.*

RELATIONSHIP AND RELEVANCE: HOW TWO MIDDLE-SCHOOL TEACHERS APPROACH THEIR STUDENTS

Monica McGlynn-Stewart, PhD, professor, School of Early Childhood, George Brown College

When I walked into Kelly's and Kendra's classrooms for the first time, I was immediately struck by the relaxed, yet purposeful way their students worked. They smiled at one another, appeared to get along well, and worked cooperatively. Classroom discussions were lively, with most students offering an answer or opinion. The teachers were warm and supportive, and everyone seemed "at home" in the classroom. I spoke to the teachers several times over the first years of their teaching to try to understand how they had achieved these positive learning environments.

Both teachers are now teaching in large, diverse urban schools in Central Canada — neither teacher expected to be a literacy teacher. Kendra specialized in teaching Mathematics and Kelly in Physical Education and Health during their pre-service education. While they have taught these subjects over the first four years of their teaching, they also have been the home-room literacy teacher.

Like all new literacy teachers, Kendra and Kelly worry that they don't know enough about literacy or how to teach it effectively. This concern has motivated them to continually seek out new learning opportunities in the form of teacher resources, workshops, courses, and mentoring from more experienced teachers.

Forming positive relationships

In order to build relationships with her students, Kendra takes the time to talk to them about their interests and activities outside of school. Doing this builds trust that allows the students to take learning risks in the classroom.

While the students are working, Kendra schedules mini-conferences to check in with the students to see how they are doing. The content of the conference may be an academic issue, but it doesn't have to be. It is the regular, predictable, personal contact that is important.

In addition to this in-class check-in time, Kendra has organized an after-school homework club for all the Grades 7 and 8 students. For some of the students who come, this is a time for needed academic help; for others, it is a time for extra encouragement and emotional support.

Kelly, too, uses mini-conferences to get to know her students and to build trusting relationships with them. She knows that if the students are not feeling safe socially and emotionally, then effective learning is unlikely to occur. She establishes the goals for her program by trying to put herself in her students' shoes: "If I was in Grade 8, and feeling really insecure with myself and socially awkward and going through puberty, I wouldn't want to be singled out in class and made to feel stupid."

The importance of classroom community

In addition to building positive relationships with individual students, Kelly and Kendra work hard to establish supportive classroom communities. According to Kelly, achieving this begins with the students' belief that the teacher likes the class and wants to be with them. "I like helping them and I like being here," she says, "and I think the kids can pick up on that energy." Kendra makes sure that there is always time for the class to enjoy one another's company through celebrating accomplishments, playing group games, or doing Tribes activities (a professional development program). Both teachers use classroom jobs, such as tending to class pets or dealing with recycling, to give their students a sense of ownership in the classroom.

Kendra and Kelly find that the more organized and clear they are, the more organized and less anxious their students are. Fostering this includes putting a weekly and daily agenda on the board so the students know what to expect and ensuring that materials are accessible so the students can get what they need.

Finally, Kendra and Kelly believe that if they want their classrooms to function as positive communities, then they need to be models of appropriate, respectful behavior, and gently but firmly call the students on their behavior when they are less than respectful to one another.

Relevant curriculum content

Kendra uses newspapers to link current events to concepts in the curriculum. She brings in articles, but also encourages the students to bring in articles and to form opinions about what they are reading. "It's not just show and tell anymore," she says. In addition, at the end of each math unit, the students need to complete a project that demonstrates their understanding of the usefulness of the concepts "just to show them that things have a real-life application — it's not all about tests."

Kelly works to connect what she is teaching to what is going on in the world and to her students' immediate lives. She says, "I try hard to make it applicable to their lives and their interests." If the students are reading *Twilight* and love making comics on the computer, she works that into her literacy program. She is always on the lookout for opportunities to teach "life lessons," to point out how what they are studying matters in their everyday life.

Early in their teaching careers, Kelly and Kendra have discovered the benefits that result from focusing on positive relationships and classroom communities, and relevant content and teaching practices. This respectful approach, coupled with their ongoing professional development, will ensure that they continue to grow as teachers and to deepen their understanding of literacy teaching and learning.

7. Be willing to innovate, adapt, experiment, change, and grow

Focus: Remembering and growing from our mistakes

David Booth

As beginning teachers, we often start by transmitting information and procedures, and then move toward a holistic and transformational understanding of how we will affect students. We may be nervous or afraid of difficult students, and want to achieve as much success as possible in this context and at this time with every student; we may have pigeonholed students as being achieving or non-achieving individuals, but we need to help them realize all of them can learn.

- The successful teacher isn't afraid to make changes to mix things up throughout the year. A stagnant learning environment might lead to disengaged students, so don't be afraid to begin with small changes, such as rearranging the room, redecorating the bulletin boards, etc.
- It is impossible to reflect on our teaching lives without recurring personal flashbacks to times when the learning went awry. As vulnerable teachers, we may be haunted by those painful student lessons frozen in time, but we must try to banish them with our extensive professional experiences, to come to understand why we did what we did, so that we can move forward in our theory-informed practice and research.
- Peter Duffy's goal for his book, *A Reflective Practitioner's Guide to (Mis) Adventures in Drama Education — or — What Was I Thinking?* was certainly achieved: "a counter-narrative to the success stories that permeate our field's literature." Reading about teaching philosophies and practice that have been transformed through reflection and research gives us hope for the possibilities of our own growth, and reminds us that risk is at the heart of teaching.

Duffy describes the painful processes involved in the recounting of disappointment or of disruption in a lesson, and then the integration of new insights and changed practice. Conversations about our professional growth allow us to take our students' "felt" responses into account as we move forward; they become adjuncts and advocates for our own learning; the student responses generate new learning for us as co-constructors of professional knowledge. It was helpful to me as I reread the book to note similarities and differences among the teaching/learning concerns, and to recognize my own misdirections. I am a card-carrying member with fifty years of misadventures to draw upon.

As drama educator Dorothy Heathcote taught us, we can and do change as we work, reflecting in action, through to the next development in the lesson, and then reconsider our efforts as we regroup for the next session, the next time, the next event. We stand on the shoulders of those who shared their misadventures with us, who worked with us to find new options, new ways of making meaning in this art form. Emily Dickinson wrote, "I dwell in possibility," and that may be what reflection really points us toward—the options, the choices, and the potential we somehow recognize in our students as we struggle to teach so they can learn.

We can engage in classroom research as professional development. Teachers in many areas have opportunities for professional development in a variety of venues: school teams can explore together a curriculum area, finding research that offers new thoughts and directions for classroom practise; teachers can engage their students in an action-based research project, where they become active participants in an inquiry that can add to everyone's understanding; teachers can work with a visiting colleague from a university or central office, looking at new ways to interact with a complex aspect of the curriculum; teachers can offer to work on developing guidelines with district, provincial or state departments of education; teachers can share information or resources from courses or conferences they have attended.

We carry memories of children at risk forever, and often they act as change agents for our teaching. As we meet new students with similar problems, we scan our past recollections to redesign our responses from the always looming shadows in our teaching psyches. We need to learn from our unsuccessful episodes with children and families as we try to invent new teaching selves, just as when we view a videotape record of who we used to be, and shudder, even tremble, at our past teaching personas and behaviours.

Rather than forgetting these children or being afraid of meeting them in the future, we need to reuse these memory icons to help locate us in the present, to support our new professional knowledge of helping children and parents inside the school community.

In spite of our best efforts, we are sometimes unable to offer enough supportive strategies to a child in difficulty to ensure a successful school life. And it may be that some children will need other environments, other structures, in order to progress. But to paraphrase the psychoanalyst D. W. Winnicott, we have to be "the good enough teacher," and for me, therein lies the struggle. I need to know that I did all that I could at that time in those circumstances with that particular child. By remembering that experience, I look at every new child differently. I have the opportunity to grow wiser because of that special child.

As teachers, we read and take courses and talk to other professionals. Knowing what we couldn't do, didn't do, and might now do, is how we grow professionally. Next time, perhaps, we will prepare differently for the meeting with the parent: we will review the child's portfolio of work, highlighting examples of her or his progress; we will create an action plan for school and home that works toward the child's social growth; we will find a booklet or an article (or an outside agency) that offers help for the parent; I will interview the child in order to have her or his own words to point towards change; I will have a practice interview with the principal to smooth out the wrinkles in my own approach; and after the interview, I will debrief with a school leader to move toward a professional response to the situation. And if the child leaves, I will follow up with a supportive note to the family, wishing them success in finding a more effective placement for the child they love.

The case studies that every teacher carries forever are not records of failure to disturb our sleep. Instead, they are signposts, computer icons to click on, which signal future possibilities in interacting with children and parents. Schools are integral aspects of a family's community. And those families come in all kinds of configurations, with all types of needs and wants. I still think that most children have satisfying and nurturing school lives, and that most parents recognize the inherent values of the schools where their children spend most of childhood.

The "felt imperative" to help every child in our care is a good one for every teacher to experience; perhaps it has to be tempered with our professional sense of having done everything we could at that time for that child, strengthened by

The full essay for this focus can be found in Cases for Teacher Development, *edited by Patricia F. Goldblatt and Déirdre Smith.*

the knowledge that the experience will nudge us toward new understandings in our relationships with the children and their parents, in the place called school.

EMBRACING CHANGE IN NORTHERN CANADIAN RURAL AND INDIGENOUS SCHOOLS

Shelley Stagg Peterson, professor, OISE/University of Toronto

My experience with kindergarten, grade one, and Aboriginal Head Start teachers in northern rural and Indigenous communities in two Canadian provinces has convinced me that mutual respect as a foundation for building trusting relationships is key to stimulating change in teachers' practice. Mutual respect takes the form of starting with what is important to teachers, the needs that they identify. In the case of my Northern Oral Language and Writing through Play (NOW Play) project, the collaborative action research projects are based on teachers' concerns that their students' oral language was not at levels needed to support literacy and all learning. Teachers wanted to know more about how to support children's oral language.

Mutual respect is inherent in university researchers' ongoing support over three years; support that honours teachers' knowledge and experiences and encourages teachers to build on what they are already doing or to try out a version of what colleagues share about their practices in collaborative action research meetings. It is important that university researchers respect participating teachers for the risks they take in opening up their classrooms to researchers from distant urban universities and make their practice the focus of research discussions.

The role of a university researcher supporting collaborative action research for change is not to do workshops, nor to provide advice, but rather to highlight ways in which teachers' practice aligns with and extends previous research based on classroom data. In the NOW Play project, the foci of these conversations are video recordings of children's interactions during various play contexts. Trusting relationships are built when teachers and university researchers are co-creators of tangible tools and approaches that evolve through discussions of the data that teachers and university researchers gather.

A teacher in the NOW Play project talked about the change process as being gradual and requiring her ongoing, active involvement in a focus group conversation.

The oral language assessment tool was a long way from being a usable thing when we first started those discussions. And that's been a big surprise for me, how that has developed…going back, looking at your class, trying it with a few kids in your class, and then coming back in that conversation that happens around the table. Yeah, that was interesting, how that came together.

When the tangible tools are shared publicly, participating teachers come to see themselves as researchers who make valuable contributions to professional knowledge beyond their northern communities.

Focus: Two adaptive teachers
Rich Coles

Suman and Anna are young teachers in the early years of their careers. Both have classes in English/Language Arts. Their students read a selection of short stories, young adult novels, and poetry. Anna selects most of the reading materials for her students. After reading, the students complete a series of questions or a book report. To prepare her program, Anna thought about her own experiences reading in school, talked with her colleagues, and read some professional materials. Over time she became more proficient developing, refining, and modifying the reading questions and the book report assignment.

Suman wants her students to make deeper transactions with the texts they read and to become more engaged in their learning. She selected some of the reading materials but also developed with her students effective and practical strategies for selecting a wide range of materials such as picture books, short stories, novels, books of jokes and riddles, poetry, spoken word, and popular song lyrics. Their reader responses to these works have included: drama activities, visual arts activities, online blogs, dialogue journals, and author profiles.

Anna and Suman followed the same procedures in different facets of their teaching. Anna first developed routines for classroom management, assessment, and evaluation. Over a period of a few years she applied these procedures with greater efficiency. Suman developed, refined, and incorporated new strategies for classroom management and assessment and evaluation. Both teachers are continuing to learn during their teaching careers. To some extent, Anna is what Hatano and Osura call a "routine expert" whereas Suman is an "adaptive expert." Routine experts develop a set of competencies and then apply them over time with greater efficiency. Adaptive experts refine, sometimes change, and add to their core competencies. They continue to expand the scope and depth of their expertise. Anna based some of her classroom practices on her own learning experiences. This *apprenticeship of observation* describes teachers developing practices based on their own experiences. However, even in the classroom of an exceptional teacher, observations alone do not lead to a deep understanding of the complexities of teaching. Teaching expertise is not simply a collection of disconnected facts. Rather, expert teaching involves knowing when it is appropriate and how to apply important concepts and procedures.

When Suman wants to adapt new procedures,— for example, small group discussion — she grapples with learning the new discussion procedures. She is challenged when refining these procedures for her particular group of learners. These processes lead to innovation in her teaching.

Our worlds are constantly reshaping and changing. Think about your world when you were sixteen, starting university or teaching. Adaptive expertise today is essential for success in teaching and in non-academic settings.

For more on this subject, see Thank You for Being Late: An Optimist's Guide to Thriving in the Age of Accelerations *by T.L. Friendman; G. Hatano, and Y. Osura; "Commentary: Reconceptualizing School Learning Using Insight from Expert Research" by G. Hatano and Y. Osura, in* Educational Researcher, *32(8); and* Schoolteacher; A Sociological Study, *by D.C. Lortie.*

STIMULATING A CULTURE OF INNOVATIVE THINKING IN EDUCATION
Catherine MacKinnon, PhD, university instructor

> As our world shifts from a manufacturing economy to the ever-increasing information age, teachers are demonstrating through their practice the need for balance between 'learning' and 'knowing.' We now realize that what students know is less important than what they can do with what they know. Teachers are charting a new course to arrive at an innovative culture

of thinking. In fact, *Harvard Business Review* (March-April 2017) states that within our global economy today, financial capital is no longer the most precious resource for any competitive advantage. It is human capital, having a work force which can generate ideas, critically analyze those ideas, and then translate them towards successful outcomes.

At Niagara University's College of Education, I had the opportunity to teach a course on Leadership and Innovative Thinking in Education. The class consisted of a group of Master's students who were also full-time classroom teachers. The **Essential Question** driving the course: What does innovation in education look like? In the book *Creating Innovators: The Making of Young People Who Will Change the World*, Tony Wagner asserts that the skills students need for careers, continuous learning, and citizenship are vital to their well-being as adults. Skills in critical thinking and problem solving, collaboration, adaptability, initiative, curiosity and imagination, along with effective written and oral communication are, as Wagner defines them, 'survival skills.'

The course on *Leadership and Innovative Thinking* followed closely on the heels of the 2016 presidential election in the United States. Class discussions often turned to the recurring trend of news reports that were being supplanted by "alternative facts" and "fake news" stories. Sandra, a grade five teacher in the course, revealed that her students, while captivated constantly by various media sites, often lacked the skills to correctly analyze and interpret what they were reading. As national attention to fake news, and what to do about it, continued, Sandra took the issue to the classroom. Taking up the challenge, she came up with a creative solution to strengthen her students' ability to tell 'real' news from 'fake' news, and ultimately assist them in becoming less vulnerable to getting fooled by what they read in the media. Here is Sandra's version of how to fight fake news in the classroom.

To begin, Sandra emphasized an inquiry-based approach to learning. She first asked students what they would look for and need to know to determine if a story contained credible sources of information, or, if the story made false claims designed to persuade or influence them. She began by exploring various social media sites with her students and discussed the difference between a persuasive opinion piece and a reported news article.

To start the game "Ring of Truth," Sandra grouped her students in pairs. She sent each group of students an article to read on their iPads. Students were given five to ten minutes to read the article and decide if the story had the "ring of truth" or not. They had to read the article carefully, use their judgment, and examine its source. Students who thought the article was '"real" rang a bell on their desks. Students who were non-believers remained silent. It was not ringing the bell that gained points in the game but deciding correctly whether the story was real or not. Most importantly students had to explain why they thought an article was fake or real to obtain points.

In supporting students to look carefully at what they were reading, Sandra gave the class a seven-point check list to follow:

- How current is the information?
- Does it have a copyright?
- Do you know who the source is? Is the source valid? (example, *National Geographic*, About.com., or questionable, Wikipedia.)
- Does the information make sense? Do you understand the information you have read?

- Can you verify that the information agrees with two or more other sources that are reliable?
- Have experts in the field been connected to it or authored other articles on the subject?
- How does the article compare to what you already know?

In a follow-up to her lesson, Sandra had students choose two real articles on a given topic and then write a fake article of their own. The challenge for students was having to use subtle changes to make their own fake news story believable. After completing this task students presented the three articles to another class in the school. Students were given time to do some research based on the presentations and then decided which article of the three used "alternative facts." Again, students had to explain their choices and give reasons why they thought an article had been "made up."

The "Ring of Truth" game gave Sandra's class an opportunity to explore real world issues, develop critical thinking skills, and practice effective written communication. Perhaps more importantly, the exercise was helping students to become wiser citizens through community and global engagement.

8. Support critical and creative meaning making

> "Great teaching traffics in enduring puzzlements, persistent dilemmas, complex conundrums, enigmatic paradoxes. Great ideas have legs. They take you somewhere."
>
> Elliot Eisner

- We can build a classroom culture of collaborative discovery.
- Welcome puzzlements; they open us to new avenues of thought.
- Value student-generated questions; they can lead to true learning.
- Wandering is the first step in arriving at valuable questions.
- Wondering moves us into different ways of seeing and being.
- Opening ourselves to possibilities creates mindfulness.
- Pondering a puzzlement focuses and directs our energies.
- We need to explore big ideas, for they will take us further.
- Hidden truths emerge through active exploration.
- We can value the imaginative responses of all.
- We need to view creativity as a vital factor in problem solving.
- The suggestions of others can strengthen our own thoughts.
- Inquiry is an ally in examining issues, dilemmas, and conundrums.
- Expression through word and image generates new puzzlements.
- Recognize the unexpected connections students will make.
- Reflection allows us to alter, adapt, rethink, and grow.

Critical thinking

We want to encourage critical understanding in our classrooms, to create situations in which students can engage in thoughtful, critical, and collaborative conversations about a text, their responses to it, and those of their classmates. We want to build a collegial atmosphere that allows for problematic issues and challenges that involve critical thinking as a way of moving towards deeper understanding. We can offer our students tools for critical understanding, the knowledge and strategies for responding thoughtfully and critically to issues that arise in and out of the classroom. We want critical understanding to become a habit of mind. This approach requires a school culture that supports such an action-oriented

In David Booth's book It's Critical, teachers from various grades describe their methods for implementing critical understanding in their classrooms.

process, but this attitude and way of thinking towards social change can be developed in individuals in incremental steps. For example, even when writing their life stories from personal memories, students can come to recognize how aspects of culture, power roles, and social relationships are brought to light.

Consider the importance of critical understanding on the Internet. Students are surfing the Web and constructing their own individualized texts, evaluating sites, processing information, and interpreting data, so that they can connect themselves to the world. Critical understanding is now seen as a mainstream strategy. We want to encourage students to become more critical in their use of all media, including the Internet; therefore, we need to teach them to be active and critical readers and viewers, who can make the most connections possible.

Interactive learning that is transformative

Teachers can incorporate learning strategies that will engage students in thoughtful dialogue and discussion as a class, in groups, and with partners. These opportunities may challenge the students' personal thinking and that of their peers in meaningful ways, so that they are constantly reflecting on their learning, increasing, altering, modifying, and deepening their understanding through collaborative and cooperative events.

These experiences can be transformative in their lives: the student builds on others' talk, takes turns, recognizes points of view, carries the conversation forward, modifies and adapts ideas, links to the ideas of others, explores and questions, accepts or adopts the role of group leader, initiates conversation with the teacher, looks for alternative solutions and suggests new lines of discussion, reveals feelings, shares personal anecdotes, and relates new information to be known. This interplay among learners supports meaning making in every discipline and creates shared understandings as individuals recognize how their own views and perceptions affect the thinking of the other participants in their learning.

CRITICAL PEDAGOGY: THOUGHTS ABOUT THEORY AND PRACTICE
Muhammad Enamul Huque, PhD, arts and education consultant

> The useful teacher's traits involving pre-secondary education in multicultural nations may include the knowledge of critical pedagogy and its adaptability in classrooms. They can contribute to students' academic success and enhance their qualities needed for developing informed, engaged, and compassionate citizenship.
>
> ### 1. Theory-linked inspiration
> Critical pedagogy followed the tradition of critical education in the early 1980s as a new field that Giroux (1997) portrays as "language of possibility." With links to the idea of social justice it accommodates the "critique of racism, sexism, and other marginalities."
>
> Its "political" dimensions may discourage some teachers from adopting it for their classrooms. However, education is not a value-neutral or apolitical enterprise. It has key players with vested interests that shape the curricula, applications, resources, and beneficiaries. Therefore, Freire and Macedo (1987) suggest, "it is necessary for educators to assume a political posture that renounces the myth of pedagogical neutrality" concerning the

marginalities mentioned above. For social transformation "teachers are in no way powerless [because] ... the classroom is a microcosm of the wider society" (Cummins, 1997) and small changes there affect the world beyond.

2. Signposts for the journey: From theory to practice

Cho (2013) correctly points out that terms like "social justice" are abstract concepts; therefore, their application into "concrete forms of alternative education" poses real challenge for teachers. Incorporation of "multiplicity" in teaching is a way of meeting this challenge, and "the main way to insert multiplicity into critical pedagogy is through inclusion"

Usually a "curriculum" is the backbone for classroom teaching, but it "is not just a matter of what someone is supposed to know, but also what they are supposed to do with it" (Inglis, 1985). The idea of *Identity Texts* may contribute to the "doing" part of curriculum. According to Cummins and Early (2011), Identity Texts are multimodal creative works (represented in individual or combined forms involving written, spoken, signed, visual, musical, and dramatic works) produced by students within the "pedagogical space orchestrated by classroom teacher[s]" where students' identities are positively reflected.

Creativity, each student's identity, and its positive portrayal are important elements of Identity Texts, and they can make positive contributions to students' academic success and beyond. For example, creativity is a key for overcoming adversity, and an ability to define and present one's identity in a positive light is a skill that can play a critical role in any form of discourse within or outside classrooms.

Strategies for promoting critical thinking

My classroom observations in multiple schools around the Greater Toronto Area associated with research projects and my living experience as a "visible minority" immigrant in Canada have contributed to the preparation of this list:

* **Choose an identity-sensitive topic** (e.g., "My family's journey as a refugee").
* **Include a role for each student's first language, if other than English, in work assignments** (tools like Google Translate can facilitate the process).
* **Use a variety of media** (e.g., handmade or electronic books, audiovisual presentations, scripted videos, puppet theatres, spoken words, embroidered quilts, and so on can carry equal weight to serve the unique needs of students).
* **Include non-European cultures, traditions, and philosophies** (e.g., geographies, histories, time periods, arts, oral/written expressions, foods, customs, religions and so on of a wide range of nations can be accommodated with critical perspectives).
* **Make bias-free uses of technologies** (e.g., no automatic rejection/ acceptance of old/new technologies for the task in hand without an evaluation of their appropriateness).
* **Value all forms of human talents** (e.g., students' inherent strengths/ weaknesses can play a role in designing, implementing, and evaluating their works. We may recall here Howard Gardner's *Theory of Multiple Intelligences*).

* **Make room for contributions from family and beyond** (e.g., parents' and grandparents' wisdom, knowledge, and life experiences can be tapped to enrich students' work).
* **Remember students' needs** (e.g., work assignments may reflect students' needs, hopes, and problems where applied and observed creativities can enrich their problem-solving skills).

Focus: Creative meaning making
Rich Coles

> "Creative learning results in deeper understanding, not just memorization of surface facts. Creativity involves knowing how to think, reason, and argue-and how to explore further, ask the next question, and find the answer. When you learn this way, you're more able to use your knowledge in the real world."
>
> Keith Sawyer, *Zig Zag: The Surprising Path to Greater Creativity*

When you hear the word *creativity* what comes to mind? Great works of literature, visual texts and photographs, sculptures, architecture, music, drama or dance, mindboggling mathematicians, renowned chefs, prominent engineers, trend-inspiring fashion designers or innovative urban planners. From your own knowledge and experiences, you can easily provide many names for each of these examples. Although many of these celebrated creative individuals and groups — e.g. Picasso or the Beatles — are well-known, creativity does not require fame or high-level achievement. Many famous people are not creative. Many individuals are creative in their daily lives but are not famous. Think about someone you know who is creative in her or his daily life but not famous or well-known. In education, the focus is on developing the creative potential of all learners, not just those who are known for their performances or their inventive products. And for many years creative scholars have generated convincing evidence about the relationship between creativity and learning.

Numerous definitions of creativity have two common components: originality (new, novel, original, unique) but also task-appropriate. Lip syncing an Adele song would not be considered novel or unique. Serving small pebbles in a sandwich is new and unique but not appropriate. Social, cultural, and historical context determines if something is original or task-appropriate.

Teachers play a vital role in cultivating students' creativity in the classroom. They create an environment that is stimulating but also provides time for quiet reflection. Classrooms have many resources for multisensory engagement and are safe places for taking risks, pushing boundaries, asking questions, and being wrong. Students use their imaginations in all subject areas to develop flexible and divergent thinking (original, surprising or unexpected ideas) as well as convergent thinking. Creators, innovators, and artists are often divergent thinkers. CEOs from numerous industries identified divergent thinking as a critical factor for success.

Young children know how to be divergent thinkers. They can generate many imaginative solutions to a problem. George Land gave more than 1,000 children tests dealing with divergent thinking. In the 3-to-5 age group 98 percent scored in the top-tier "creative genius" level. Five years later only 32 percent scored in this level. After an additional five years only 10 percent of the same young people achieved a score in the top level. More than 250 000 adults have taken the same tests. Only 2 percent attained the top level. These findings are not surprising since divergent thinking is often disregarded in schools.

Creative teachers are supportive, energetic, open-minded, flexible, curious risk takers, and frequently display a sense of humour. They are comfortable with change and demonstrate divergent thinking. Creative teachers design inquiry or project-based learning experiences for students to acquire deep knowledge in each subject area. A deep knowledge of a topic in a subject area is essential for creative expression. Creative teachers provide meaningful feedback that takes into account advances in students' developing creative ability. This feedback facilitates the acquisition and growth of creative metacognition, which, according to R.A. Beghetto and J.C. Kaufman in "Classroom Contexts for Creativity," is "a combination of creative self-knowing (knowing one's own creative strengths and limitations, both within a domain and as a general trait) and contextual knowledge (knowing when, where, how, and why to be creative)." Students collaboratively investigate complex problems of personal interest. Teachers integrate the arts which develop abilities such as observation, expression, reflection, exploration, and persistence, that are valuable in other subject areas. They acknowledge that creative work takes meticulous effort over a period of time.

With an increasing demand for creative, innovative, and entrepreneurial people, educators need to rethink schools that standardize knowledge, skills, and assessments. Memorizing facts and procedures can produce a Trivial Pursuit whizz, but to create a new product, idea, invention, poem, song, drama or app requires deeper knowledge and creative thinking.

Perhaps there needs to be a shift to a new innovative paradigm for learning in this century. In this paradigm teachers and students set challenging goals. Learning experiences are personalized where students investigate elements of an inquiry that are personally interesting and relevant. Teachers guide children and youth to think about improving their performance and knowledge building rather than completing a task. Learning focuses on ideas, collaboration, creative and divergent thinking, artifacts that demonstrate a developing expertise in a domain rather than a collection of decontextualized information. Students learn from mistakes rather than just trying to avoid them. Technology is used to enhance and expand learning beyond the school into the global community. Teachers participate in active research projects to discover, discuss, and create innovative answers to their personal questions (e.g., How do I expand my repertoire of questioning techniques? How can my students become collaborative learners? What are useful strategies for middle-school writers to revise their written drafts?). Teachers are afforded time during the school day for their professional learning.

Advances in technology, globalization, and cyber-communication are changing the ways people are learning, doing business, and communicating. Creative abilities are essential as people endeavour to adapt to these new realities.

> "We maintain that for students to understand what they are learning, they must come to that understanding in their own unique and appropriate (i.e., creative) way."
> Ronald A. Beghetto and Jonathan A. Plucker, "The Relationship among Schooling, Learning, and Creativity: 'All Roads Lead to Creativity' or 'You Can't Get There from Here'?" in *Creativity and Reason in Cognitive Development,* edited by J.C. Kaufman and J. Baer.

> "Conceptually, imagination is rather simple. Patterns flow into each cortical area either from your senses or from lower areas of the memory hierarchy. Each cortical area creates predictions, which are sent down the hierarchy. To imagine something, you merely let your predictions turn around and become inputs."
> Jeff Hawkins and Sandra Blakeslee, (2004)
> *On Intelligence*

9. Strive to be engaging with students

Relevance connects the students to the learning

Students need to become engaged with the content, or with the skills they are acquiring, or with the exercise of learning. Relevance can mean that the students are connecting their lives to the topic or issue at hand, or that they are learning skills that will benefit them, or that their involvement in the activity will strengthen their understanding of learning. Interestingly, students want to be challenged, to enter the puzzling processes, to activate their brains, their emotions, and their bodies. They need to feel secure with their initial entry into the event, and then move into a dynamic of collective awareness as the community moves forward. And every student needs to find success attainable and self-worth accumulating as integral to well-being. There needs to be a future hiding in the clouds above.

Often the teacher's observed level of engagement can motivate students into active participation in the learning events. How we encourage this response is a large part of the art of teaching. In a whole-class instruction time, we may be demonstrating a science experiment, showing a teaching film, explaining a new mathematics concept, reading a story aloud, but much of the learning success of these direct instruction times relies on involving the students as the lesson proceeds, finding ways for the students to interact with the topic or theme, asking questions for clarification, adding personal experience, taking quick surveys, finding information on the computer. As well, after the instruction time, response activities can move students to use what they have experienced or learned, and to activate their own understanding of the content of skill acquisition process.

SCIENCE IS REAL IN DEBBIE'S CLASSROOM

Farveh Ghafouri, PhD, professor, Seneca College

I met Debbie in her kindergarten classroom on a chilly October morning to invite her to participate in my dissertation research project. With sparkles in her eyes and a big smile on her face, Debbie welcomed me with about twenty pictures and a story of children's recent discovery of a dead squirrel in the park behind the school. Our conversation attracted five children who left the drama centre to loudly and impatiently talk about the photos of the mysterious dead squirrel. Our excitement then brought in two more children who interrupted everyone to grab my hand and drag me to a desk where their drawings of the squirrel were piled up. I smiled and listened while selfishly knowing an excellent teacher and classroom would soon be at the heart of my research.

There are many theoretical models to frame a "good" pedagogy. More recently the Ontario Ministry of Education (2014) suggests engagement, belonging, expression, and wellbeing as the four foundations of a good pedagogy for learning. Revisiting Debbie's pedagogical approach, it is impossible for me to single out one of these foundations to write about. So, I start with "one" characteristic which I think brings all the four foundations together.

Being fully *present* with children. Teaching with joy of being, wondering, puzzling, discovering, playing, and laughing with children ... every day. Joy of investigating all questions, theirs and hers, with commitment, humbleness, openness, and excitement. A meaningful and authentic *being* with each and every child, because Debbie was a child inside her heart and mind, full of curiosities and playfulness on a journey where learning, play, and life are tangled unpredictably. Being present with each child was her pedagogy to create a sense of ownership and responsibility towards learning and being in a classroom, where each question was serious and had to be investigated, individually or in group, each fantasy needed a stage to be pretended and imagined, each conflict was offered a space to be discussed, maybe resolved maybe led to more conflicts.

Debbie's class was loud, busy, messy, some days less organized, and desks were covered with works-in-progress. Debbie's class was full of questions, surprises, and discoveries ... full of life. A pedagogy of risk taking to open space for unpredictable complex encounters and learning: to investigate a dead squirrel for about ten days, hatch and care for chickens for over a month, open the classroom windows and offer children a bench to climb up

The Five Dimensions of Engaged Teaching, by Laura Weaver and Mark Wilding, focuses on how to improve teaching practices by being a more mindful and emotionally aware educator, and offers ways of improving these and related skills.

and see the world outside; just a few from many risks that Debbie was taking every day. She pushed the boundaries of predefined *do's* and *don'ts* which underestimated the power of teachers and children in decision making, in owning their learning, in being *present*.

In Debbie's class, rights of children and teacher were tangled and lived through opportunities to express oneself, to feel well, to be engaged, and to be a part of it all. At the core of her pedagogy was a strong sense of ownership and responsibility: this is *my* class; this is *our* class.

THE HUMAN LIBRARY: BECOMING A BOOK AS PROFESSIONAL DEVELOPMENT
Maria Martella, owner of Tinlids — Best Books for Young People

Not sure what you should read next? Why not try the Human Library? A library made of people.

The idea is to invite people to "borrow a human book" for half an hour. The human book tells a story (based on the theme of the event) and the "borrower" is invited to ask questions during or after the story. I was asked to be a human book at a school board event last month. The theme was "Indigenous Cultures."

As a human book you are allowed to tell your story orally, or silently with pictures. You could act it out, sing, dance, and bring objects for display. It's your story to tell, so you can present it any way you wish. I chose to show pictures of where I had been, the people, the landscape, the books I talked about, and I brought in the moccasins that I learned to make while I was there.

Before the event was publicized, I had to submit my book title. I chose my title, *The Lasagna at the End of the Ice Road*. A catalogue was created listing all of the human books, a photo, their book title, and a short blurb. The available check-out times were also listed. As a borrower, you simply browse through the catalogue and find a title to borrow.

My story is a true one, about my travels to James Bay schools for three years each spring. I was invited to bring books to the schools and present book talks for students, parents, and teachers. It was part of the "Books in Homes" program which gave a $30 coupon to each student to purchase books for home. My story was about the power of letting children choose their books by offering a lot of choices. It's about putting real books in front of students who don't have access to a bookstore, library or home full of books. My story started with a twelve-hour train ride and another day to arrive at a fly-in Cree community. I travelled on an ice road and yes, there was lasagna. I talked about how connections are made when we share our own story with others who may seem very different at first. In the end, we are all so similar. And who doesn't love lasagna — even caribou lasagna?

As readers, we make our connections to the story, based on our own experiences and what we need or want to take away with us. When a borrower reads a human book, the same thing happens. Every borrower connects with the human book differently. As a human book, I also found myself telling the story slightly differently each time. Everyone has a story to share, and a human library is a creative and fun way to share it.

10. Set high expectations for every student

Good teachers strive for high-quality work from their students. They want them to take risks, try new things, discover, experiment, and not be satisfied in just completing the assigned work. Formal tests are only one way of recognizing growth. Teachers need to present challenges for students and then support them in working toward success. Caring for students includes wanting them to strive toward deeper, wider learning, to not be content with first drafts, to seek more than they were asked to do, to become involved in the very act of learning. We can follow Lev Vygotsky's zone of proximal development:

> The *zone of proximal development* (ZPD) has been defined as:
> "the distance between the actual developmental level as determined by independent problem solving and the level of potential development as determined through problem solving under adult guidance, or in collaboration with more capable peers" (Vygotsky, 1978, p. 86).
>
> Lev Vygotsky views interaction with peers as an effective way of developing skills and strategies. He suggests that teachers use cooperative learning exercises where less competent children develop with help from more skillful peers — within the zone of proximal development. Vygotsky believed that when a student is in the ZPD for a particular task, providing the appropriate assistance will give the student enough of a "boost" to achieve the task
>
> Saul McLeod, *Zone of Proximal Development*

A PERSONAL REFLECTION ON MY TEACHING LIFE
John Mazurek, teacher and university instructor

Based on more than three decades in and around teaching, here are five things I've learned about good teaching:

1. Be true to your character. I'm a bit of a contrarian by nature. I try to see complex issues and projects with a sober eye to the long-term. Who will my students be in thirty years? How is what we are doing together today, this week, this month, this year going to help them to "fish for themselves and with others" in the future? I'm distrustful of high-minded theories that skimp on practical plans for action. Equally, "recipes for success" that have no grounding in research or which blithely cite research of dubious rigour exasperate me.

This is my touchstone, my starting point, and it's consistent with who I've always been as a person. I believe every good teacher has their own authentic starting point.

2. Be a flexible learner. I have always been a keen participant in sports. However, as a child and adolescent, I didn't have many opportunities to design and construct things. I missed out on that aspect of problem solving. Experiences like camping and crafts were likewise not part of my life. As a teacher, I've had to stretch in ways I could never have imagined in order to learn along with and for my students. In the process, I've gained facility, even expertise, in new areas: classroom design, children's literature, community-building games, sculpture projects, historical city walks, puppet making and puppet plays, to name a few. I've survived a white-water canoeing expedition and led studio classes in intricate South Asian dance. During my first year of teaching, I was expected to use a Gestetner machine to make copies of phonics worksheets. Thirty years later, in a fully digital classroom, I was providing my students writing feedback via audiovisual messaging.

3. Be a critical learner. Focus on instructional practices and frameworks that will significantly impact student learning. Understand deeply the research behind what you're doing and asking your students to do. Avoid fads and manic change.

Over thirty-plus years, a few ideas and practices have met the above standards and been very influential in my work with students. These include: cooperative learning (effective group work) in its myriad forms; tribes community building; self- and peer assessment; daily independent reading and vocabulary research; writers' workshops; literature circles; and with learners in the primary grades, guided reading. In each case, I required a minimum of three to five years of focused practice to develop true facility, i.e., to integrate a particular innovation with my existing repertoire in ways that maximized student learning. There were always negative consequences for both my students and me if I tried to implement too many "new" strategies too quickly.

4. Be mindful that time is a precious commodity. For a classroom teacher, it takes devotion, skill, sweat, and long hours to build rapport with students and parents; to plan thoughtfully and thoroughly; to consistently provide opportunities for engagement, novelty, and creativity, as well as for meaningful, individualized assessment. Students won't sustain effort on tasks that don't lead to learning, joy or satisfaction. The same applies to teachers. Think carefully about how you invest your time and what you are asking students to do with theirs.

Workshop leaders and consultants sometimes promote practices that they themselves would not be able to sustain in a real classroom over months and years. Additionally, administrators may have a limited understanding of what successful implementation looks like, how long it actually takes to get there, and how innovations can and cannot be integrated with each other. I have seen these factors lead to burnout at the classroom level and cause some teachers to give up on formal professional learning.

While I believe I have mostly avoided these pitfalls and, in the best interest of my students and myself, developed my teaching repertoire consistently and gradually over the course of my career, this has required me to ignore, downplay or delay some of the change projects that have been promoted in my schools and districts.

5. Be in the almighty "zone of proximal development." Student learning thrives when there are realistic, attainable challenges. The teacher's task is to ascertain what constitutes a realistic, attainable challenge, for a given student in a given moment. Assessment is all about finding these constantly shifting targets and acting on them. It's about constantly relearning who your students are, not collecting forensic evidence for a report card.

Whenever students and parents have described me as a "challenging, but fair" teacher, I've surmised that I've been somewhat successful in my assessments and planning for those learners. It's been validation, if you will, that my behind-the-scenes work has been worth the effort. Students are motivated by appropriate challenges far more than by teacher admonitions or cheerleading. Besides, I've never considered myself capable of sustaining an effective cheerleading role with twenty-five, thirty, sixty or ninety students over the course of a year.

11. Reflect often

Focus: Reconsidering our teaching
David Booth

"Examining your practice is one of the best ways to improve it. There is no one 'right' way to reflect. Just as students have multiple learning styles, so do we when it comes to reflecting. Reflection should not be a chore; if the approach seems burdensome then regroup and try another way. In the final analysis, the ability to critically examine one's professional practice in a constructive manner is a healthy and rewarding component of an effective teacher."

Jennifer L. Hindman and James H. Stronge, *Virginia Journal of Education*, February 2009

We want teachers to move toward self-directed growth and professional development, where feedback is focused on what a teacher understands about the progress required in his/her teacherly life. They are more likely to find inward strength for change, a desire to keep growing and learning, to create a stronger version of who they might become. We can use formal feedback evaluations if we establish a context for how we will accommodate these opinions and observations in the developing picture of who we can be. As more accountability procedures are put in place, as standardized test results are used to consider success in teaching, we will have to keep grounded in our understanding of who we are as teachers, and keep our students first and foremost in our professional lives.

As you tune in as a self-observer, you have opportunities to reconsider your teaching actions, your own attitudes, and your disposition as an educator; you can suspend self-judgment and open your mind to possibilities, to other ways of being, to finding alternative solutions to challenges, to build your own sense of efficacy.

You can begin by noting which areas or aspects of your teaching are causing you to feel stressed or overwhelmed. What may not be working in your classroom approach or in your interactions with students? Could you chart which times in your schedule are fraught with tension or dissatisfaction, which students are struggling against the culture of your classroom? By examining successful events, you may find better ways of handling the tough times. Whom can you talk to for advice or guidance over a complicated issue, on staff or online?

There are professional books and articles written by teachers on every problem or challenge in teaching, and by reading about similar situations, you may discover how to alter your own problem. Self-reflecting can be a regular part of your week, in a journal, with colleagues, or in an online group. When we confront an issue, we have a hope of finding solutions. Training in mindfulness, "paying attention in a particular way: on purpose, in the present moment, and nonjudgmentally", as defined by Jon Kabat-Zinn, is being implemented in many schools with students, and the processes of reflective mindfulness can work as well with teachers. To respond thoughtfully is a very different action from reacting immediately in the heat of the situation. Can we simply pause and consider how we are being perceived in this interaction, and either reframe the discussion or postpone further talk after we and others have time to think about the issue that is causing the friction? The true question is probably, "How can we reconsider these concerns so that all of us can move on with insight and clarity, and a respectful awareness of everyone?"

Feedback from trusted others is our prime means of changing, but that success dynamic relies on our wanting the feedback and on how we receive it. It doesn't help if we find ourselves incompetent or imperfect with nowhere to turn. Some schools have developed helpful guides for students to illustrate and share their views on how school is affecting them— their learning, their social lives, their work habits, and how teachers might assist them more effectively, instead of judgmental comparisons of different teachers. Teachers may undergo formal assessments by administrators and peers, or even by outside companies hired for this purpose.

FINDING PATHS FOR REFLECTION
David Booth

Enhancing Practice through Classroom Research, by Catriona McDonagh, Mary Roche, Bernie Sullivan, and Máirín Glenn, deals with the importance of professional development in every teacher's career, and describes in a practical way how to improve classroom practice through research and reflection.

Reflection is a much-used word today, but we can reclaim it as teachers if we accept the personal processes it supports. Jean Koh Peters and Mark Weisberg, the authors of *A Teacher's Reflection Book*, discuss the overwhelming "mind-less" activities that too often sap our energies as teachers. The expression "we build the boat while we are in the water" seems to fit much of how our daily routines in large school press on. But "mindful" reflection" can be "an intentional, non-judgmental review of experience... witnessing that experience, examining it, illuminating it and exploring it... which often leads to fresh perspectives and renewed energy."

Over the years, teachers in my courses have taught me so much about different ways of rethinking and reworking our teaching lives. Because I taught courses in children's literature, we tried a variety of forms for course reflections. My favourite was having graduate teachers keep a notebook of the significant quotations from the books they were reading throughout the course. How they organized those selections was up to each student, and I still have two copies that were given to me many years ago. G. Anson-Hill wrote his quotations in a most beautiful calligraphy, with delicate drawings representing each book read, on handmade paper, hand-sewn to hold the signatures together, and designed as an alphabet book. Pat Chesterman collected hers in a book she had designed as a calendar, a birthday book for special friends and family. In beautiful handwriting, she places each quotation beside the week of special days, with a drawing that highlights the author's words. Some reflections need to be kept safe inside special places that will hold truths for thirty-five years.

Stress is omnipresent in our lives. Managing our stress with proactive strategies means we recognize the issues having negative impact on our lives and we handle the surrounds of those issues with intentional plans. Reflection is personal; you need to work in your own way, with methods that fit your rhythms of your work and your home life. You need to care for yourself as well as your students:

- Different strategies will be of use at different times depending on your stage in life. Choose what works at present.
- Choose colleagues and friends you can trust to be supportive, good listeners, in person or online, so that you are not bound by others deciding what you should think about.
- Read books or articles in print or online as springboards that extend your thinking, that allow you to non-judgmentally reconsider or extend your learning.
- Consider meditation, workouts, long walks, deep breathing exercises, to create a frame for rethinking teaching practice and behaviours you want to reconsider.

- Perhaps guided reflection would be helpful: a retreat for the purpose of stepping outside to better see inside your life, time with an instructor who understands the process, or journal writing.
- Some school districts are implanting mindfulness programs in the school day, with strong results in the area of self-management by students, and with teachers who are entering into the process as well.

THREE WAYS TO REFLECT WITH PURPOSE

Michael Paul, blogger, Edutopia, 05/06/2016

Like many teachers, reflection is a natural and regular part of my life. I spend a lot of time and energy reflecting (often it feels like too much time and energy!); I think about Student A on my walk home from work, Lesson B while laying down going to sleep, Colleague C as I take my dogs around the block at night, Meeting D over a bowl of cereal at breakfast. While there are many meaningful benefits of this natural and routine reflection, I often do it without planned purpose.

Make it a part of your lesson plans

This year I began adding a blank Reflection section at the bottom of each of my lesson plans. I still print my lesson plan to have them nearby during a lesson in order to stay organized and use planned questions or prompts. At the end of each lesson I then have a space to write down my reflections of the lesson. This is a generative process. I look back on my lesson to see what I will do differently in the future. Sometimes the reflections are specific to a particular lesson, like adding extra time to a think-pair-share activity or to reword directions of an assignment. Other times I draw larger conclusions that apply to the unit or my teaching in general, like to incorporate more cold call discussions or design a tracking system for which students I worked with during that particular day. This helps my lessons and my teaching to evolve and become more focused towards student learning.

Peer observations and reflections

Like the Beatles said, "I am going to try with a little help from my friends." Reflection is great alone but can be even more powerful when done with others. Over the last two years my middle school social studies colleagues, including HighFiveHistory's own Jason Deehan, and I have set up peer observations. Our group, led by department head Marlene Perez, created a schedule and a protocol to follow. We decided on a technique of having the observing peer write down a series of clarifying and probing questions based on their observations of the lesson. Then after the class, we sit down and discuss the questions — with no unsolicited advice or judgement.

The reflection that came about was informative. It is amazing to "see" your class from another person's viewpoint and to reflect about details from the class you don't always notice with your own eyes. I have come away with many aha moments from these reflective discussions — how I lead discussions, who I call on, how I move about the classroom, how the class flows. What makes this peer-led reflection so powerful for me is the safe space that my peers and I have created between us. By focusing on questions, and not feedback or judgement, we have allowed ourselves the room to reflect, with a little help from our friends.

Seek out student input

I have always been open and honest with my students, and I try my best to create a trusting relationship with them. This means at times pulling back the curtain on my teaching and showing them what I do and why I do it. It also means seeking out their opinions of lessons and activities, to get a feel of the class from their perspective. I do this informally by talking with small groups of students who happen to stay a little late or I discuss it with the entire class at the end of a unit or project. I also do it formally by creating student surveys. I use surveys at the end of certain units, especially when I am trying something new, and in the middle and end of the year as a general look back. What started out as paper and pencil feedback forms has turned digital with the use of Google Forms. What hasn't changed is the valuable feedback, and opportunity to reflect, that comes of seeking out student input.

Some of the most transformative moments of my teaching have come out of these student feedback surveys. What I have come to learn, especially with middle school adolescent students, is what you think you do as a teacher and how you intend to be, is not always as important as how the students interpret what you do and construct who you are. Similar to the shift in teaching and learning, it's not what a teacher teaches as much as what did the students learn. To reflect, or to look back, as a teacher is not just looking back at yourself in the mirror but looking back at yourself from the eyes of your students.

Prompts for reflecting

- When do you feel best about your teaching?
- List five things you really enjoy about teaching.
- How would you define "a "good" teacher?
- What keeps you energized in your teaching?
- What are the contexts for supporting an excellent teacher?
- What changes would you want to make in your teacher preparation years?
- When in your own life have you observed excellent teachers? Who were the teachers you admired most, who inspired you as a teacher? What were the particular characteristics they demonstrated?
- What does "learning how to learn" mean to you? Consider how this notion might be reflected in classroom practice.
- What do you notice about this classroom environment that makes it conducive to developing student voice?
- When you look into other classrooms as you walk down the school hallways, which ones appear to be filled with the energy of learning? How are the desks arranged? Are there shelves for books? Are the walls filled with student work, or with tattered posters advocating rules? Are there a Smart Board, computers, art supplies, book nooks? Do you notice quiet times for read-alouds, group activity, independent feedback sessions, interactive discussions, directed instruction for the community, guests, intergrade activities? Do you ever hear laughter, singing, media voices? How can your classroom reflect the best of these hallway visions?
- What characteristics do you possess that may be a hallmark of excellent teaching?

Through a collection of stories of teaching experience, *A Teacher's Reflection Book,* by Jean Joh Peters and Mark Weisberg, offers insights into how to reflect on and develop teaching practices, with particular emphasis on listening skills.

2

Know Your Students

In Kevin Major's *Hold Fast* a student is disciplined for fighting on the playground and the principal states that he will have to inform the student's parents that their son has been expelled.

> "Sir," I said when I finally got started, "you needs to read your stupid records. You couldn't recommend a lousy thing to my parents. Both of them are dead."

12. Know, respect, and advocate for each child

Be aware that students have lives beyond the classroom, and their reaction to your lessons may be the result of events happening in their own lives and may not be reflective of your teaching methods.

Life stories

It is the business of schools not only to pass on the stories of the past but also to encourage young people to tell the stories of their own lives, the stories of their own making. For many of the students this respect for and understanding of story's central place in our lives may never have been fully valued.

Students are in a privileged position as they develop into storytellers and storymakers, not fitting easily into stages or ages, but working with stories in order to understand the process of building life narratives, telling their tales out loud to find out what they have said and how they could say it more effectively. But do we stifle their story impulses in school with unnatural silence, even sometimes removing recess from a crowded curriculum? When and to whom will they tell their tales, honing them, tuning into those who are listening, learning what works in storytelling, learning what compels the listener to listen? And when will their crafted life stories connect with literature, where they can borrow the shapes and cadences, the words and phrases, of the professional authors they have loved in print or have heard read aloud by generous parents and teachers?

As storying teachers, we can find ways to both inspire and enable our students:

- to call upon their memories of life experiences as starting points for building stories;
- to turn their stories into tales worth telling to others;
- to make the stories of others into their own, not through memorization, but through reworking, retelling, and reliving them until they are deeply embedded in their story chests;
- to be guided and inspired by other memorable story experiences told by significant tellers who matter;
- to seek opportunities for listening to and telling carefully crafted personal life tales in natural and authentic ways that serve well the teller and the told, investing each story with meaning and art;
- to gain insight into their own stories through the process of sharing in the story circle, deepening their own storytelling practice and transforming themselves from within the tales they tell of their lives thus far;
- to be strengthened by the storying process so that competence, confidence, and self-esteem will accrue and be part of other activities.

A LETTER FROM PARENTS

Dear Teacher,

First of all, we would like to tell you how much our son Adama enjoys being a student at the school. He leaves with his grandma every morning with a positive attitude, often composing a song or experimenting with new dance moves, in between admiring and naming the flowers they pass on the way.

He has never complained that he does not want to go to school, one of the strongest indicators we see of how well he has adjusted to his new life on this side of the world. We are extremely proud of him and all that he has accomplished since he started school here six months ago. We acknowledge and appreciate the extra academic supports he has received, as well as the kindness and consideration that has been shown to our son. However, recent email communications between us regarding Adama's lack of participation in a class discussion and his nervousness in reading class has given rise to some concerns which we feel compelled to address. Adama's father in particular feels passionately that you do not have a full understanding of the magnitude and type of adjustments and challenges faced by our young boy who very recently moved here from The Gambia, West Africa.

We were particularly concerned by a lack of cultural sensitivity recently when Adama was reluctant to speak about why he and his father came to Canada. We were astounded and Adama confused as to why you sent him to the hallway, especially since only days earlier I alerted you to the fact that The Gambia was under a state of emergency and on the verge of civil war. You should know, that all of Adama's years prior to coming to Canada were spent in a vibrant, hot, mainly sunny, colourful, family-centred, multilingual, communal, Muslim, semi-urban, black-skinned, largely oral, low-tech, musical, economically challenged country and former British colony, steeped in a rich history. He has had to adapt to a multitude of changes both outside and within the home and school, not to mention changes within himself through his self-identity.

Adama is used to a very different style of education. Learning is very much by rote in the early years in Gambia. At his age, he is unfamiliar with being called upon to speak or write about personal information about his family, participate in group work, and express himself in writing. He is bravely trying to establish his place in this new world and with that naturally comes a certain amount of anxiety. We do our best to provide him with a comforting and loving home where he feels safe to express himself and learn. We are so very proud that he has gone from speaking almost no English on arrival to having a good mastery of popular language.

Recently we were invited to participate in an anxiety workshop as a result of you "identifying that anxiety is a concern" for Adama. We welcome opportunities to learn about possible strategies to help Adama overcome his hesitance to participate fully in the classroom, but we see this as part of the larger picture of his experience this year. We see him as a whole person and that how he felt in the "how did we end up in Canada" situation was connected to the way he needs reassurance in reading class. Avoidance and saying "I don't know" and looking for constant reassurance are, in fact, common manifestations of anxiety in both adults and children who are newcomers.

Our awareness of a general lack of cultural consciousness at the school intensified this month when it became apparent that the school is not participating in African Heritage Month to any significant degree. This is so disappointing for us as a family as we had anticipated that despite a lack of African studies content in the curriculum, at the very least the month of February would be a chance for Adama to celebrate and be proud of his African roots. As you know, this kind of cultural self-identification can be essential for a child's development of self-esteem and confidence.

As parents, we would be negligent if we did not advocate for our son in this regard. A recent study revealed that black children in our local school districts continue to be disproportionately streamed into programs below their potential and suspended with much more frequency than others. We will not allow Adama's free spirit to be worn down by any school system. We have all heard the horror stories about police carding and racial profiling, Trayvon Martin and the dangers of 'walking while black'. Adama needs all of our support and encouragement if he is to develop into a confident, responsible and happy young man.

In keeping with the Buddhist and other Eastern philosophies which the school is embracing at this time, we accept the place where Adama is at this moment in time and hope that with mindful encouragement from you and the rest of the staff, he will continue to grow and gain confidence. He is a very determined and intelligent young boy.

Sincerely,
Adama's mother and father

13. Maintain a sociocultural responsiveness to students

Is Everyone Really Equal? An Introduction to Key Concepts in Social Justice Education, by Ozlem Sensoy and Robin DiAngelo, will help teachers with concepts such as social justice, institutional change, and language power, and promotes opportunities for affecting school change.

The Dream Keepers: Successful Teachers of African American Children, by Gloria Ladson-Billings, offers profiles of teachers who work with the unique strengths that every child brings to the classroom.

GOOD MUSIC

In *Home of the Brave*, Kathleen Applegate beautifully describes the feelings of youngsters new to a country, to a school, to the social fabric surrounding them. Kek, from Africa, is in an ELL class in Minnesota. Even when teased by his classmates, he remembers home:

> I draw a bull with great curving horns, like the finest in my father's herd.
> I even give him a smile. But it takes me a while to decide on his coat.
> In my words,
> we have ten different names for the color of cattle.
> but the writing chalk is only white.
> I am working on the tail
> when someone in the back of the room says, Moo.
> Then more say it,
> and more,
> and soon we are all a class of cattle.
> At last we can all
> understand each other.
> I think maybe some of the students are laughing at me.
> But I don't mind so much.
> To hear the cattle again is good music.

Focus: A culturally diverse society

Rich Coles

Children and youth in schools reflect our culturally diverse society. It is not uncommon particularly in urban or surrounding areas to have young people from twenty-five or thirty cultures and indigenous youth attending the same school. Lamar, Tanya, Laavanyah, and Tsering are youth from different cultures in the same class. Their cultures are not homogenous but rather consist of subcultures based on features such as class, ethnicity or age. From experiences shared with their families, friends, and other cultural members, their often unconscious cultural learning enables them to know how to act appropriately in different social settings and to predict the actions of others. They use symbols such as gestures, objects, signals, and language as they endeavour to make sense of their worlds. All aspects of their cultures are related and to know a culture requires understanding the various parts. Their cultures include traditional practices but are also dynamic and ever-changing as when they exchange ideas and symbols with other cultures. These young people are also members of multiple cultural worlds, one being their school.

Lamar, Tanya, Laavanyah, and Tsering have diverse linguistic literacies, histories, cultural practices, and culturally mediated ways of coming to know. Their school also has a culture. In the past many classroom cultures have been dominated by White middle-class norms of acting, knowing, and being successful in school. Unsuccessful students with diverse, working-class or Indigenous backgrounds were often thought to have deficiencies to overcome. This deficit thinking necessitates that these students learn White middle-class language and

The Reason You Walk, by Wab Kinew, is a personal account of one man's year spent reconnecting with his father and his First Nations culture, and trying to reconcile a painful past with the potential of the future.

norms in order to achieve success in school. Cultural incompatibility between the structures, pedagogies, and attitudes of teachers towards diverse learners can interfere with students' academic success.

Culturally relevant pedagogy involves teachers knowing about and monitoring the academic needs of their students and believing that they can achieve academic success. Teachers learn about their students' cultures and communities and use this knowledge to integrate those cultures into their daily learning. Culturally relevant pedagogy helps ensure that students' cultural competence continues to develop, and students are consciously aware that it is valued by their educators. In addition, students are challenged to question the status quo of the knowledge they encounter, whose interpretations are valued, and the social order of their worlds.

Culturally responsive teaching uses students' cultural identities — e.g. prior experiences, cultural knowledge, performance styles, discourse, communicative frames of reference — to make their learning meaningful and relevant. It connects in meaningful ways home and school experiences as well as classroom learning with the students' social and cultural worlds. Teachers must know about and value diverse classroom cultures and use their understanding when designing active, integrated learning experiences. Such teachers' classrooms are caring, safe learning environments with multicultural resources, materials, and creative displays of student learning.

Sociocultural consciousness is an awareness of one's own and others' sociocultural identity, an understanding of how culture and social class influence thinking and behaviour and the relationship between schools and society. Do schools advantage some learners based on race, life experiences, social class, gender, sexual orientation while disadvantaging others? How do schools and teachers deal with existing social inequalities? An affirming attitude toward students from culturally different backgrounds reveals an acknowledgment that in a diverse society there are multiple ways of thinking, behaving, talking, and coming to know. Teachers' attitudes toward students greatly shape their expectations and students' learning. Affirming attitudes have been shown to support young people's learning.

Constructivist views of learning affirm that students use their background knowledge and experiences to actively build knowledge as they investigate new ideas and concepts in learning activities. Teachers assist learners by bridging what they believe and know to new ideas and concepts. They also monitor their students' learning. The constructivist perspective posits that all students are capable of learning and there are multiples ways of generating meaning. Constructivist learning develops problem solving, critical thinking, and collaboration and acknowledges multiple perspectives. It also provides spaces for teachers to employ scaffolding teaching strategies, demonstration of new strategies or procedures and occasions for students to practice developing skills. Constructivist learning pedagogy facilitates active learning in authentic real-world contexts. And this learning also builds on and emphasizes social justice principles from a critical pedagogy stance.

Learning about students involves teachers knowing about their students out-of-school as well as school experiences, interests, strengths, favourite school subjects, and preferred learning styles — e.g., collaborative or individual learning. What are their students' aspirations and what brings them happiness, fulfillment, anxiety, and fear? This deep, multilayered understanding benefits teachers when they are designing meaningful learning experiences for their classes.

Culturally responsive teaching practices integrate these notions into classroom pedagogy. Teachers have their students investigate topics from multiple perspectives, use assessment procedures that foster learning, and develop a classroom culture that is caring, academically challenging, and inclusive.

Recently some scholars have questioned whether "relevant" or "responsive" are suitable terms for the broad growth of research and teaching based on these theoretical perspectives. Django Paris and H. Samy Alim in their article "What Are We Seeking to Sustain through Culturally Sustaining Pedagogy?" contend that prevailing pedagogy and teaching practices have not kept pace with the dynamic social and demographic changes in today's society. Nor do they "go far enough in their orientation to the languages and literacies and other cultural practices of communities marginalized by systematic inequalities to ensure the valuing and maintenance of our multiethnic and multilingual society." Paris presents **culturally sustaining pedagogy** as an alternative. It extends resources pedagogies that honour the linguistic and cultural practices in poor diverse communities while resisting and opposing deficit approaches. It seeks "to perpetuate and foster—to sustain—linguistic, literate, and cultural pluralism as part of the demographic project of schooling." Culturally sustaining pedagogy focuses on the multiple and developing nature of youth identity and cultural practices. But youth culture also has the potential to be oppressive and produce inequalities. For example, rap battles (improvised verbal sparring) are often dominated by male participants and frequently contain derogatory terms. Culturally sustaining practice "requires that our pedagogies be more responsive of or relevant to the cultural experiences and practices of young people—it requires that they support young people in sustaining the cultural and linguistic competence of their communities while simultaneously offering access to dominant cultural competence." Culturally sustaining pedagogy can facilitate the development of equity and inclusivity in schools.

The demographic of today's classrooms is diverse and dynamic. Thinking and writings about language, literacies, cultures, cultural practices, and education for multiethnic and multicultural societies is also dynamic and ever-changing.. The literature in the field may focus on students of colour, Latina/o or Asian communities, the working poor or Indigenous people. But there are also many first- or second-generation children and youth in our schools who have a strong connection to their heritage culture but also want to be part of the youth culture and the broader culture of their new country. This can lead to family tensions around issues of appearances, dress, and social practices such as dating. New arrivals have the task of learning a new language, new cultural practices, and new schooling procedures. Their conversations and writings give them voice to express their fears, anxieties, and sometimes profound sorrow over leaving family, friends or a loved and cherished pet, perhaps in dangerous conflict zones or camps for displaced people. They wonder: Will I be accepted and have any friends? Will there be others who look like me, talk like me, and really get me? Will I be successful in school when I know so little of the language and have missed so many years of

---

See "Culturally Sustaining Pedagogy: A Needed Change in Stance, Terminology, and Practice," by Django Paris, in *Educational Researcher*, 2012, 41: 93, and "What Are We Seeking to Sustain through Culturally Sustaining Pedagogy? A Loving Critique Forward, by Django Paris and H. Samy Alim, in *Harvard Educational Review, Spring* 2014."

school? At the same time, the voices and actions of such kids also often express joy and excitement about their new homes, sometimes new climate, and their new communities and schools.

The research and literature about these issues provide theoretical building blocks for classroom environments and practices. When these notions come to life in a classroom there are possibilities for Lamar, Tanya, Laavanyah, and Tsering to reach their potential and fulfill their aspirations.

INDIGENOUS WAYS OF TEACHING

Sandra Styres, professor of Indigenous studies, OISE/University of Toronto

This essay by Sandra Styres is from *50 Years of Impact: Ontario Institute for Studies in Education*.

As far back as I can remember I have always wanted to be a teacher. However, as sometimes happens, life took a detour and I ended up working as an executive assistant for the managing partner of a large law firm. After a few years I realized that I wasn't making a difference either in my community or in any one individual's life. About the same time I was thinking about this I took a call from a friend who was a programs officer at Grand River Employment and Training — a community organization on Six Nations of the Grand River Territory. They were looking for someone who could design and implement youth community-based programs and inquired if I would be interested. I decided to make the change and began designing programming for young single mothers who had dropped out of high school and lacked job experience.

In implementing these programs my passion for teaching and working with students was reawakened. I felt invigorated and I thoroughly enjoyed watching lives transforming as opportunities were opened to them and that they saw that their lives mattered — their stories were important. After listening to the stories from these and other youth concerning the barriers and challenges they faced in school I realized that I wanted to make a difference *before* they dropped out of school and not just intervening after they had fallen through the cracks in the system. Thus began my journey into becoming a teacher, particularly in the field of education. I realized that we needed to change how we train teachers to become teachers.

Graduate school gave me the opportunity to broaden my horizons while also taking a step back and thinking more deeply and critically about the complexity of the issues I was exploring. It gave me the space to ask questions — of myself and others. I began the search for a university where I could continue my true life's work.

I knew that OISE has an international reputation as Canada's leading centre for graduate studies and research in education. I noted that OISE offers comprehensive interdisciplinary and collaborative programming pathways in education across diverse contexts. OISE is seen as one of the most research-intensive faculties of education across Turtle Island and it is well known that faculty diligently work at developing extensive partnerships with schools, communities, NGOs, and government agencies seeking to understand education across diverse contexts. As a member of OISE now, I feel that I am in a place I can play a significant role in education.

As Indigenous people, we see ourselves in terms of relationality and the roles and responsibilities we have to those relationships. So perhaps relationality and understandings of self-in-relationship are more appropriate descriptors of what I see as my roles and responsibilities within the greater

OISE community. Relationality refers to the quality and state of being relational — that is to say, the ways we are all in relationship to each other and to all of Creation. I understand my self-in-relationship within the greater OISE community in a multi-layered and iterative circular framework: community, OISE, and the University of Toronto.

I believe that it is important to foster an understanding of whose traditional lands we are on and why that acknowledgment is important for everyone. As well as promote respect for the historical and contemporary cultural development of Indigenous students' learning experiences at OISE/University of Toronto. To promote the validity of Indigenous philosophies and knowledges along with culturally aligned research methodologies and ways of doing research with, not on, communities. As well, to encourage positive, respectful, and collaborative working relationships between the university (including students) and the Indigenous community (locally, nationally, and internationally.

I want to continue working with Indigenous students, opening up spaces for them to be able to engage in meaningful and relevant research in ways that honour and respect Indigenous ways of knowing and being. To be an advocate for Indigenous students who are trying to navigate a foreign structure that, many times, does not make way for or understand Indigeneity within mainstream structures. I want to continue to work with non-Indigenous students and faculty who are interested in working within the context of Indigeneity in good and respectful ways.

14. Support a learning pathway for every student

CREATING PATHWAYS TO SUCCESS

Pathways to Success: An Education and Career/Life Planning Program for Ontario Schools, Policy and Program Requirements, Kindergarten to Grade 12, 2013 (Ontario Ministry of Education) describes a comprehensive education and career/life planning program for Kindergarten to grade twelve designed to help students achieve their personal goals and become competent, successful, and contributing members of society. The policy's goals are to:
- ensure that students develop the knowledge and skills they need to make informed education and career/life choices through the effective application of a four-step inquiry process;
- provide opportunities for this learning both in and outside the classroom; and
- engage parents and the broader community in the development, implementation, and evaluation of the program, to support students in their learning.

Year-end maps: towards paths of enlightenment and commitment
Dr. Bryan Wright, philosopher of education

Mapping learning affords reflection for individual students and can guide learners to deeper understanding of the ideas and concepts encountered over the course of time. Year mapping can strengthen the relationship between the teacher and student as well as provide an avenue for thoughtful reflection and expressions of past learning in the classroom. These thoughtful reflections afford students the time and space to re-cognize their unique connections in school classrooms between and amongst their peers, teachers, concepts, ideas, and approaches to learning. Teachers and students can revisit memorable lessons, skills and events from the year in the class spent together, and this mapping strategy allows both students and teachers the chance to relate to and revisit chosen subjects and lesson experiences, which may be depicted in collages and/or graphic organizers which groups of students can create together. Often there are emotional connections revealed as students reexamine their school lives, and different interpretations can cause individuals to rethink their responses.

The power of mapping is revealed when the students come to understand how they learn what they come to know, whether it is through discourse and conversations prompted by teachers and instructors, or reliable sources of information available through different channels. Many of the rich sources also may contain nuance and lines of flight opening in other universes unimagined when explored further as a group.

One key aspect of the year mapping strategy is to prepare a plane for deeper learning, or metacognition. Through summarization of key experiences and direct reflection on knowledge learned, the student develops an early awareness of their learning strategies and begins to fashion tools with which they can analyze their world. Further, learners craft, develop, and present coherent presentations, individually and collectively, which may then be collected together to reflect the scope of learning experienced. This giant collective map can represent the learning experiences of the whole class. It is essential that we reflect on our learning and teaching and celebrate life, and looking back can offer glimpses of how to move forward.

When should students work in groups?
John Myers, instructor, OISE/University of Toronto

For the promotion of learning through purposeful talk, the following kinds of tasks are suitable for designing grouping activities for pairs or larger groups.

Tasks involving exploratory talk. Sometimes you may want students to struggle with new information by talking through ideas. Small group brainstorming to generate ideas and reactions to a provocative question posed by a teacher (or another student) are two examples. **Point of View-Pair Share**: The initial prompt "As you read the story about the flood imagine having a farm in the path of the flood water. How might you feel?" directs each student to imagine themselves in the situation.

Tasks involving checking for understanding. Students may be more willing to express uncertainty in a small group or with a trusted partner than in front of a whole class. That's why the often-used "Any questions? Any comments?" directed to an entire class may not work. **Think-Pair Paraphrase Share:** One partner responds to the teacher's prompt about the main point of the passage. The second partner paraphrases the response, "Are you saying that . . . ?"

Emotionally arousing events tend to be better remembered than neutral events. See *Brain Rules: 12 Principles for Surviving and Thriving at Work, Home, and School,* by John Medina.

Tasks involving problem solving and/or decision making. Members of a small group talk through a problem or issue in order to achieve a consensus and in so doing achieve a deeper understanding. **Think-Pair Consensus Share**: "What is the message in the poem?"

Tasks in which a variety of abilities are required. Different students may bring different talents and experiences to a task. Using roles can help here. For example, if students create a propaganda poster for World War I, some students can draw while others can work on the caption. While working from strength is important, your ultimate goal is to help students develop strengths in many areas of learning.

Tasks involving review of previously encountered ideas or material. If you ensure individual accountability, students can review material in small groups prior to a quiz or major test. If you used direct instruction or another whole class approach to initial learning, change the approach for review. After all, students who mastered the work the first time do not need review, while those who struggled with a teacher-centred approach the first time are not likely to learn through more of the same. This advice is reversed if the initial teaching used a group learning format. Depending on what is to be reviewed there are many think-pair-share options. One of the variations could be **Think-Interview Share**: Each partner asks questions of the other about the content of the reading. This could be done in role. "Please explain to our viewers how a combination of diet and exercise promote good health."

As a substitute for individual practice in a direct instruction lesson. Sometimes individual seatwork makes it difficult to help students who are struggling, especially the "closet confused" who do not want others to know of their difficulties. **Think-Rally Table Share**: Partners take turns writing or performing a task going back and forth several times as in a rally in tennis; for example, contributing arguments with evidence to support an argument in a position paper on an issue such as "Who won the War of 1812?"

As a vehicle for reflection on the learning. This works in the same way that people talk after a movie, play, concert or other event. It promotes synthesis of information. **Think-Unpack-Suggest**: Partners explain their reasons for their thinking and responses. Then each student, pair or larger team of four (pair of pairs) suggests an alternative procedure for use next time they face a similar learning task. "Next time I will try to get into the role of the character in the short story from the beginning so I can more easily figure out the motivation for his/her action."

SUPPORTING GROUP WORK

The following is an account of two teachers exploring the potential for effective grouping.

John and Sue taught in an inner-city K–8 in the west end of Toronto. As a result of a curriculum project sponsored by their school district they decided to teach "A Child's Introduction to Government and Law" in their grade six classes. Their original interest had to do with the many opportunities students would have to write and since their school had many ELL students they saw writing as a priority.

The unit was centred around a group lost at sea on "Shark Island" who realized that until they were rescued they had to figure out how to survive. While there were indeed many opportunities to write, the focus of John and Sue's planning shifted to showing students how to work in groups since democracy depends on groups of people with different backgrounds, experiences, and interests working together and getting along.

Sue's background was physical education and as a coach she recognized the power of teamwork in which students worked towards a common goal yet were individually responsible for their individual work such as playing their positions in Sue's sport, soccer.

John was visually impaired and from his early teaching days realized that he could not really manage a child standing at the front of the room and droning on. He found that if he gave students engaging, curriculum-related tasks that allowed them to talk he could monitor their progress by "working the room."

So, over the course of the unit, the two teachers had students work with each other while they:
- decided on priorities for surviving on the island (food, shelter etc.);
- came up with some laws for dealing with potential situations;
- turned some of the key laws into a "constitution" which eventually became the class rules.

Their experiences and attendance at some timely workshops refined their work in groups to what we now know as "cooperative learning," a subset of group work in which students' academic and social success were based on:
- face-to-face interaction through talk (talk also served as a "prewriting" activity which helped even the ELL learners be clear on their thinking);
- positive interdependence in which tasks were structured so that students had to work together to achieve a common learning goal;
- individual accountability so that no one could get away with slacking on the job.

In the government and law work much of this happened through the use of interdependent roles needed to complete tasks or "jigsaw" grouping in which the class was divided into teams which were responsible for exploring various aspects of island life and bringing recommendations to the island as a whole.

There were a couple of pieces of evidence that these approaches to structuring groups cooperatively worked. First, the grade seven teachers knew who were in our grade six classes since our students did not have to be taught how to work effectively in groups. Our students were skilled in forming groups, establishing group norms, working interdependently yet also handling their individual contributions.

Three years later John ran into some of the students from that first year in a nearly Toronto high school. "Are you still doing Shark Island?" they asked. "Yes," he replied, and they smiled.

TEACHER VOICES

- If you as teacher care about what you are teaching, the students may catch your passion.
- The teacher's own beliefs about teaching and learning generate motivation in the students.
- Promote interactive activities — group projects, partner problem-solving, media work, sharing times. Learning for students is often a social act.

- Motivation is intrinsic and personal. Offer choices whenever possible of texts, activities, and response modes, remembering that the learning styles of different students can determine success if they are accommodated.
- Involve students in the planning of different aspects of the classroom programs. Community is built upon a sense of ownership.
- Take an interest in how each student is progressing. Celebrate success, and recognize solid effort.
- Help students to keep on track with a schedule and time frame.
- Value the three interactive patterns in a classroom: individual, group, and community.
- Assign members for groups in different ways: student choice, social connections, interest in the topic, mixed ability, single or mixed genders.
- Give clear directions for group members. Wait for their questions asking for clarification.
- Have check points every so often, where groups explain their progress or problems, and others offer support.
- Interact with each group in a supporting role.
- Assign leaders if one member appears to dominate.
- After group work, always have a brief report time, so students that understand their contributions matter.
- Individuals may not always feel at ease speaking to the whole class. It is useful to have some discussion time before asking for individuals to speak to the class.
- Independent projects can be shared in groups if students are nervous about presenting.
- Assess individuals and their group separately.

15. Recognize ages and stages

Among Chuang-Tzu's many skills, he was an expert draftsman. The king asked him to draw a crab. Chuang-Tzu replied that he needed five years, a country house, and twelve servants. Five years later the drawing was still not begun. "I need another five years," said Chuang-Tzu. The king granted them. At the end of these ten years, Chuang-Tzu took up his brush and, in an instant, with a single stroke, he drew a crab, the most perfect crab ever seen.

A great deal has changed both in school and outside school in the last decade, especially in the field of literacy — reading, writing, media, and speaking and listening. Just consider the impact of technology on the literacy practices of everybody — students, teachers, and parents. More books are sold online by Amazon than in paperback. Many schools are full of computer labs and/or laptops, Smart Boards, digital cameras, blogs, glogs, vlogs, and some inventions were no doubt just marketed today. The world is now one globe educationally, and students can have access through the Internet to people, places, and Information from international sources. How will this change the literacy goals for schools educating students for the 21st century, for both boys and girls?

Students are always in different stages of development while placed in one classroom: some are avid voluntary readers while others are still struggling; some write easily with good command of transcription skills while others lack confidence to put pencil to paper; some speak up in book discussions, eager to share their responses while others draw back and remain silent. Most want to work independently, manage their own learning, and follow their own interests. As they attempt to find their own voices, they discover the complexities of relationships and the tentative nature of their roles in a school community.

The lives of these students are changing every year, and these developments are reflected in both the content of what they read and in their attitudes toward writing. Family patterns are changing; young people are becoming more critical of parents, adults in authority, and siblings; they depend more and more on peer groups, and have entertainment stars, sports heroes, and friends as role models; future careers are talked about, and they begin to look forward to their own independence, testing their positions at every stage. Many are developing a sense of history and of their own place in society; they are becoming concerned with justice and the unfair treatment of minority groups. Of course, their physical development is a central factor influencing their lives, relationships, and identities.

Students entering the middle years are expected to read and write independently and more often, to read longer and more difficult texts in a variety of curriculum areas, to read faster and more selectively, to write coherently with their own voices, to remember more information and to make integrated connections with the curriculum. There are new words and terms to learn in all the different subject areas; some of the texts may be outdated, inaccessible or poorly written; readers of widely differing abilities are expected to read the same resources with few support structures.

We want to encourage students in all these classrooms to work responsibly together as a community. If we collaborate with them in negotiating how we will explore the curriculum as language learners, we can observe from the inside out how each student learns best and select our strategies carefully, so that young people do not spend their time attending to what they already know or pretending to be learning when they are completely lost.

WHY NOT ASK THE STUDENTS?

Beverley Strachan, instructor, OISE/University of Toronto

As educators, we understand the complexity of teaching and learning. We try to define the craft of teaching and recognize the complex nature involved in this process. We value time to learn from and with others as we share practices and personal and professional connections in whatever community we are part of. We reflect on our practice, we talk about our teaching, and we refer to research that has been done about what 'good teaching' looks like, sounds like, and feels like. We approach teaching with inquiring minds to help us make sense of the 'heart and art' of teaching. Maybe we should be asking our students what they think. This is exactly what one teacher did!

The teacher decided to visit some of his former Grade 4 students four years after he had been their teacher. The students were just graduating from Grade 8 and about to enter secondary school. He filmed his students as they responded to two thought provoking questions: *What are your memories of Grade 4? What are your wishes for Grade 9?*

As I transcribed their responses, I noticed that there were some common themes apparent in both the students' past memories and their future wishes. Many of the thoughts and feelings the students experienced in Grade 4, and wanted to replicate in Grade 9, were about how they connected with their teacher and their peers. Content and curriculum were not specifically mentioned but how the content was presented was noted.

I chose to present the themes and responses in chart form. They are all truly interconnected and are not in any particular order. The responses could easily be placed in multiple areas of the chart to reiterate the complexity of teaching and learning. Many thanks to Andrei, Teeya, Leanna, Stephanie, Vishal, Zaid, Amber, Hanna, Chris, Dennys, Louai, Hassan, and Jaeda, who all responded to these questions.

Students want their teachers and peers to:	Grade 4 Memories	Grade 9 Wishes
Care	"I remember that our whole class…we were always doing stuff together and so we were always having fun and you were always like smiling so nothing bad ever happened." "I remember when, at the end of the year, you gave us those Frisbees that said something good about us all and since I remembered you from my old school, I had the one with my old school's name on it."	"I hope that they're nice and kind of like you because you're always happy."
Respect	"I remember that in Grade 4, there was always a good, positive learning attitude in the class and everybody was respectful to each other."	"I would like the teachers to be respectful to us and help us when we are struggling in any problem and encourage us to further learn and not discourage us from anything."
Connect	"I remember we would always have fun together and we would always work together and always like interact." "It was an amazing class actually. It was my favourite one, too since I just moved to the school. The teacher was amazing! He was a great teacher and all of my classmates were great. They helped me through the year."	"I think about Grade 9 as a great year because the teachers are going to help you to make your career and help you through your future. I think that the teachers are going to be nice to you if you are nice back to them and work hard and show yourself that you are improving."
Listen	"I remember when every morning we would go into a circle and we talked and listened to each other."	"I think that it's important for the teachers to be nice and caring to the students so like when the student is talking, they don't just ignore them and be rude."

Communicate	"I remember the relaxed kind of inviting classroom. I remember the tables…we had group names so it was kind of like a big family. Also, the mutual respect, the right to pass really, I think, helped open up like when we were having class conversations."	"I just hope that in Grade 9 I can have a teacher that I can communicate with and that can be nice to me and cooperative and help me get my work done and I can do the best that I can."
Motivate	"I remember going on the computers and working and making our own CDs." "Everything was great! Things I remember — when we went to that park — our field trip. That was pretty good. And then, all of the Mac Books and the laptops we got to use — that was great!"	"I want to have fun and I don't want to always have to go to a classroom where everything is negative."
Manage	"I remember the chimes that we had — it was a good way to control the class when we needed to talk about something."	"I want my Grade 9 teacher to be understanding and caring to the students and know when to say no and be half strict, like not 100% strict…like they know when to have fun and when to stop." "Don't be too hard on them because then they are going to hate high school…throughout…they're going to hate their whole high school career."
Facilitate	"I remember that we would always get into groups each month and each group would make their own name and every day one group would get to sit on the couch and chairs and get to play with the koosh balls."	"I'd like the teachers to prepare us for what's ahead in the future."
Understand	"What I liked…our teacher always gave us time to think. He always helped us out if we had any problems and always helped us when were stuck on questions."	"In grade 9, I would like the teachers to have a really good understanding of what the kids need and everything and help us out whenever we're stuck."

| Teach | *"From Grade 4 I remember a lot of good things because our classroom was very exciting everyday that I went to school. I always liked going to school because I knew you would always have something fun planned for us but I would also learn from it, too."* | *"Just give us work that we can do."* |

There is one very thoughtful and articulate response that is not recorded on the chart. This student is giving us all something to think about as we move forward in our ongoing journey of understanding what teaching and learning are all about and how we can respond to the question, *"What do our students think?"*

> *"I think for grade 9, having teachers that actually have the passion or want to be there and care about getting across to students and making them not just learn what's in the textbook but something other than that like more life skills and the ability to communicate with others and making it fun or more understandable so you would actually want to come to school and enjoy being there with your teachers and friends."*

We all need people in our lives who care for us, respect us, connect with us, listen and communicate with us, motivate us, help us manage if need arises, help facilitate celebrations and challenges we may experience along the way, understand us, and teach us.

Focus: The complexity of gender issues
David Booth

In *Guys Write for Guys Read: Boys' Favorite Authors Write about Being Boys*, edited by Jon Scieszka, male writers remember their own boyhoods. Naturally, teachers are present:

> I was a huge fan of professional wrestling. My guys were The Sheik and Bobo Brazil. The only way I could find out about these wrestlers was through the newsstand wrestling magazines.
>
> So, I'm at the library, and I see a whole shelf of different magazines. As I go to check out my books, I summon up all my courage and ask the librarian if the library has any wrestling magazines. That is what I thought I asked; instead I think I asked her to show me what her face would look like if she sucked on a lemon for a hundred years. She looked like she was about to stroke out at the mere mention of wrestling magazines in her library. She made me feel stupid and I never went back.
>
> Patrick Jones, "Wrestling with Reading"

There are diverse opinions about the origin and even the nature of the problems that we find in such an incident. Most important, the education of boys is closely connected to the education of girls, and school and education policies on

---

Reading, Writing, and Talking Gender in Literacy Learning, by Barbara Guzzetti and colleagues, examines the issues concerning literacy and gender.

Drama Education in the Lives of Girls: Imagining Possibilities, by Kathleen Gallagher, presents a case study of adolescent girls who learn to become the authors of their own experiences.

Even Hockey Players Read! by David Booth explores the stereotypes connected to boys' reading lives, and offers directions for offering new definitions for boys' literacy.

gender will directly influence both. If we focus on the problems of boys, do we endanger the efforts of so many in the struggle to bring equity for girls into our society? Or do we see these initiatives as dialogues that are attempting to move us all forward into strengthening the life of every child as an individual? What if we consider the issues not as a "war" but as an inquiry into the dynamics of how boys and girls construct their gendered literacy lives?

How can we who work in schools respond fairly to the needs of boys in relation to the needs of girls, and to the diversity among groups of boys and girls? Fortunately, we can benefit from the educational reforms that grew out of changes in attitudes toward girls: we can apply those principles of gender equity to the educational needs of boys, even though in many ways, that very system of schooling formerly marginalized girls and privileged some boys. What conditions, then, influence or exacerbate these problems for so many boys and for many girls?

We know that no single category includes all boys or all girls. We don't need to reinforce or add to the stereotype of classifying all boys' behaviours, tastes, and attitudes into one single frame. But as we look at studies and reports that examine boys and girls and their learning styles and special interests, their growth patterns and their stages of intellectual development, we do notice some differences. These differences are not in all boys or in all girls, but enough of them to cause us to reflect about our demands on their young lives.

The debate about literacy and gender is lined with emotional minefields and requires careful negotiation. Even the terms reveal multiple definitions: *boys*, *girls*, *literacy*, *gender*, and *masculinity*. We need to engage in thoughtful conversations about issues of gender and school success.

16. Create strategies for supporting differentiated instruction

Family Tree
I am how I am because Grandma was born wired, and my dad, Carter Pigza, was born wired, and I followed right behind them. It's as if our family tree looks like a set of high-voltage wires strung across a field from one steel tower to the next. Grandma all the time said I was just like my dad, "bounding off the walls twenty-four hours a day." But he hasn't yet bounced in our direction so I guess he is still bouncing around somewhere else. But someday he might spring back and just bounce right through our front door. I wish he would because I only just heard[*d?*] about him now, and I'd like to see for myself what he is like.

Jack Gantos, What Would Joey Do?

Good teachers have always supported children with individual needs, abilities, and interests. And there is little wrong with the teacher working with the whole class some of the time. We like to think of the classroom program as including demonstrations by the teacher for the class, seminars with teacher and students who are sharing information and ideas, workshops where groups are learning specific strategies and tools, presentations by students who have important work to share, by guests in the room and on Skype, and reflective discussion and writing, in all kinds of arrangements that benefit as many as possible and as often as possible. And, of course, the teacher reads to the whole class, leads them in song, runs with them at gym time, shows videos, and uses the Smart Board to share strategies. But even during those events, we observe the students — their behaviours, their attitudes, their individual focusing — so that we can assess and organize future learning events that will support our students in learning.

All the teachers who find time, opportunities, and techniques for supporting those students who need us most, are professionals who care for the students in their classrooms, as best they can, with the knowledge they have. We differentiate our teaching so that students can differentiate their learning. The list that follows shows what effective organization and management can offer the teacher who wants to support growth in all their students.

1. We will need to know each of our students: their abilities, their skills, their fears, and their talents.
2. We will need to assess their individual challenges, so that we can support and strengthen their learning.
3. We will need to adapt our lessons, our models of instruction, and our activities to respond to their needs, interests, and learning styles.
4. We will need to find and develop strategies for including all our students in the teaching/learning situations, providing choices where possible.
5. We will need to incorporate new technologies so that students can find support for their literacy tasks: computers for reading, writing, and researching, and programs that read the print text aloud, that read our writing back to us, that highlight inconsistencies, that note spelling difficulties.
6. We will need to scaffold instruction, to make small achievements possible, and take time to work with those students with different levels of experience.
7. We will need to organize opportunities for whole-class community building, for small, flexible groups based on need and/or interest, and for individuals to work at their own pace and competence level.
8. We will need to be "kid watchers," to notice how each student is progressing and to alter our programs for maximum impact.
9. We will need to become reflective teachers, unafraid to change our habits, our behaviours, prepared to search for new ways and different resources to reach our students.
10. We will need to engage in professional conversations with our colleagues, participate in workshops, take courses, read journals and books in print and online, about education and young people.
11. We will need to involve our students in our planning, and listen to their voices as we build a sense of ownership for them in their program. Then they may be more likely to reveal their concerns and ask for assistance, learning to take charge of their own progress.
12. We will need to incorporate assessment into our planning and teaching, through formative and summative assessments, using objectives and/or outcomes, rubrics, benchmarks, and exemplars.

WHAT I WOULD DO NOW: SUPPORTING DIVERSE LEARNERS IN READING AND WRITING

Shelley Murphy, PhD, special education instructor, OISE/University of Toronto

A tough transition to make

My image of a student with ADHD is thirteen-year-old Marcus, a student I taught during my early years as a teacher. Marcus was a bundle of energy and humour. He talked quickly and incessantly, and he had a sparkling kind of mind. He was original, creative, and intelligent. His behaviour, however, was another matter; he would often act, it seemed, without regard for the consequences of his actions. Academically, he struggled, especially in reading and writing.

At the time I had little, if any, awareness about the academic implications of ADHD and the kind of instruction that could support his success. I assumed that if students had ADHD, it simply meant they would have a harder time managing their behaviour, which would end up making *my* job more difficult. More difficult it was, but much more so for Marcus. He had a challenging time regulating his attention, remembering instructions, completing assignments, and keeping his behaviour in check.

With more experience and training, I have come to realize a number of things. Many of Marcus's struggles (including his disorganization and inattention) were not matters of deliberate choice. They were, instead, a result of cognitive challenges related to his ADHD. I also realize now that there were many ways in which I could have supported him better.

Prompts for supporting students

- On which students have you made a big impact?
- What characteristics do students find in an excellent teacher?
- What defines a "good" class? A "good" student?
- Do your students feel like members of a community that supports growth, teamwork, and creativity?
- Do you incorporate strategies on the first few days of the school year for students to learn about each other, to practice respectful ways of speaking to each other, to realize this will be their home community for the year?
- Similarly, do you have ways of supporting closure at the end of the year, a letter to each student, a collective card for all with good memories written on it by everyone?
- Do you participate in cross-grade interactive sessions with your class and students from a younger or older class?
- What do you see as the benefits of using a social networking format with your students?
- Are you helping students to develop open-mindedness and collaborative skills?
- Are students developing their communication skills?
- What are the benefits of bringing the students' outside activities into the classroom?
- How might you show that you value the expertise that your students bring to their learning?
- How might you include students in the assessment process?

Teachers have begun to share their teaching experiences and suggestions in books such as *In the Best Interest of Students*, by Kelly Gallagher, and *The Essential 55,* by Ron Clark

- How are you accommodating learners with special needs in your regular classroom program?
- How might you modify or change the intervention programs currently in place in the school for at-risk learners?

3

Develop Your Teaching Strategies and Techniques

MY JOURNAL

Wally Karr, student

May 1

I have changed my password again on my laptop. I don't trust my dad.

We are back in school after our drama trip to New York. I never dreamed I would take a drama class in high school, but there are lots of girls in it, and since I am shy, it makes sense to get to know some of them in a safe way. I was worried I would have to wear tights and work in bare feet. Not at all. We always begin the class with a game, and Mr. Swartz makes us change partners each time. I like the ones with music blaring in the background; I don't have to talk as much. Then we improvise different ideas he suggests, usually in groups, and when they are polished, we put them together as a class. I am amazed at how intense the scenes become, and how hard everyone works to make the dialogue seem real.

We created a play for the spring assembly; each class had built a scene that fit into the theme of leaving home. Drama works! That's why I volunteered to go on the school trip to New York. (Dad paid the cost.) I couldn't believe how well-behaved everyone was on the bus trips. I guess everyone who came wanted to be there. I had never seen a real play before, and we went to three of them! Mr. Swartz really seemed to enjoy the whole experience. He brought his partner Wayne and the VP along as chaperones, and they treated us as friends. (I was wrong about the VP. She was great with us.) They even paid for the Chinese food on the last night.

Later, I told my friend that he should take drama next year. I like math and English, but drama helps lift the weight of all the other classes off your shoulders. I think I will take music next year. I already play the recorder. (My dad says "badly".)

17. Establish clear learning objectives, outcomes, and standards

We like the phrase "a culture of opportunity" to describe what can happen in a classroom. Each student needs to feel "I can get better here, I can learn, I can be safe." A student was walking by a Reading Recovery Classroom with his buddy and whispered to him, "See in there? I can read in there."

Curriculum goals can be complicating forces in a classroom, unless the teacher discovers ways of clarifying what is expected. There is content for various subjects, there are the skills required to be a successful learner, and there are pedagogical strategies that can affect the first two. Separating these facets in your planning may help you cope with what seems as a heavy burden of content to be covered. What do they need to know, what do they need to find out, what skills do they need to achieve these goals, and how can I as a teacher support this learning? Of course, each one of these has a cause-and-effect relationship with the others: how I teach will affect how they learn; what they discover will add to their information content; how they go about actively engaging will strengthen their skill sets.

Strategic teaching involves organizing and planning for student growth and success. The more structures in place, the greater the freedom for the teacher to be among the students, negotiating, mentoring, questioning, conferring. Routines also give students a sense of order: they know where their novels are, where their writing folders are kept, where they submit completed work or work that requires revision. The time table for the day or the week is posted, including names of visitors or changes in rooms. Expectations are clear, and students understand that structure and order support them as active, interactive, and responsible learners. The teacher and the students are in charge of the program and the environment, and everyone helps to manage the place called classroom.

- By collaborating with colleagues, you benefit from their experiences, you build resources together, you share books and websites that save time, you help yourself and others.
- Plan your program carefully, with large-scale goals and big ideas, accompanied by daily lesson outlines. Find a strategy for planning that increases larger units of the curriculum, and then facilitates organizing your lessons. Check with other teachers for their methods of organizing the program. It may be helpful to add stick-it notes to your plans for things you want to continue or change for the next event, and for students who may need extra help or consideration.
- Always differentiate your plans for a variety of learning styles, for students who need extra time, or for those students with issues in English as a second language.
- It helps to share your learning expectations with the students, so that they can see the direction of your plans and feel confident about what they have to explore and learn. You can list the success criteria, construct a rubric with the students, to provide a map for their time on task.
- It is helpful to take a few moments at the close of the lesson to summarize, or have the students reflect with questions, about this learning event.

A RESOURCEFUL TEACHER
Judy Caulfield, PhD, teacher/university instructor/storyteller

If we are lucky, we will encounter throughout our life teachers who inspire us and who give us confidence in the direction of education for the next generation. Jen is one such teacher, in a French Immersion classroom.

Jen seeks out resources for her students — beyond the limited trade books and publishers' materials — that will give them opportunities to engage in French meaningfully. Indeed, she often creates original print materials for them. Inspiration for her students to engage in dialogue and activities comes from a variety of sources. For example, Rick Mercer's rants on his television show, *Rick Mercer Report*, provide ideas and connections to real-world issues for Jen's students. Each year we hear snippets of the rants her students have created. They rant about what makes a difference in their lives: from the annoying sound a fork makes as it scrapes food off a plate — why can't their families eat more quietly? To the absurdness of buying electric cars which cost more than a house — energy saving for the rich! They plan their rants and choreograph them for videotaping on iPads much as Mercer does — stopping to make a point and then moving on. Jen gives them a structure and opportunity to find and use their voice — in French!

Jen's Honours degree in environmental studies clearly informs her teaching practices. Her students explore the outdoors through the lens of different subjects. For art, she has exposed her students to the land art of environmentalist Andy Goldsworthy and then taken them into the nearby woods to collect objects from their own environment in order to create their own land art. A visit to the War Plane Heritage Museum provided an opportunity for them to connect to history as well as to engage in science experiments. Her students have the opportunity to learn collaboratively and to be physically active, all the while finding meaningful expression in French.

Jen's students' experiences are so far removed from the Cours Moyen textbooks that I used in high school. I could figure out the pattern and could easily fill in the blanks in the exercises, but I could not express my own thoughts in French — nor was I asked to or expected to. How I envy these students their opportunity to learn and to develop, and to express their ideas in French with a teacher who cares to make education real, exciting, and relevant. Jen is the kind of teacher I hope my grandson encounters. She is the kind of teacher I hope our student teachers have as a mentor. She is the kind of teacher whose passion for teaching and learning shines through.

Focus: What are your students really doing?
Rich Coles

International literacy scholars Ken and Yetta Goodman have taken great delight in visiting classrooms around the world. As they roamed the classrooms they would ask the young people, "What are you doing today?" A common reply was "work." When Ken asked for clarification, "Why are you doing that work?" or Yetta would ask, "Tell me what work you are doing?" the responses were often puzzled looks and shrugs. Clearly these young people did not have a clear understanding of learning goals or specific success criteria. Effective teaching and learning requires a clear understanding of learning goals.

Grant Wiggins and Jay McTighe in *Understanding by Design* propose a "backward design" instructional design process based on three stages: 1) identifying desired results; 2) determining acceptable evidence; and (3) planning learning experiences and instruction. They begin with the goals (e.g., content standards/curricular expectations) for the unit of study. What should the young people know, understand, and be able to do as a result of their investigation of this topic? Since each topic has a great deal of content, they differentiate knowledge within a topic as *worth being familiar with, important knowledge*—facts, concepts, skills, and *enduring understanding,* the "big ideas" that students have a deep understanding of and retain after they have forgotten some of the details.

Next, they ask how the students will demonstrate and provide evidence of their understanding and proficiency. Teachers collect evidence using a variety of formal and informal methods over a period of time. Students demonstrate they have achieved the desired understanding and they are able to apply their knowledge in appropriate contexts.

Finally, after clearly identifying the desired results and the evidence of understanding, teachers now plan and design the learning activities and instruction for the unit of study. What activities will enable the young people to acquire the required knowledge and skills? What will need instruction, scaffolding or coaching? What materials, resources, and technology would be appropriate for achieving the goals?

In their book *Essential Questions: Opening Doors to Student Understanding*, Wiggins and McTighe propose using essential questions to frame a teacher's key learning goals and to stimulate students' thinking and inquiry. Some essential questions extend beyond the topic — e.g., "In what ways does art reflect, as well as shape, culture?" Topical essential questions refer to a specific unit of study — e.g., "What do ceremonial masks reveal about Inca culture?"

ORGANIZING FOR NOVEL STUDIES

Doug Caldwell's middle-school language arts class is going to investigate the essential question "Who is a true friend?" Each student selects a novel from the text set that includes: *Raspberries on the Yangtze* by Karen Wallace, *Twisted* by Laurie Halse Anderson, *Slam* by Walter Dean Myers, *Stargirl* by Jerry Spinelli, and *Gym Candy* by Carl Deuker. These young-adult novels vary in complexity and involve friendship from different perspectives. Doug poses the essential question and the class briefly discusses different aspects of friendship. Who are your friends? Why are these individuals your friends? What's the difference between a casual friend and a BBF (Best Friend Forever)? Why do people stop being friends? The class divides into small groups based on their novel selection. Before each learning activity Doug clearly discusses the learning goals and specific success criteria which are also posted on the Smart Board. Each student keeps a learning log to record information, ideas, and reflections dealing with the essential question. In the computer lab, the students design a web page with many attractive features to record their information and ideas based on their inquiry. Each group has a form for online posts and asynchronous discussions. The class also displays their many creative artifacts dealing with this investigation. Evidence of individual and group understanding, thinking, and questions are revealed in their learning logs, written work, dramatic presentations, artistic displays in the classroom, and the website.

Some of the learning activities involve: reading and discussing the selected novels with their group and also engaging in discussions with members of other groups. The students are encouraged to suggest other novels for this inquiry. Each group locates and records famous quotations, poems, and songs that relate to the essential question. The groups generate an outline of a real life middle-school learner on a large piece of paper and write words and phrases around the figure about friendship qualities and characteristics. Students create a character poster for one character in their novel. The poster displays a drawn picture of the character and a written explanation of why this person would be a good or poor friend. Each young adolescent generates a "character mandala" for one of the characters in their novel. The students create short video clips based on scenes from their novels. For a culminating activity, each group plays a part in designing and contributing to the class wiki dealing with the essential question. Each student also writes a personal reflection about this inquiry. The reflections reveal their growing understanding about personal relationships and friendship. They also comment about their experiences, what they liked or disliked during this inquiry. And they students express some thoughts about making this unit of study more engaging and meaningful.

Before each activity in this inquiry Doug presents the learning goals and success criteria. There is time for discussion and questions. Sometimes the students make constructive suggestions about learning activities that would help them achieve the learning goal. Or they suggest modifications to the success criteria. Visitors to this classroom are informed about the "big ideas" and the daily learning goals for the students' learning. They also observe the collaboration, enthusiasm, and deep learning taking place.

AN INSPIRATIONAL TEACHER

Barbara Smith, PhD, instructor, OISE/University of Toronto, and chair of the board of Headwaters Academy

> When I think of what separates a proficient from an exceptional teacher, I think of what exceptional teachers do, and I think of Tanisha Nugent Chang.
>
> A great teacher knows that a one-size-fits-all model does not lead all students down the path to success. It takes more. Exceptional teachers are distinct in my mind because they are the people who inspire kids and their colleagues. They can inspire in many ways. They can be teachers of character, by being that individual who cares and can be trusted. Many are teacher-leaders, leading by example, and directly supporting others. Even though it is not as common for teachers to take on the role of action researcher, I admire these brave explorers for making the extra time to make meaning. The teachers who take part, and coordinate extracurricular activities are also a special breed. The teachers who boldly go beyond the limits of commercial products have insight in spades.
>
> When I first met Tanisha Nugent Chang, she was a grade five math teacher, but soon after she became a mentor teacher, the math coordinator for the school, and our dean of teacher development. As her principal, I reduced her teaching load to half in order to free her up to support more students and teachers in the context of real classrooms.
>
> In Nugent Chang's words, "I think a teacher should take pride in what they do, that is, to show up to work on time and work hard. They should care about *all* the students and most of all love the subject that they teach…I am

driven to keep learning about how to teach mathematics so that I can help students learn…Throughout my career, I have been driven by my passion. I am excited and open to new ideas that make my classroom better. I strive to help open doors of success for my students, to defy ceilings, whether they be social, academic or cultural. I want to be that teacher that kids will miss and the staff will welcome back. I want to continue being a positive force, a hard-working professional and a highly respected leader."

What makes Tanisha Nugent Chang an exceptional teacher is that she motivates and engages students by treating teaching and learning as a collaborative process and by showing students that their thoughts and opinions are valued. It can be really good motivation for students to feel that they're working *with* their teacher to develop their understanding.

I wrote the following quote for part of Ms. Nugent-Chang's performance review at the William E. Dora, Jr., Charter School for the Performing Arts:

> Division was more than simply a task to solve a word problem in Ms. Nugent's class. It was a context for building powerful math habits. The deep examination of the problem prepared the students well for their application activity that involved negotiating using UPS to solve a math problem. Three different groups worked on three different math problems — recorded them on poster paper and then presented each poster to their classmates. The "talking math" and student-directed task was brilliant! The only suggestions I can think of that might augment this experience would be to reduce the number of students in groups (2), so that folks would be forced to talk more…. The beauty of this experience was that so much was learned with only four questions used in a deep and targeted way! Take a picture of their posters for your portfolio.

Tanisha excelled as a mentor. Rather than use the conventional coaching model where the teachers were observed and given feedback and resources for making improvements, Tanisha met with one teacher at a time each week for an hour to co-plan a class, and then another hour to team-teach with the teacher. At any given time, Tanisha would have upwards of five or six mentees. The school math scores increased by close to 10%, an extremely rare occurrence in DC charter schools.

Ms. Nugent Chang was also the founder and dance instructor for the Ire Contemporary Dance Company, where she teaches boys and girls ballet, modern, jazz, west African, Caribbean folk, and reggae style dance. The company debuted "On this Island" that featured the integration of dance with Caribbean history. Her work was featured in the *Washington Post* in February 2013.

Becoming the Math Teacher You Wish You'd Had, by Tracy Johnston Zager, and *The Four Roles of the Numerate Learner,* by Mary Fiore and Maria Luisa Lebar, offer practical advice for improving your math program.

18. Recognize the dynamics of the classroom

The Ontario Ministry of Education Literacy and Numeracy Secretariat produces the Capacity Building Series to support educators. These reports about a range of topics can be located at http://www.edu.gov.on.ca/eng/literacynumeracyinspire/research/capacityBuilding.html

TEACHERS AND STUDENTS: MOVING INTO A LEARNING PARTNERSHIP

In many of the classroom communities that we have observed over the years, a positive partnership between teacher and students has had a supportive and enabling effect on how the learning developed. The goal is to build a curriculum that addresses both what each student wants and what each student needs. Skills are not ignored — they are taught as students need them in their quest to communicate and make meaning.

When the teacher moves from being the disseminator of knowledge to becoming the facilitator of the learning process, teachers and students move into partnership and share the responsibility for selecting and organizing tasks. The daily program can allow various types of learning to occur simultaneously so that teachers can meet individual needs. A range of instructional strategies, resources, teaching styles, and activities will accommodate the interests, abilities, and backgrounds of both the teacher and the students; it will also provide opportunities for students to work alone, in flexible groups, and as a whole class.

Within a classroom setting that supports inquiry, questioning, and discussion, students and teachers are co-learners. A sense of democracy is felt by students who begin to take some responsibility for their learning, who can co-construct the rubrics of assessment, who have a say in the texts they meet and the response modes that evolve, and who help shape the way the classroom functions.

OPEN SPACES

Cathy Marks Krpan, PhD, mathematics professor, OISE/University of Toronto

When I observe effective teachers of mathematics, there is one characteristic that they all have in common. It is the *space* they provide for their students to voice their ideas, reflect on their thinking, and explore mathematical concepts. This may seem simplistic. But I argue that it is not. Space is time. It is the precious real estate in the classroom schedule of which we never have enough.

Ineffective teachers rush through their space, filling it up with lots of math worksheets that students complete, on their own, following rigid rules and formulas which they have memorized with limited understanding. Ineffective teachers believe that if their students complete the math, their students understand the math. Teachers who hold on to their space want to control everything. They strive to control the strategies and solutions their students produce — rendering mathematics to be monotonous, predictable, and uninteresting.

It takes a lot of courage as a teacher to share your *space* — the *space* which you would normally fill with your mathematical ideas, your mathematical explanations and your questions. Effective teachers realize that sharing their space with their students means that lessons will take longer, but what they also know is that their students' learning will go deeper. Effective teachers realize that deep learning is messy; sometimes students' answers are hard to follow and their strategies may not replicate those that are found in commercial math resources. But, these incredible teachers explain that the messiness is the joy of mathematics; it is the freedom to explore and think.

Effective math teachers share the space eagerly with their students as they facilitate rich discourse and help their students to value mistakes as part of learning in mathematics. For these teachers know that it is by listening to their students' ideas that they will gain insight into their students' thinking. They know that just because their students do the math does not mean that their students understand the math. They also know that by providing wide spaces in which students can explore, pose questions, and share their mathematical ideas, they are helping their students to celebrate the beauty of mathematics on a daily basis. When the teachers I have observed collaborate with their students in the excitement of inquiry, their students see themselves as mathematicians and value mathematics as a meaningful part of their lives — all of this because their teachers cared enough to share their space.

The classroom as a community
What is really exciting about a classroom community is discovering that what is achieved as a group usually exceeds what individuals could have achieved alone. Students are shocked and surprised into knowing.

Benefits that accrue from including voice and choice in the classroom
The classroom must be a safe place where all participants feel respected as they engage in social, academic, and emotional learning; move towards acceptance of others' viewpoints; overcome anxieties, personal and student-related; and develop self-efficacy.

So much learning can grow from a classroom where students have part ownership in how authentic communication can function on a day-to-day basis.

Strong motivation to learn
As students express their thoughts and feelings, they build a sense of competence and a developing belief in their own abilities to learn, increasing motivation.

Rich resources, rich perspectives
Students need to encounter rich resources to develop their global understandings, to increase their frames around important topics and issues through technology, books (both fiction and nonfiction), newspapers and magazines, and guests (in person and online) so that they can gain insights, alter perspectives, be challenged on current thinking, and engage in deep inquiries.

Student empowerment
When students feel empowered, they can change who they think they are in the classroom and move toward who they can become. This is not easy for some of them. They have honed their reputations over years and often been emboldened by teacher responses to their behaviors.

When the eighth-grade boy known as a bully is put on a team to help reduce bullying in the junior years, he has a chance to morph into a new disposition; he can now be the one who helps, and even in that short period of time, he will have a memory of how others saw him in a new light, and he may call on that role at another time in his life. And consider how his teachers change in their understanding of him, and how that can affect his attitudes with them. Altering how students see themselves in our eyes is a struggle worth engaging with.

Cathy Marks-Krpan writes comprehensive support books for teachers. See *Math Expressions: Developing Student Thinking and Problem Solving through Communication,* and *Teaching with Meaning: Cultivating Self-Efficacy through Learning Competencies.*

One of the best books about developing school communities is *Building Community in Schools,* by Thomas J. Sergiovanni.

IN MEMORY OF MY TEACHER
Joan O'Callaghan, instructor, OISE/University of Toronto

Stupiditas delenda est! (Stupidity must be wiped out.) If the words seem vaguely familiar, it is because the last two were first uttered by the Roman senator and orator Cato the Elder in reference to the Third Punic War. Cato's famous phrase was *Carthago delenda est!* (Carthage must be wiped out.)

Cato's phrase, borrowed and modified by Edwin R. Procaine, has resonated with me through the decades since the years that I spent as a student in his English class at the Brantford Collegiate Institute and Vocational School in my hometown of Brantford, Ontario. Known to us all fondly as Earp, he would thunder, "Stupiditas delenda est," at any student who offered a particularly unintelligent answer to a question.

Ed Procaine had a profound influence on me. I was in his English class for three years and I loved every one of them. Under his direction in the school drama club, I played such roles as Look in George Bernard Shaw's *Arms and the Man*, Alice in Shakespeare's *Henry V*, and the leader of the Women's Chorus in T. S. Eliot's *Murder in the Cathedral*. Heady stuff for high-school kids and typical of Earp's high expectations. We didn't let him down.

From him, I learned much of what I know and believe about teaching English. His scholarship was impeccable. I still have some of my texts from those years, and reading through my notations is a revelation! He demanded excellence and would settle for nothing less. Although there was another gentleman who taught senior English and who was more generous with the marks, I don't believe any of us would have traded the opportunity to learn from our beloved Earp for the higher grades dispensed by his colleague.

Earp had a marvelous sense of humour! "Stupiditas delenda est" was joined by "Non es dignus" (you are not worthy) if we happened to pick up the wrong dictionary, and "You base football player" taken from the pages of King Lear and directed to the members of the senior football team who were in our class. He managed to infuse our classes with laughter and learning, but never at the expense of anyone's self-esteem. I find myself even now echoing some of the lines for which he was known in the school.

He inspired me to take my BA in English language and literature, and then challenged me to complete an MA in English, which I did. I entered the teaching profession, with certification in English and dramatic arts. Earp joined the faculty at the fledgling Althouse College (University of Western Ontario). Years later, when I joined the faculty at MacArthur College (Queen's University) and then OISE as a sessional instructor in English, it was a source of pride for us both.

I was fortunate enough to know him on a personal level after I graduated. He was a collector of Canadian art, recognizing the work of the Group of Seven early on. He willed his impressive collection (372 pieces) to Memorial University in Newfoundland. He was also a talented dramatist, writing plays and acting as an adjudicator for Theatre Ontario. I attended some productions with him and accompanied him to art galleries as well. His death in 2011 was a great personal loss. Edwin R. Procaine, *requiescat in pace*. Your legacy endures.

Creating the Dynamic Classroom, by Susan Schwartz and Mindy Pollishuke, offers solid strategies for developing a dynamic classroom.

Focus: Good teaching

Carol Rolheiser, director, Centre for Teaching Support and Innovation, and professor, OISE/University of Toronto

> "Teaching is teaching, regardless of the grade level. That is why all teachers must continue to be learners."
>
> W. H. Moore

Picture yourself in a conference room. The room is abuzz with activity. The wall real estate is occupied by flip chart paper, scribbled with visuals and notes about learning outcomes, learning activities, assessments, and instructional design challenges. It might be easy to assume that this is a group of K-12 teachers or teacher candidates; but no, this is a Thursday afternoon in the Centre for Teaching Support & Innovation (CTSI) at the University of Toronto, and this is the culminating activity of a two-day Course Design/Re-design Institute for thirty university professors. Their courses reflect a diverse faculty group, from first-year instructors to seasoned veterans, and from graduate seminars of fifteen students to large, undergraduate introductory classes of hundreds of students. As well, they reflect a wide array of topics, including an Introduction to Philosophy, Critical Thinking about Narrative, Restorative Dentistry, Statistics for Managers, Developmental Neuropsychology, and so forth. Across those diverse disciplines and programs, however, there is commonality. Instructors' discussion of teaching and design approaches are informed by their individual reflections, engagement with our instructional team, and discussion and feedback for one another. Collectively we are striving to create significant learning experiences for the almost 89,000 students we teach across three campuses of the University of Toronto.

This is one of many examples that emerge from our work in CTSI; we provide support for pedagogy and pedagogy-driven instructional technology for all teaching staff and teaching assistants across the university's campuses and divisions. Along the way, we look for a range of opportunities to support instructors in their courses, be they face-to-face, online, hybrid, or through Massive Open Online Courses (MOOCs). Weekly you might see staff from CTSI working with instructors in a workshop, providing one-on-one consultations, engaging with a cross-discipline community of practice, organizing a pilot technology initiative, linking instructors for engagement in peer mentoring for teaching, supporting teaching-related inquiry and the dissemination of results (e.g., SoTL or the Scholarship of Teaching and Learning), or leading a symposium or other community event. Ultimately, our goal is to help university educators develop and realize their teaching aspirations. Those thoughtful educators are invested in creating transformative learning for their students, whether it be through inquiry that leads to disciplinary competencies and skill mastery, or experiential learning that leads to engagement and meaningful contributions to our broader communities.

Professional learning is not just for "new" instructors, but rather reflects the building of instructional excellence at all stages of careers. Our CTSI staff support university instructors as they document their teaching successes, innovations, and challenges, and provide feedback as they build their teaching dossiers that are integral to annual review, tenure and promotion processes. However, the work of our centre is not just about encouraging individual instructional expertise — it is also about how we build cultures within departments and divisions, and across the university, that support effective teaching. It is our belief that teaching in higher education is no longer a sole endeavour — it takes a team and a team mindset. That team includes registrars, educational developers, librarians, technology professionals, student support staff, teaching assistants, and a host of others who are working to maximize student engagement and success. CTSI serves as a hub where we work to create bridges across units and services, in order to strengthen partnerships and to serve as "boundary spanners" in support of more powerful teaching and significant learning.

Across the country and around the world, we see the emergence of teaching and learning centres in higher education. While each centre's mandate is different, each reflects a commitment to higher-quality teaching and learning. In our context at the University of Toronto, the work of CTSI reflects our broader institutional goals, and an emphasis on the synergy that is possible between our teaching and research priorities, both of which are career-long undertakings, nurtured from the day that one is hired, supported *by* others, and carried out *with* others throughout one's career.

As leader of CTSI, one of the realizations from my forty-plus years in education (K-12-higher education) is that my understanding of what it means to be a "good teacher" has evolved. In particular, my work with university faculty has taught me to think more about the verb, rather than the noun. "Good teaching," therefore, is about the dynamic intersections of learning — it is about connecting, questioning, collaborating, and improving to better serve our students. This is the work of CTSI and of teachers across the University of Toronto. And, it is what educators at all levels are striving to achieve when they simply state: "I am a teacher."

19. Invite and support student voice

A CONCERN THAT ALL VOICES BE HEARD

Students will recognize when they have voice as participating citizens, and through their inquiries they will discover who is marginalized and what they can do to ensure that all voices are heard, so that they can begin to make a difference in the world. Students can develop insight into what they as individuals can do to have a voice and to help others make their voices heard. They begin to recognize the importance of the factors that affect them as speakers and listeners — culture, background, language, personal and social identities, passions and interests, aspirations and abilities. As they and we participate as individuals in a cooperative, inclusive setting where student voices and identities are welcomed, an awareness of community is built.

REFLECTING ON CLASSROOM TALK

How have talk patterns changed since your own school education?
- Consider these oft-used interactive modes with students in today's schools: interviewing, asking questions, solving problems in groups, reading aloud, retelling life stories, sharing inquiries, explaining science experiments to others, working in role, and using intergrade groups for reading. Which `processes are you including or strengthening\ in your classroom?
- As we discover more about how children activate learning, what changes do you foresee happening in the talk patterns of your school?
- Opportunities for natural talk are expected and welcomed in our classrooms. But can we discover more useful situations that require students to talk in pairs, in small groups, and as a class, so that the listening and speaking grow naturally from activities that the students regard as real and important?

- How will technology affect speaking and listening in your program? For example, do your students make use of taping to replay significant moments from their text discussions? Could you use the new gadget that plugs into a computer and records voices? Are students using graphic technology, such as PowerPoint, Prezis, and iMovies, for presentations in your classroom?
- Think like a dialogue coach. Our own talk patterns and behaviours can be the source for future change. You might record and assess a conversation between yourself and one student or a group of students.
- Are there techniques you could use for promoting accountable talk in groups, such as always requiring feedback time after discussions?
- Can you find occasions where you can elevate the discussion, highlight the significant moments in students' conversations, deepen the points the student have made or redirect the discussion to extend their meaning making?
- Let's assume that you observe students engaged in talk. What would you include on a future observation list so that you could better reflect on their behaviour and patterns of conversation, and apply your ideas when you set up other interactive situations for promoting student voice?
- How can you relate talk to reading aloud for the students, so that they come to understand the importance of interpreting the written word, as if they were speaking, and of finding their voice inside the words of the text?

INTERVIEWS IN A SMALL LANGUAGE SCHOOL IN JAPAN

Eri Hachiya, language instructor, Hiroshima, Japan

I teach English at a private language school in Hiroshima, Japan. The students, ages several months to fifteen years old, are learning English as a foreign language. I usually teach them in classrooms, except for an interview activity held in the summer.

Every year in the summer, I take my students (grade three and older) to the Hiroshima Peace Memorial Park to undertake this special activity: Interviews with visitors from all over the world. The task is that each student meets at least three people in the park to ask them where they are from, what they like in Japan, and some other questions, if possible. For this activity, the children have learned some basic expressions using chants and songs, and also to prepare further questions.

On the day of the interview, students are divided into groups of four or five. Many of them are often too shy to stop someone in the park and start up a conversation. But once they begin, they are brave enough to carry on with the interview. When they are finished, their faces reflect joy and excitement having been able to communicate with foreigners using the English they have learned.

In the next classroom lesson after the interview, the students are supposed to report to each other who they interviewed, what countries the interviewees were from, and what they found out from the activity.

Usually the students say that they met people from more than ten different countries; it was often their first experience talking with someone from certain countries. Also, they say that most of the interviewees were very nice and friendly.

In this interview activity, the children have an opportunity to get to know someone from another country in an authentic situation. This gives them a reason as to why they are studying English, and also motivates them to study more. Many of my students are interested in and simply just enjoy learning English, perhaps because they know that English is a powerful international language, and learning it is cool. But in reality, it is also true that they have very limited opportunities to communicate with someone in English in their daily lives, even though they live in Hiroshima, where many foreigners visit. It is no wonder that children in more local areas often feel that they don't even need another language other than Japanese because they feel that they will never use it in the future. So, I believe, by giving children a chance like this activity, they start to open their eyes to the world and understand that each one of them can be a communicator in the world.

It is my hope that my students will look broadly at the world and grow up to be people who can create a more peaceful world through positive communication and a better understanding of others. I myself want to contribute to it by helping children learn English.

DISCOVERING VOICE

Think back to a time in school when your voice was actually heard, when you realized that you as an individual had something important to say and others were listening.

Student voice represents the individual and collective perspective and actions of young people within the context of learning and education. Student voice is about giving students the ability to influence learning to include policies, programs, contexts, and principles, including issues of equity and justice.

Good teachers want to examine and explore the power of incorporating student voice in our classroom communities. Assisting learners in developing their own authentic voice can help them to develop confidence in their own capacities, to realize their own potential, to maximize their abilities, and to take a self-determined path of personal growth. Since student voice increases engagement and promotes a willingness to take part in classroom and whole-school activities, we as teachers want to find strategies for promoting and valuing student voice in our classrooms. Can you think of two blocks or challenges that can occur in classrooms that may silence student voice?

MS. NAKANO

Angelica Galante, PhD candidate in languages and literacies, OISE/University of Toronto

Many multilingual international students enroll in English language programs in Canada to prepare for postsecondary studies. When they first arrive in the new country, one of the first people they talk to in English is their teacher, who often briefly welcomes them and starts teaching a well-planned lesson. After a few weeks, realizing that academic studies and social life in Canada require communication with locals, many of these students feel they need to "conform" to the new culture and ask teachers to teach them "how to speak and behave like a Canadian." Little do they know that a single definition for "Canadian culture" is unrealistic. Yet, what many teachers fail to do is to highlight to their students that the languages and cultures they bring to Canada make rich contributions to this diverse country; however, Ms. Nakano (a fictitious name) makes sure to validate and celebrate her students' languages and cultures as assets for communication, particularly in a multicultural country such as Canada.

In his book I've Got Something to Say, David Booth includes the voices of excellent teachers who have inspired students to free and add their voices to the classroom learning.

I had the honour to have Ms. Nakano as a participant in one of my research studies. As a researcher, my goal was to observe how her students learned English, but Ms. Nakano's classes were so engaging that I could not help observing how she delivered the instructional program. Rather than overtly teaching students how to write essays in English or how to communicate effectively with Canadians, Ms. Nakano took a different approach, one that would consider students' prior knowledge in any other language or culture as a springboard for learning the target language. A typical class started with Ms. Nakano asking students about how to say things in their own languages and do things in their own cultures. She would even encourage students to speak in their own languages and teach their classmates a few words in these languages before engaging with English texts. For example, in a class with focus on networking in English, one Colombian student taught a Chinese student how to greet in Spanish, following the cultural norms of giving a kiss on the cheek. I observed that students showed an intrinsic excitement to learn about each other's languages and cultures. In addition, because students felt included in the lesson, they were then able to make comparisons to the English language, facilitating learning. Ms. Nakano always showed high interest in her students' languages and the stories they had to share, which encouraged them to participate in class and increased their interest in learning English. Ms. Nakano explicitly told me she enjoyed reversing roles, that is, letting students have the role of the teacher while she simply facilitated their learning.

Welcoming students' languages and cultures in the English class, giving up the role of the sole authority figure, and showing empathy and interest in what students had to say, are three main qualities Ms. Nakano has as a "good" teacher. Without a doubt, her students will be ready to integrate into the Canadian multicultural landscape.

TEACHER VOICES

- Support English language learners.
- Let them use their home languages when they need to.
- Connect their past experiences to their school work.
- Allow them to learn from interacting with each other.
- Don't dumb down the texts or the assignments; simplify them.
- Support students' reading and writing with technology.
- Offer them different ways for expressing their ideas.
- Consider the message of a student's work before commenting on the usage errors.

20. Incorporate inquiry groups into the curriculum

INQUIRY MODES

Think of a school where the students spend a week, or even months, exploring a topic or theme that interests them, sometimes as a class, or in groups, or, occasionally, as individuals. What will they read, write, construct, observe, record, paint, revise, make, present? How will we organize their time and help them track their experiences? What resources, including technology, books, magazines, and films, will we search for to deepen their experiences? How will they share and reflect at the close of the inquiry? What will they remember and take home to put on top of their dresser? How will we account for and represent their learning? How are they employing inside and outside school those strategies we keep talking about? What have we taught them about how literacy works, in all its modes and shapes? Good schools everywhere are looking at all of these components as basic to learning, and inquiry education (in its new and wider definition) is a mainstay of every successful school program.

PROJECT-BASED LEARNING

> Students go beyond the textbook to study complex topics based on real-world issues, such as the water quality in their communities or the history of their town, analyzing information from multiple sources, including the Internet and interviews with experts. Project-based class work is more demanding than traditional book-based instruction, where students may just memorize facts from a single source. Instead, students utilize original documents and data, mastering principles covered in traditional courses but learning them in more meaningful ways. Projects can last weeks; multiple projects can cover entire courses. Student work is presented to audiences beyond the teacher, including parents and community groups.
>
> *Edutopia*, August 11, 2005

"…our notion of inquiry as stance is perspectival and conceptual — a worldview, a critical habit of mind, a dynamic and fluid way of knowing and being in the world of educational practice that carries across professional careers and educational settings."
Marilyn Cochran-Smith and Susan L. Lytle, *Inquiry as Stance: Practitioner Research for the Next Generation*.

An inquiry model can grow from a curriculum need, from an interest the whole class has, from a group's having coalesced around an issue or from an individual whose passion for a topic needs to be recognized and explored. Beginning with students having a say in the topic, the theme or the issue, we can move them into an inquiry model of learning, following these general phases of exploration:
1. selecting a topic;
2. forming an inquiry group;
3. building background knowledge;
4. classifying and categorizing information acquired;
5. interpreting and assessing data;
6. presenting and sharing the inquiry;
7. reflecting on processes and products.

Focus: iPad Inquiries

David Booth

A school in Timmins, a mining community in Northern Ontario, was part of a research project conducted by Tina Benevides of Nipissing University exploring literacy development through the incorporation of iPads into the daily reading and writing events of an all-boys classroom. With each student being supplied with an iPad for the year, I became a partner in the project, helping to set up the e-resources that would act as a library of novels for small-group and whole-class reading, organizing some of the units the students would explore, and visiting the class as a guest teacher, where I could demonstrate literacy strategies that the iPad could support. These relate to promoting both the reading of texts and the enriching and expansion of the big ideas that fiction explores.

I wasn't prepared for the power that technology puts in the hands of youngsters, and I became part of the learning process with the boys and their teacher, Suzanne Chartrand, caught up in the ease and accessibility of the world of information that this wireless tool can offer. The boys were given some hands-on workshops by the technology consultant, and within moments they had found the games that connect them to the pop culture of the techno generation, and swiped their way across the screens into more text forms than I knew existed.

ELECTRONIC HEROES

I wanted to explore research strategies using the Internet with the iPads. I asked the boys to find information on the Internet about a hero who interested them. I wrote their responses on the SMART Board. Their heroes ranged from Batman to Terry Fox to J.F.K. As the list grew longer, I asked the boys to classify their responses, and they came up with these categories: political heroes, celebrities, artists, sports heroes, war heroes, people who demonstrated courage, and when one boy shouted out "Jesus," we added religious heroes. The lists they had discovered on the Internet could not have been found in any one reference book.

As they dug deeper into what defines a hero, a student called out, "Nellie McClung," I asked him to tell us why she should be included, and he read information about her in a halting voice. Then he shared other names from his list, suddenly stating, "Dr. Booth, these are all women, and they are Canadian." This was a lad who felt that he had limitations as a reader. His discovery represented for me the value of this kind of freewheeling research, like years ago when I would walk among the stacks in a library and discover books I had not known about, that I would not search for in the card catalogue, backpacking in "idea countries" and surprising myself into new discoveries.

These boys had stumbled upon Greek myths, athletes who had passed on, comic heroes, law makers, and ordinary folk who had behaved in extraordinary ways. They tried dozens of websites, used hundreds of cue words, and argued and debated the qualities of heroic action.

Then, the moment arrived that we as teachers hope for in every teaching situation: a student asked whether Leonardo da Vinci could be classified as a hero. There were comments back and forth, until one boy informed us that the artist had painted the Mona Lisa, and that alone should classify him as a hero. There was consensus, and his name was added to the list. I asked the class to find a picture of the painting on their iPads, and when 22 boys held up images of the Mona Lisa in a classroom in Northern Ontario, far from the Louvre in Paris, I felt that I was in a Fellini film. When one student said, "I heard that there is a secret code in her left eyebrow." 22 left eyebrows appeared on their screens, and a new inquiry was born.

Focus: Curiosity and learning
Rich Coles

Being curious is a daily feature of our lives. Why is the tasting menu at a favourite restaurant so irresistible? Why does it seem there is always pop-up road construction when someone is pressed for time to make an important appointment? How do filmmakers create so many alluring special effects? How can a small electronic device be so powerful? Why do some rational people transform into maniacs when they get behind the wheel of a vehicle? What facets of deep learning spark your curiosity? What aspects of curiosity may well facilitate deep learning?

Parents know that young children are constantly trying to make sense of their worlds. They interact with physical objects and with people. These experiences expand their intellectual and social development. Young children try out different activities and see what happens. They are aware of the reactions of adults around them. Their curiosity takes place in a social setting.

Young children demonstrate their curious nature by the seemingly endless questions they pose. With age the questions expand from inquiries about aspects of their world to questions about things they cannot see. Susan Engel suggests that "curiosity, the engine of intellectual development, is possibly the most valuable asset a child brings to her education." But as young people progress in school they ask fewer questions and have fewer opportunities to communicate their curiosity. Their robust curiosity appears to diminish in formal educational settings. Why should there be places for students' curiosity during their schooling?

Young people are already curious when they arrive at school about topics of interest to them such as the wonders of science, games, technology and social media, video gaming, social issues, various sports, popular culture, music, and dress. Curious learners who seek out new information and experiences demonstrate enhanced learning. Intrinsic motivation engages them in topics of personal interest. Their deep learning, for example about polar bears, is stimulated by pleasure and curiosity. Their developing knowledge about a topic of inquiry makes them more confident as learners. Curious children and youth play with ideas and concepts, try different approaches, take risks, and learn from productive mistakes. They listen attentively to others and respect the sometimes esoteric and abstruse percolating ideas and notions of others.

Teachers play a critical role in fostering curiosity. They accept that many learners are going to follow different paths to deep understanding rather than the widespread top-down standardized learning approaches. Teachers provide time and opportunities for learners to engage in meaningful learning. They do not dominate classroom talk and pose numerous factual questions. Their questions model critical and creative ways of thinking about ideas, concepts, and information. Student questions kindle intrinsic motivation, activate their current thinking, include many members of the class, and provide insights into their learning. Asking great questions is a characteristic of today's top technical inventors and innovators.

Students' learning is also influenced by their beliefs about themselves as learners. Children and youth with growth mindsets believe that their abilities and skills change during their schooling and that their efforts influence their learning. Others with a fixed mindset believe that certain abilities and skills cannot be changed (Dweck, 2016). Teachers demonstrate a growth mindset when they believe all children can learn, praise their hard work, effort, risk taking and willingness to take on challenging, difficult tasks.

In classrooms that foster curiosity teachers scaffold students' learning. They guide students' investigations of new ideas and topics based on their interest, wonder, and curiosity. Teachers also express their curiosity, excitement, and self-direction when they talk about new ideas and try innovative ways of coming to know.

How would you respond to this question: Imagine a school where _____? Our imaginations allow us to envision a number of responses to this question. W.L. Ostroff posits that "Imagination is the basis of all our creative action—any-

For more insights into curiosity and learning, see "Children's Need to Know: Curiosity in Schools," by Susan Engel, in *Harvard Educational Review*, 81:4, 2011; "Stimulation Seeking and Intelligence: A Prospective Longitudinal Study," by A. Raine, C. Reynolds, P.H. Venables, and S.A. Mednick, in *Journal of Personality and Social Psychology*, 82:4, 2002; *The Innovator's DNA: Mastering the Five Skills of Disruptive Innovators,* by Jeff Dyer, Hal Gregorsen, and Clayton M. Christensen; and *Cultivating Curiosity in K-12 Classrooms,* by W.L. Ostroff.

thing we make or alter or envision or combine—and therefore, it is at the root of all intellectual life, from art to science to technological innovation."

Imaginative young people demonstrate enhanced cognitive development and academic success. In class, they tend to be better problem solvers, have more self-control, and be more cooperative. Coaches have their athletes use their imagination to envision success shooting free throws, snapping wrist shots or making difficult wedge shots. The athlete's envisioning of these skills improves performance. When designing learning experiences for their students, teachers can envision the details of the activities and their young people participating in the learning experience.

Children and youth are constantly trying to make sense of people, events, experiences, concepts and information in their lives. Nourishing curiosity that facilitates their deep learning is essential in all subject areas.

21. Demonstrate effective classroom management

"Discipline climate is also consistently related to higher average performance at the school level. In 48 participating countries and economies, schools with better average performance tend to have a more positive disciplinary climate, even after accounting for the socio-economic status and demographic background of students and schools and various other school characteristics."

United Nations. Organization for Economic Co-operation and Development. *What Makes Schools Successful?* Paris: 2014

Focus: You there, be quiet

David Booth

Each year, the most frequently requested workshops by student teachers are those involving classroom management, or what is commonly called discipline techniques. We buy all sorts of manuals on this topic — videos, kits, texts — but the solution to classroom management problems really depends upon the health of the community in the individual classroom. There are hundreds of strategies that can help teachers move towards becoming an enabling and supportive leader with the youngsters in their charge, but the change begins with the teaching self, and the way that self is presented to the class. And of course today's schools are complex places where we are dealing with so many issues, interruptions, absences, illnesses, and mobility that building a classroom community is a much harder goal. And yet there are so few alternatives.

- Establish ground rules with input from your students. Note those guidelines that are determined by administration (hall behaviours, class, attendance, bullying reports); then, with the students, work out classroom behaviours and expectations, alongside consequences. Keep the rules to a minimum, and stress fairness and responsibility. Help the students with clear homework procedures, manners for working in groups, expectations for different kinds of talk times, where to keep books and writing folders, when computers will be used, and so on.
- For me, the work has always been the answer to discipline problems. By changing the instructions, modifying the content, motivating the youngster, we can eliminate so many problems. I need to accept the variety of conditions these young people bring to the classroom, and they need to know and accept my frailties. And we need to know when our help is not enough and not to be afraid to ask for assistance. While sending a child to the office can be a temporary measure so that the others can continue, it solves no problem. Such is the complexity of managing thirty children at a time, each with different needs. Operating successfully as a participant in a classroom community seems to me to be a vital life skill. We need to find out what we can do to facilitate this process.

- Over the years, I've learned to move the desks around so that we could work easily together, to create a classroom where children made most of the decisions, to care about their working conditions so that we could accomplish what we needed to and what we wanted to, and to recognize that sometimes things just didn't work out. Like all teachers, I have had many sleepless nights turning over failures in my mind, playing out the scene a hundred different ways. But one of the great secrets of teaching is that we can begin again every day, we can let that child know there is still hope in this classroom. And we can move forward, bruised and wiser, rebuilding the place called school, remembering that bruises, in time, fade.

- In Ralph Conors's *Glengarry School Days*, we read about a rural school where the mixed-grade children face a succession of different and untrained teachers throughout the year. Why do we feel such satisfaction when the oldest boy in the room takes on the bully supply teacher to protect a younger child from a whipping? Because I am sure we have all confronted that unfairness in our lives at school, and we know something should be done about it but we don't know what, and we feel powerless.

- We teachers are adults assigned the tasks of guiding the children along the way, like mutants or clones gone awry, with bits of significant others clinging to us — a hint of the parent, a mirror image of a favourite aunt or uncle; the nasty neighbour who allows no noise after dark, the youth group leader, the tutor, the babysitter, the actor, the comedian, the interviewer, the coach, the warden, the government clerk, the therapist, the driving instructor, the waitress, the friendly giant. And the children come in all varieties, supposedly ready to respond when and about whatever the teacher decides, no matter how their day began, or what was said, or what was done.

- We need to be clear that there are differences between "strict" or "tough" and "mean." Students are quite able to cope with a teacher with a "tough" reputation, if that teacher is "fair" and respectful of students. If boundaries are clear and articulated, then all of us know what is expected in the running of this community. If students can be involved in problem solving and decision making, and if they can have a sense of ownership in the classroom culture, they are more likely to accept the norms of behaviour. If the challenges are intense, we have to find ways of reframing the classroom mood — a class meeting, rewriting the goals of this classroom community, clarifying school expectations and how we could go about changing them, changing the timetabled event to a different topic, asking students to write down their thoughts on handling the issue in a better way.

- Some students act out their perceived personalities. If they were publicly considered difficult last year by their teacher, then they may maintain that role this year. Always be consistent, but do not confuse consistency with routine. Maintain the tempo of the classroom and don't play favourites. Offer redirecting behaviours when confronted with a difficult student, and be consistent and fair with the boundaries the class has developed with you. It may help to find out the cause of the behaviour, and help the student to interpret the reasons for his/her actions, approaching the incident with curiosity and a need to learn more. It may be the student doesn't understand his/her own reason for the difficulty, and needs a pause time.

- We support our students best when we manage our emotions as wise, caring professionals, sharing what is appropriate, helping them to manage their own emotional states, their own stress levels, and taking time to include methods of self-management in our classes, such as brainstorming ways to cope with turmoil, creating a quiet apace in the classroom (a peaceful corner) or conducting a mindfulness workshop. A student involved with the class project of individual research using computers in the library, after an hour of inquiry, shouted out, "I can't stand this machine any longer. Aren't there any books in this library I can read?" The librarian quickly stepped in and said that he could go and read quietly in her office, which he did. That librarian acted with compassion and organizational strength, and the class continued to work on their inquiries.

- What are the most effective ways of maintaining order in a classroom, and in a school? The answer lies somewhere in the building of a community to which we all belong. For a teacher, it is about relationships; for a student, it is about fitting into the community as a respected and contributing member. We need a classroom culture that nourishes and supports us, as teacher and as student. Living in a confrontational setting each day is not healthy; we need the students to know how to participate, and want to participate because it is worth it. The more we understand their lives, their situations, their stages and ages of development, the better chance we have of building a community culture of collective learning that is managed by peer expectations, by feeling secure in a place where we have shared, common goals, and where each of us matters.

- And we need to remember that we build such a community, that there are processes to support group awareness, that teachers can facilitate how students interact with one another. Meaningful conversations require trust and mutual respect. There are strategies that will help you to develop a collaborative, cooperative community of learners, increasing performance and satisfaction. We want to influence behaviours and attitudes, not demand change. As a teacher, my responses to any student's inappropriate challenges must correct the situation, but also demonstrate my respect for all students; I am a professional.

The Classroom Management Book, by Harry K. Wong and Rosemary T. Wong, includes fifty procedures for creating a well-managed and productive classroom.

22. Employ technology effectively

As teachers, we enjoy sharing the foibles and fractures of our daily lives in school with the students, parents, and other teachers we meet. Somehow, laughing at ourselves creates more opportunities for honest dialogue among the adults who supervise the lives of children. We are great fans of the Wayside School stories by Louis Sachar, in which our school lives are twisted and mocked and full of fun. The thirty classrooms in Wayside School are stacked on top of one another (rather like my faculty, OISE/UT), offering a teacher in the school, Mrs. Jewls, an opportunity to take out her frustrations on the advent of technology in the classroom:

> "Watch closely," said Mrs. Jewls. "You can learn much faster using a computer instead of paper and pencil." Then she pushed the new computer out the window. The children all watched it fall thirty floors and smash against the sidewalk.
> "See?" said Mrs. Jewls. "That's gravity! I've been trying to teach you about gravity, but the computer showed you a lot quicker!"

Do you look for ways that you can engage your learners using technology? Most of us are familiar with tablets, tutorial videos, and the like, but are you comfortable using those as means for learning?

TECHNOLOGY AND LITERACY

Everyone we know working in the areas of education and literacy spends hours each day reading and writing on the computer, yet often celebrates the book as the most important centre of the student's world. Some schools have one computer at the back of each classroom, while others have a computer lab down the hallway; some have a trained librarian with print and computer resources to assist teachers, and others have a laptop computer for each student and a Smart Board for the teacher. Schools are trying to give their students opportunities to become computer-literate, to learn about technology but more important to use technology to support and enhance their own learning events.

Now we have youngsters at all levels working with word processors, chat lines, blogs, emails, text messages, web searches, Photoshop, etc. And all these activities are literacy events. Boys and girls are reading, and especially writing, more than ever in the world's history. But what we can consider is the quality of the literacy events they are engaging in, the kinds of learning processes they are exploring, and what languaging options they may be minimizing, or even missing.

The disparities between the plugged-in or wireless electronic home and the traditional school contribute to the alienation many students feel about what goes on in their classroom. How can we build on their digital literacies as we re-conceptualize how we could teach reading and writing in ways that would help them to value the intertextuality of the many different literacy experiences in their lives? We can be plugged in at times, and still gather together and sit in a circle, to listen to a tale 2,000 years old.

The texts that most students read and enjoy at home are print and electronic. Our choice of texts in the classroom needs to reflect the multi-modality seen on the Web to appeal to students' reading behaviours. Yet computer use can be balanced by programs involving print resources that connect the students to the worlds they inhabit, while at the same time stretching their abilities and interests.

We now have e-books, e-magazines, e-stories, e-comics, e-information, and e-poems, not to mention e-video games, the most popular of the texts designed and created for children. Reading has now been redefined to include making meaning with a variety of text forms, or combinations of forms.

WHAT ABOUT VIDEO AND COMPUTER GAMES PLAYED IN SCHOOL?

Many parents are still nervous about their children playing computer games in school. As in everything, balance matters, but computers, in one form or another, are part of the daily lives of most students. There are dozens of games that can be played onscreen using the Internet or prepared programs. With the computer, children can search and discover several games, then make a "game plan" for others to follow, keeping track of the results or printing the outcomes.

Board games such as Pictionary and Scrabble, which involve reading and spelling, can motivate students and encourage learning, and can also be used in cooperative learning lessons to encourage working in groups. A principal we know purchased twenty board games last summer for his middle-school classrooms. A father we know plays a board game with his two children (ages five and seven) almost every evening after dinner. They must have fifty of them, and the two children read and count in ways with the games that are difficult to imagine with school texts.

Playful approaches and games may be among our strongest allies. Computer programs are beginning to offer us intriguing ways for building word strength with spelling and vocabulary games and puzzles, as well as offering support for struggling handwriters and spellers. It is significant that many of the games onscreen offer openings to limited readers for taking part in print-based activities, with less frustration and defeat than in much paper-and-pencil work.

In *Literacy and Education*, the New Literacies authority James Gee says that many features of electronic games facilitate learning:
- they allow players to take on a new identity;
- they are interactive, and players must perform some action in order to receive feedback;
- they are scaffolded into well-ordered problems;
- players form hypotheses and gain competencies in the early stages of a game that will be used and built on in later stages;
- they offer multiple ways to learn, provide an opportunity for active learning, and encourage experimentation and discovery.

> Implementing effective uses of technology in the classroom is supported by books like *Power Up*, by Diana Neebe and Jen Roberts, and *When Writing with Technology Matters,* by Carol Bedard and Charles Fuhrken.

LOOKING BACK, LOOKING FORWARD: BEST PRACTICES FOR INCORPORATING TECHNOLOGY INTO YOUR CLASSROOM

Tina Benevides, PhD, innovative tech educator, Hands: TheFamilyHelpNetwork.ca and Nipissing University

With the ubiquitous nature of mobile technologies entering our classrooms every day, we are able to enhance the learning of our students in a very real way. For example, a class can visit the Louvre with Google Earth to look at various works of art when studying an artist such as Vermeer or Van Gogh. Or we can Skype with the International Space Station during a science lesson to listen to astronauts speaking about their research. Students also have the opportunity to become publishers (e.g., on YouTube, blogs, vlogs, Twitter, Instagram) and have their voices heard across the world.

In 2011, David Booth and I experienced the magic of placing iPads (which had just been released) into the hands of grade seven boys in Northern Ontario. Immediately, we realized that this device had the potential to change our educational landscape. Lessons no longer needed to be static and didactic; rather, they have the potential to be flexible and interactive. When teaching future educators, I always challenge them to consider if they have hit their M.A.R.K. That is, are the learning opportunities designed to be Meaningful, Authentic, and Relevant to the Kids. If the answer is no, then I ask them to reconsider their lesson(s). This is particularly important today, when the opportunities to reach beyond the classroom walls into the world, have never been easier.

Technology is also allowing our most vulnerable students to share their thinking and understanding. With the release of e-readers in 2010, children who struggled with reading had the opportunity to read a book that might otherwise have been too challenging by using the text-to-speech function. This is only one example of how mobile technologies today are being used to assist all learners at all levels. No matter what stage you are at in your comfort level with technology integration, the following list has been developed from my experiences with established best practices in this evolving area.

TOP TEN LIST FOR INTEGRATING TECHNOLOGY IN YOUR LEARNING ENVIRONMENT

Tina Benevides, professor, Nipissing University

1. Have a purpose.
Why are you incorporating the technology into your lesson(s)? What are your goals for incorporating technology? It is important to clearly outline your purposes for incorporating the technology so that learners are meaningfully engaged and do not view the technology as optional.

2. Put pedagogy before technology.
What are you already doing in your learning environment that could be enhanced by the use of technology? Is the technology simply an addition or a true integration that will allow for authentic and meaningful learning experiences? Will the technology enable learners to connect their outside lives and interests with their education inside of the classroom?

3. Set clear expectations.
Consider the expectations and routines that you will incorporate with respect to the use and handling of technology in your classroom. It may be a good idea to include your students in a discussion of these expectations and the appropriate uses of technology. It is also important to involve your students in a discussion of digital citizenship and digital footprints. We also need to consider the privacy of our students. Before placing any personal information (e.g.., pictures) in a public format, it is essential that you confirm your Board policies regarding privacy.

4. Challenge yourself to try one new tool per month.
New technological tools and applications are being released daily and it can be difficult and challenging to keep up with all of these new advances. I suggest visiting several websites that list appropriate tools and apps for the lesson(s) for which you would like to incorporate the technology. In this way, you will be able to decide which of these tools and/or apps might best suit your students and your lesson(s).

5. Practice, practice, practice!
Play in the sandbox and get others involved. I have found that the best way to ensure success with technology integration is to make sure you are comfortable with the technology yourself. Why not invite your colleagues, friends, and/or family members to play in the sandbox with you? This discovery time will enable you to avoid any delays and/or pitfalls when introducing the technology in your classroom.

6. Make it accessible.
Technology should not be a tool that is only permitted at certain times of the day. In fact, the wonderful advantage of mobile technologies is that they are mobile! If learners are permitted to have the technology at all times (as

long as expectations for appropriate use are clearly defined), then the tool will virtually disappear and the authentic learning will become the focus. In this way, students will quickly realize that the technology is simply a tool that can be used to assist them to connect the inside world of the classroom with their outside world.

7. Let your students take the driver's seat.
Never be afraid to let your student's take the lead with technology. Currently, it is very difficult to keep up with our students in their understanding of mobile technologies. They have grown up with these tools and can often show us new ways of using the technology if we just let them! I think it is important that today, more than ever, educators need to be facilitators of learning environments where students are allowed to use technology to answer their own questions. In addition, allowing your students to take the lead will foster a sense of empowerment that will take them outside of the classroom walls.

8. Connect with other educators using technology.
When in doubt, try connecting with other educators (globally) who are integrating technology as well. There are thousands of educational websites, blogs, vlogs, journal articles, and YouTube videos that you can visit for assistance. Another wonderful way to network with other innovative and passionate educators is through professional development courses and/or educational conferences. These professional development learning opportunities will allow you to connect with and perhaps collaborate with like-minded educators.

9. Collaborate with colleagues to develop cross-curricular opportunities for engaging with the technology.
What cross-curricular opportunities are available in your school? Are there other colleagues in your school who would be interested in collaborating in a cross-curricular lesson that employs the use of mobile technology? How could you integrate your lesson ideas with other subject areas? The options are limitless.

10. Have fun!
When you are having fun, it can only catch on!

23. Ask open-ended questions and welcome student questions

Focus: The art of questioning
David Booth

STUDENT-GENERATED QUESTIONS

We have a much greater chance of having our students invest themselves in the learning experience if we help them to take ownership with their own questions. They may begin to participate in the text-inspired meaning making if they believe that their questions really matter, and that others are interested in grappling with them. This practice may result in those same students questioning ideas as they read, wondering why they are occasionally breaking down in making sense of text, and allowing them to use their own questions to move them forward as they seek answers, information or clarification. They read as real readers do, moving back and forth between their own lives and the worlds created by the author, wondering, pondering, challenging, inquiring, rereading, searching, summarizing, and always questioning. It is the way humans learn, and the way readers read.

But student-generated questions may lead to deeper comprehension, as readers begin to consider the effect the text is having upon them, when they can give voice to their own concerns, rather than us trying to second-guess what they should be able to answer by inventing thought-provoking questions the night before. When we as teachers are solely responsible for asking all the questions, there is little chance that many students will be engaged in a rigorous negotiation of the text and their inquiries.

TEACHER-GENERATED QUESTIONS

How will we ever help young readers to become independent thinkers who will choose to engage with a topic if we don't allow them to predict as they read, to practice inferential thinking, to question the text when complex questions are not easily answered? When will they learn to draw their own conclusions, to seek out further information, to ask a friend for an opinion on a difficult issue that arises because of the text? How will they learn to become curious about the ideas generated by the author? And our guilt-ridden teacher voices asking, "Why did I spend so much of my time inventing questions that I thought they should ask, when they might have brought forward much better ones?" Lists of predigested and impersonal comprehension questions are no longer part of our classroom teaching. However, manuals for published programs can often offer ideas for giving the students thoughtful and deepening literacy strategies, or suggesting book sets for increasing the reading repertoires of the students, or presenting significant background information for supporting the text.

- We have questions to ask, but they will grow from our conversations about the text, from the honest revelations of the students' own concerns, as we try to guide them into deeper interpretations. But now we attempt to ask honest questions that are driven by their inquiring dialogue, as we would in a conversation with peers during a book club session, based on listening to their interactions rather than to our own scripted agenda.
- We want the students to engage in thoughtful considerations about the topic and its connections to their lives, not struggle to find the responses they think I want. I like the description educators Gay Su Pinnell and Irene Fountas give for using this strategy: "The teacher's questions are a light scaffold that helps students examine texts in new ways."
- We can model and demonstrate how effective questions work, showing the need to listen carefully to others, revisiting points in the text that support a particular comment, and supporting effective responses of the students.
- Try asking no questions during a text discussion but note down the ones you might have asked in the past. Or tape-record a text talk session with you and the children and play it back to analyze the types of questions you asked and the effect of them on your students' contributions.

International authority on writing Lucy Calkins gives us such important advice on the art of self-questioning as we write: "Our job is to ask questions of children so that children internalize these questions and ask them of themselves and their own emerging drafts."

- Rather than initiating questions, build on the questions and comments of the students by offering open-ended responses after they speak, encouraging further contributions, and helping to focus and deepen the dialogue.
- Consider using prompts rather than recall questions in your interactions with the students during group sessions and individual conferences, and in your responses to their reading and writing journals. These prompts can expand or deepen the offerings of the students, helping them to clarify or expand their thoughts and nudging them into expressing their opinions and ideas. We have questions to ask and we need to ask them, but we want to teach our students to ask their own, to behave as proficient readers do, framing personal and public questions to promote deeper understanding of the ideas stimulated by the text.
- Separate assessment questions from your text discussions. Clearly stating the purpose of the evaluation activity, whether in practice sessions or in a testing situation, can help students understand the different purposes and to learn how to handle both types of events.
- When students ask authentic questions as the learning event proceeds, the teacher can point out the complexities involved, and share her need for more information, learning along with the students. These student questions reveal the process of learning, and allow the teacher to adapt, to rethink the planned lesson, to move instead to seeking responses that matter to the process of learning. Both teacher and students are involved in the learning dynamic, co-partnering in the process of discovery.

Dan Rothstein and Luz Santana make the case for teaching students how to ask their own questions and assume responsibility for finding out what they want and need to know, in Make Just One Change: Teach Students to Ask their own Questions.

Apple seeds and inquiry

David Booth

In Carla Correa's grade four class, the computer is usually hooked up to the projector and the screen. When the need for information arises in a discussion, a student simply goes to the computer, types in the query with teacher support, and then the students read the answers and discuss the points onscreen. It is such a natural process. While visiting their classroom, I had read a poem about apples to the class, and a student mentioned that she had heard the apple seeds contained arsenic and so, if eaten by a dog, could cause death. I asked her to find this out onscreen and we all read the information. Another student questioned whether this was a danger to humans. The student typed in the question and we discovered the facts about arsenic. For example, apple seeds do contain arsenic, and are dangerous eaten in quantity, but you would need to finely chew and eat about 200 apple seeds, or about 20 apple cores, to receive a fatal dose.

A student wondered as she stared at the computer why Apple Inc.'s apple logo had a bite taken out of it. On she went, and the resulting information was so strange that the students asked more and more questions about this design's origins. One student then offered, "If all this began with a poem, I think we should compose a class haiku to thank Mr. Booth," which is just what they did (two haikus, in fact). This unexpected direction for learning turned my poetry visit into a learning event that changed me, the teacher, and the students. I want to follow their leads, clarifying and redirecting when necessary. If the co-creating partnership is working, we will involve my original plans, but they will be enriched and deepened.

Prompts for reflecting

- Can you identify the goals that you feel will support student growth in your class and in the school?
- How often do you play the role of lecturer, group facilitator, individual tutor, scribe, conversationalist, with your class? Different patterns of classroom involvement for the teacher offer opportunities for interacting on a conversational level with individual students.
- How do you handle unforeseen disturbances in your classroom?
- Would you like some supportive strategies for improving classroom management?
- Do you have difficulties reaching particular students?
- What do your students think about your relationships with them?
- How would you describe the culture of your classroom?
- How will you know if your students are learning academically, developing social relationships, becoming critical thinkers, appreciating others from different backgrounds, supporting community service? Are there ways of collecting data to support your successes?
- How might teachers help students to become metacognitively aware of what they are learning and how that learning might be applied in real life?
- How can you move the talk from being teacher-directed to being student-directed?
- What are the challenges of ensuring that student-directed talk is accountable talk?

4

Understand How Effective Schools Work

> Ms. Hempel was already thinking about her anecdotals. The word, with all its expectations of intimacy and specificity, bothered her: a noun in the guise of an adjective, an obfuscation of the fact that twice a year she had to produce eighty-two of these ineluctable things. Not reports, like those written by other teachers at other schools, but anecdotals: loving and detailed accounts of a student's progress, enlivened by descriptions of the child offering a piercing insight or aiding a struggling classmate or challenging authority. It was a terrible responsibility: to render, in a recognizable way, something as ineffable as another human being, particularly a young one. On average, she would spend an hour writing about each child, and then waste up to another hour rereading what she had just written, in the hopes that her words might suddenly reveal themselves as judicious.
>
> Sara Shun-Lien Bynum, *Ms. Hempel Chronicles*

24. Recognize the school as a strong professional community

Based on research and practice, successful schools have collaborative cultures in which administrators and teachers work as a team with a common commitment to learning initiatives that ensure success for all. By creating a collaborative culture among educators, it is possible to incite interest in theory and new methodologies and practices. A collaborative culture naturally establishes partnerships with other possible team members, such as parents, in a common pursuit to improve learning skills for all students.

It has been shown that if schools work as teams, there is much sharing of expertise so that all students benefit from the most effective ,instruction available. To create a unified team committed to school change, a school needs a specific, detailed and rigorous plan that has a shared vision of how it will get from here to there.

A collaborative culture provides a combination of pressure and support to help teachers deal with change and improve student learning. In *The New Meaning of Educational Change*, Michael Fullan describes this process as "the overlapping of strong pedagogical practice" with the existence and implementation of assessment. What is implicit in such a belief is that teachers need to work together with clear goals, while at the same time with clear accountability. To move from a collaborative community to a professional community where teachers overlap strong pedagogy with assessment, teachers need the ability and desire to assess their students and to respond to the results of that assessment to inform their practice.

Principals not only need to create collaborative school environments that promote professional development so that teachers can hone their practice, but also need to facilitate self-directed learning so that students at all grade levels have more choice in their learning. By taking control of their own learning, students become more independent, more in control, and ultimately make better choices in their learning. There are several factors that have proven instrumental in creating support for a strong professional community:

- building in time for school change;
- in-school professional development;
- district professional development;
- teacher motivation;
- support systems for teachers;
- the support of parents.

> *Inherent change* is when change happens almost organically. We say 'almost' because, as we shall see, the roles of leaders and the enabling conditions they foster are essential. Under the right conditions, inherent change can occur more rapidly and more easily than anything we have seen before in complex systems. This is how the new pedagogies' change process is different: it is faster because its fundamentals are natural to the human condition. It is built on humankind's need to be a) doing something intrinsically meaningful, and b) to do it socially (i.e., with the group) (Pink 2009, Brooks 2012).
>
> *Inherent change* is efficient, reaches everyone, motivates from within, cultivates group ownership and has built-in sustainability. It is organic change for complex human systems. The model of organic change is useful because, in organic systems, under the right conditions, change can spread quickly and existing systems can be transformed in very short periods of time. In educational systems, when the right learning conditions are in place, there can be a natural and organic adaptation of new pedagogies by students, teachers, and other stakeholders throughout the system.
>
> Michael Fullan and Maria Langworth, *A Rich Seam: How New Pedagogies Find Deep Learning*

BEYOND WHAT WE MEAN BY "TEACHER" AND "PRINCIPAL"

Kelly Manning, PhD, educator

These insights emerged from conversations with an elementary school principal who reflects on lessons learned during her years as a teacher, and how these lessons inform her practice as an administrator. Curious to know

---

The Hundred Languages of Children, edited by Carolyn Edwards, Lella Gandini, and George Forman, describes the transformations in the Reggio Emilia school experiences, begun fifty years ago in Italy, that have led to great changes in primary education worldwide.

In *A Rich Seam: How New Pedagogies Find Deep Learning*, Michael Fullan and Maria Langworth describe an international perspective that examines the complexities of school change, and present significant and powerful visions and examples of schools that are offering deep learning opportunities for diverse student populations.

where she developed an awareness that she can have a moral influence in improving the lives of children, she recalls a student teaching placement in an economically challenged school, just outside of London, England. She confides, "I'm not even sure if up until that point I realized what I had to offer kids". Acknowledging the importance of teaching her students the fundamentals of reading and writing, she recalls that many of these students had needs that went beyond the academic. Vividly recounting the first day of her teaching placement, she remembers being confronted by a small child who was anxiously looking for his brother. Noticing that he was "all disheveled" with no socks and wearing pants that were too short, she thought, "Okay, who's this child? I'm going to need to know him." She continues, "I got to know this family really well and [I] think of them still. . . . I think the discussion always comes back to ethics, and how we show compassion for the children that we teach."

As a principal, she shares these stories with teachers and encourages them to consider the needs of their students that go beyond the curriculum. These needs include food and clothing and having someone to listen to them. Recognizing that her message may be unconventional, she explains, "Sometimes you have to go above and beyond what we would call *teacher* and sometimes it is a difficult thing because not everybody is in agreement with what your role might be".

During a teaching practicum in a Multiple Exceptionality classroom, the principal came to understand that students need to feel a sense of belonging. She recalls how the educators in the classroom worked as a team to ensure that the children felt that they were part of a community, and that they were loved. These educators taught her that she had to pay close attention to the students who were "always telling us something" in what they said and did, "or just through their demeanour". She learned that she had to slow down and attend to the children, in order to understand what they were communicating. Being present to children, demonstrating patience, and affording them dignity and respect, reminds us that the ethics of teaching is a process, and one that requires us to reflect on our interactions. Guided by the needs of students, rather than by preconceived notions of who they are, we learn to appreciate their uniqueness as individuals, and to celebrate who they are becoming.

In her years as a Special Education teacher, she continued to be inspired by her students, who taught her to be patient and kind, and to understand that they were capable of learning, albeit at a different pace than their peers. As a principal, when dealing with parents who are distraught about their child's challenges in school, she strives to keep an open mind, and to help others do the same. She conveys hopeful messages, as she guides parents toward a realization that their children are able to succeed, but "in different ways". She helps teachers to empathize with parents when they are feeling frustration or sadness about their child's challenges. Teachers are encouraged to realize the important role they play in each child's learning.

Teaching presents us with a moral struggle to recognize and endeavour to respond to the unique needs of the child. At times this requires courage as well as a willingness to embrace a broader understanding of what we mean by "teacher". This principal's words and actions convey a belief that teachers are influential in creating schools that are caring and inclusive, where children of all abilities belong, and where they can realize their fullest potential.

This essay by Kelly Manning is taken from *Moral and Ethical Leadership: One Principal's Beliefs and Practices*, her unpublished doctoral dissertation at the University of Toronto.

PUTTING COMMUNITY IN PROFESSIONAL LEARNING COMMUNITIES
Larry Swartz, PhD, instructor, OISE/University of Toronto

Fifteen or so years into my teaching journey, I had the opportunity — and the luck — to be in a school that honed and sharpened, challenged and stretched my beliefs as my teaching journey was under way. I had the fortune to be in a school that truly valued professional learning communities.

I was hired by Paul Shaw and I was fortunate enough to be a member of Paul's staff for several years at both Floradale Public School, Queenston Drive Public School in the Peel District Board of Education.

As an administrator, Paul Shaw understood the importance of building a community. He recognized the importance of building trusting relationships with students, with parents, with the wider school community. He was determined to gather teachers who were known for their teaching finesse and expertise and he knew that having such teachers aboard the ship of which he was a captain would help to shape a school community centred on professional inquiry that would serve the students and their families, and enable each staff member to do "best" work.

Paul timetabled sessions in which teachers met once a month to sit down, talk, and examine procedures and share stories from our classrooms. He implemented a ritual of having all teachers in the school meet — during the day for half-day sessions, for professional development. This required finesse and commitment on the part of the teachers. The staff was divided into two teams, an arrangement that allowed one team to cover classes while the other attended a session. What helped to make this initiative a success was that at each of these meetings, the team of teachers focused on a particular issue that was agreed upon. We might have responded to professional reading, talked about our outside school course work, shared experiences from conferences and professional development workshops we might have attended. We asked questions of each other. We learned from each other. At these meetings, the principal's enthusiasm and the normal sharing and discussion that take place with colleagues next door and across the hall provided a forum to share our assumptions and move toward a richer language-based program.

As we continued with our research, one event particularly serves as an example of a community coming together for professional development when the entire teaching staff gathered around a long table together in the library. Paul had arranged a teleconference with the noted educator Donald Graves. To prepare for this interview, we read articles about writing and brainstormed questions to ask Graves, and the questions we raised were most likely the ones that many teachers were asking at the time about the writing process: How much choice should students have in their writing? How do we motivate students who are reluctant to write? How do we find time to confer with each of our students within a week? For one hour Donald Graves gave our gathering of teachers thoughtful attention as he answered each of our questions. Of course, we came away from the session with new questions and were given the challenge concerning changes we might make to our writing programs over time. The following year, we arranged a similar teleconference on assessment in writing with educator Jane Hansen.

I think each of us can learn something from the teacher next door, down the hall, sitting next to us at a course or at a conference. We can learn as much by disagreeing as agreeing, from questioning as much as answering, from listening as much as speaking. To be great teachers, we need to be open to learning, to gather around a table and to surround ourselves with people who also strive to be "good" teachers.

25. Join and participate in planning and teaching teams

Each teacher wants to belong to a staff where a trusting relationship with staff members opens nuanced and deeper understandings of the school's cultural values. Teachers who are part of a collaborative and cooperative staff recognize the value of being a member of a teaching team. Mentoring and being mentored demonstrates how both parties are part of the teaching/learning cycle that works with our students as well. We share information and techniques, we find new resources, we express excitement and give credit when a colleague has an article published or runs a successful school event. We hold back our judgment, we are respectful and patient, and we know how negotiation and diplomacy increase relationship success. An open, collaborative network of colleagues will allow you to discover different ways of working, and other teachers' ideas may complement yours.

Teachers Teaching Teachers
Geneal G. Cantrell, Gregory L. Cantrell
In Teachers Teaching Teachers, the authors use their decades of teaching experience to write about how to create successful classrooms based on a set of teaching principles.

- Are you part of a professional book club that meets regularly to examine a writer's philosophy or methods for changing education?
- Could you work on a shared project with someone with whom you have had a difficult relationship?
- If you examine the triggers that upset you with a particular colleague, you may discover new ways of responding.
- Involve yourself in social events with colleagues. Having coffee together or sharing treats can open up avenues of communication.
- Excellent teachers plan well.

PLANNING WITH COLLEAGUES

Lena Glaes-Coutts, vice-principal, Durham District School Board

All the best teachers I have had the pleasure to work with are teachers who plan well; and all the teachers who plan well are those who plan with others. But what is planning, really? In today's results-driven and product-oriented educational climate, there is a focus on perfection in creating plans. Boxed programs with blackline masters and templates are all the rage. But does a perfectly executed day plan or long-range plan make for greater student learning? When I started teaching, my principal demanded that I have three days of fully filled out day plans on my desk at all times. As an administrator, I am more likely to have day plans emailed to me on the day the teacher calls in ill. Does this mean that the teacher has not planned well? I would argue that it might actually be the exact opposite.

I think we can all agree that it is important to know our students. Regardless of how we gather data and information on the learners in our classes, all this information will be beneficial for creating engaging learning opportunities. This means that our plans must change in response to how our students learn and react to how we have structured the learning opportunities. There is a saying in yoga philosophy that goes something like this: "Each body is different and each day is different." I have found this to be true for teaching as well, as each student is uniquely distinct, and each day provides new and exciting learning for both teachers and students.

Besides knowing our students well, we need to not merely know but actually understand the curriculum we are teaching. What does it look like when it comes to life in our classrooms? How does this expectation link and integrate with the others, and how can we realize it so it makes sense for our learners? One experienced teacher I know expressed it this way: "I now have an exquisite understanding of the curriculum." I believe that is why this teacher consistently plans lessons and activities that engage the students; not by relying on boxed products, but by knowing the students and the curriculum and being able to mediate the two in a meaningful way.

But just as important in planning well is to leave space and time for being surprised — surprised by what our students bring to us, surprised by how they interact with the lessons we planned, and surprised by how we can all dance this dance of learning together. Some days we even need to set aside time to be amazed! Therefore the "laminated day plan" that is used from year to year, or the latest downloaded lesson created by someone else, does not lead to classrooms where learning comes alive. Sticky notes, scribbles, marks, and reflective questions and observations — such plans are organic, realistic, and continuously evolving to meet the needs of the students.

The teachers I have met during my twenty years in education who plan well have a deep understanding of what they are teaching as well as the students they are teaching. These teachers are always looking to make their teaching better and continuously reflect on what worked and what didn't work. Some reflect in private, but most seek out a trusted colleague, a critical friend, to do the reflecting and planning with. In today's technology-infused world, increasingly more of them use tech to do co-learning, co-planning, and reflecting. They use Twitter to be part of a larger learning community, co-create learning using Google Docs or OneNote or write blogs to share their experiences and invite feedback from others. They seek out colleagues with whom they can engage, who can challenge their thinking and share their own. They plan together, dialogue, discuss, and reflect on how the planning came to life and how it can be improved upon. They depend on the collective wisdom that they create together and the professional dialogue that grows their personal, practical professional.

WHO IS THE TEACHER?

Kimberly Bezaire, PhD, professor, School of Early Childhood, George Brown College

Over five years ago, Jennifer and Marie were assigned to work together as an "educational team" in Ontario's new full-day Kindergarten program. The program involved a number of innovations — a full-day schedule, play-based curriculum, and a co-operative, equal partnership between a registered early childhood educator and a certified teacher. They each admit to feeling excited, though a bit ambivalent, at their first meeting; with only several days to prepare for the children. Within the first few moments of getting to know each other, they agreed on a common goal and challenge for themselves: "Let's aim to make a space where a classroom visitor can't tell who is the teacher and who is the ECE." What a playful approach to forging this new relationship! In doing so, the educators began their journey in creating a classroom characterized by respect and a sense of agency — a social climate they built for themselves and each other and aimed to foster in children.

As an ECE professor-researcher, I was introduced to this team at a professional learning event, and was struck by the passion, curiosity, and critical thinking they brought to their practice. Sharing their pedagogical document and speaking with my undergraduate students, they bring to life new public policies aiming to integrate systems of "care" and "education." Reggio Emilia's notion of the "environment as third teacher" is a further new foundation to Ontario's Early Years Pedagogy — "valued for its power to organize, promote relationships, and educate. It mirrors the ideas, values, attitudes, and cultures of those who use the space (Malaguzzi, 1993 as cited by Ontario Ministry of Education, 2015, p. 20). By purposely and playfully disrupting power relationships in their Kindergarten — where ECEs have traditionally acted as assistants and teachers led in teaching — Jennifer and Marie created a social environment that opened up new possibilities and created a space for "safe risk-taking."

Jennifer and Marie describe an interesting comfort and tension within their relationship — where they purposely demonstrate respect and positive communication toward each other, while consciously challenging each other's assumptions and ways of enacting curriculum. "I've encouraged her to 'let go' and really focus on the children's learning process, rather than a predetermined outcome… she's pushed me to more strongly connect our daily routines to the curriculum document. We find those differences interesting."

As a team, they discuss and decide upon common goals and approaches based on how to optimize learning opportunities for the children. "At the beginning of this year, we set a goal of truly focusing on reducing transitions — and so decided to start our day outdoors." It's an approach that's noticed and questioned by others in their school community: "Teachers in the older grades questioned it, since the research says that students are most open to learning in that first period of the day. Isn't it a 'waste' of prime instructional time to have them outside? We explain that they are learning so much in outdoor play — we bring the curriculum outdoors. It's rich." Through their collaborative risk-taking, innovating, revising, and reflection, the educators describe a growing confidence in their abilities to articulate pedagogical decisions, and see their teaching as a continuing inquiry. "I'm not as nervous when a parent or colleague questions what we're doing — 'What are they really learning when they play?' 'What does literacy and math look like in the early years?' I can explain more and more clearly our choices and our own questions. It's part of the ongoing conversation in our room."

26. Learn how assessment procedures can increase learning

Focus: An integrated ongoing assessment approach
Richard Coles

Assessment is an integral component of learning. Assessment practices reveal how well young people are learning and provide insights to improve learning.

Everyone has a personal story about an assessment experience. Some of these stories took place in a school setting — a biology exam, or a history presentation — and others in a non-school setting — a driving test, or a work-related performance review. What is striking about these personal stories is the remarkable amount of detail that can be recalled even if the experience took place many years or decades ago. And there is commonly an emotional aspect — fear, panic, relief, anxiety — related to the assessment experience.

Most states, provinces or territories have documents dealing with assessment principles and procedures. Many of these documents outline advances in knowledge about learning, thinking, and technology that are being employed in many classrooms. Assessment design and practices need to address these classroom learning experiences. The key to meaningful assessment is teacher knowledge. Their funds of knowledge include: a deep understanding of their students, the curricula, the science of learning, and the nature of large-scale and classroom assessment. Their knowledge enables teachers to communicate appropriately to their students, educators, parents, and other community members.

Assessment takes place in real school settings. Children and youth vary in multiple ways, as, for example, in their cognitive, social, emotional growth, attitudes and interests, and dispositions. But their teachers know that all students can learn. In terms of assessment there are concerns about fairness and equity. Diverse student populations have different background knowledge and life experiences. Young people follow different pathways as they strive to make sense of new ideas and concepts. Students in the same grade also require different time frames as they develop deep knowledge. Distinct assessment formats (multiple choice, question and answer, essays, class presentations) favour students who excel with a particular format. Many assessments are used for multiples purposes (to measure student achievement, school programs, schools, and teachers). Such assessments provide a "selfie" of achievement in a particular time and context, whereas meaningful assessment requires multiple insights into a student's understanding from different perspectives over a longer period of time. Multiple sources of evidence also enable teachers to make clearer judgments about students' growth and to design more effective learning activities. Assessment practices have to be aligned to teaching, the curriculum, and diverse classrooms.

In most schools, students are assessed in various forms of large-scale mandatory, standardized assessments and classroom assessments. Large-scale assessments are external assessments that usually serve summative purposes (assessment *of* learning). Standardized tests make some assumptions about learning and assessment. The inference is that if a student can answer the reading question or solve the math question then the individual understands at least part of the text or has some mathematical understanding. These questions do not provide information about how the student made sense of the reading passage or solved the math problem. Numerical test scores such as reading at the 7.2 level and percentile rankings are presented as the results of the testing. Test scores are popular with the public. Today we live in the age of Big Data. Numerical data dominates most sports, businesses, marketing, investing, politics, and other aspects of our daily lives. Many believe these tests are scientific and lack teacher bias. And they are able to reduce the complex processes such as reading or applying mathematical reasoning to a simple raw score. Some parents and stakeholders feel more comfortable with a number or letter grades than anecdotal comments written in educational jargon.

But there are some concerns in regard to standardized testing. Do these external assessments reflect current knowledge about learning and various subject domains? How many topics in a specific subject area such as geometry are included on the large-scale assessment? Literacy assessments use short reading passages whereas daily readings include more lengthy narrative, informational, and multimodal texts in print or a digital environment. There are some concerns about fairness and equity. Is the data going to be used to hold back students, stream students or evaluate teachers or schools? Many outcomes of learning (creativity, critical thinking, resilience, empathy or motivation), are not addressed in these assessments. Large-scale assessments provide little information about why some students perform well or poorly, making the results not very insightful for the improvement of teaching and learning. How well do large scale-assessments predict school success and later life accomplishments? Effective assessment requires multiple sources of information to make informed inferences about a student's learning. External assessment can be one of these sources of information.

Classroom-based assessment provides multiple aspects of students' achievement leading to proficiency over time and deals with multiple ways of coming to know. Classroom assessments are primarily formative (assessment *for* learning) and provide evidence about what students currently know and are able to do. These assessments also provide teachers with information to improve learning and teaching.

CUPCAKE ASSESSING

To investigate classroom assessment, we shall visit a diverse urban middle-school classroom. Mr. S. and his Integrated Arts class are investigating how to make a cupcake. After ascertaining each student's cultural and dietary requirements Mr. S. arrives at their first class with a box of cupcakes. Each student receives an appropriate cupcake. While munching their cupcakes the students write in their learning logs a description of the taste and any thoughts about the baking process. Mr. S. circulates around the classroom listening and interacting with his class. He wants to determine the students' background knowledge and any misconceptions they have about baking or cupcakes. These insights assist him with his teaching and designing learning activities. He recalls that some students are members of the school's baking club and he is aware that others assist with family members' baking. The class is organized into diverse groups whose first task is to agree upon a name for their group.

Each activity in his baking class begins with a discussion of the learning goals displayed on the Smart Board. Mr. S. then employs a variety of strategies to determine the students' knowledge of the learning goal. He designs instruction to move the students towards competence in terms of the learning goal. For example, the curriculum states that one of the goals for this unit deals with demonstrating an understanding of frosting and decorating cupcakes. In their groups, the students examine a number of pictures of cupcakes they located on the Internet and discuss decorating procedures. Mr. S. and two members of the baking club demonstrate methods for piping and other frosting procedures. The students try piping some completely cooled cupcakes. Mr. S circulates around the room offering feedback and encouragement. He knows that moving toward becoming proficient in decorating cupcakes requires risk taking, assistance from others, opportunities for practice, and feedback information that the young

---

"The Maker Movement in Education," by E. R. Halverson and K. Sheridan, is appearing in classrooms as a useful guide to a strategy for engaging students in the creative production of artifacts in their daily lives, finding physical and digital forms to share their processes and products with others.

bakers can use. His students will acquire their baking skills when they receive information about what they have done correctly and the nature of their incorrect work. The students and teacher can discuss strategies for improving their work. And Mr. S. anticipates that many of the first or second batch of cupcakes will end up in the recycling bins.

Mr. S. has also integrated some mathematics into the lessons — for example, measurements, 2 cups/260 g/9 1/4oz, estimating and solving problems involving fractions, decimals, and ratios. They observed the reaction when a substance is heated and changes state. The young people investigated popular baking products in different cultures. And they learned about the nutritional value of many baking products.

During the class Mr. S., a knowledgeable "Kidwatcher," records some observations in his notebook with one double page for each student. His notes recorded in the natural learning environment of the classroom reveal the knowledge, skills, and strategies each of his students is acquiring. He also uses this information to adjust his instruction and lesson designs to meet the needs of his students.

Mr. S. knows that his students construct knowledge and deep understanding within a social and cultural context. Knowledge includes facts and the ability to integrate skills, strategies, and procedures for interpretation and problem solving. Understanding involves students actively making connections between their background knowledge with new information. Mr. S. wants his students to self-monitor their thinking and learning (metacognitive skills). He provides opportunities for students to make their thinking visible. Through group discussions and writing in their learning logs, students think about their thinking, knowledge building, problem solving, as they monitor and evaluate their progress. Learning also takes place in a context where the students interact, negotiate, and collaborate. From an assessment perspective Mr. S. wants to determine what his students know and when and how they are able to use this knowledge. He observes his students, participates in short and extended conferences. His students produce reports to demonstrate their understanding — for example, a paper on "The Top Ten Mistakes When Decorating or Frosting a Cupcake" or a YouTube clip on making a cupcake from scratch.

From a situative or sociocultural perspective during the baking experiences students are developing the discourse, practices, and norms associated with the baking community. They test their own developing theories and build on the knowledge of their classmates. Assessment from this perspective involves observing and analyzing how students use their knowledge, baking skills, and practices when participating in the class baking community.

During this unit of study students also engage in self-assessment and group assessment. Self-assessment (Assessment of Learning) enables students to reflect on and self-assess their progress. With a clear understanding of the learning goal and practice using checklists, written prompts such as *What happened when…?* and conferences, students are learning to assess themselves somewhat accurately and fairly. Mr. S. commonly observed that the self-assessments were often more critical than his own assessments. After each group activity Mr. S. conducted a group assessment. He would ask each group member to write in their learning log what was working in their group and one aspect of their group that could improve. Each group member described how one person made a positive contribution to their group. The groups would discuss their observations and briefly share their group assessment with the class. During these procedures, the students became actively engaged in the assessment process.

Mr. S. wants his assessments to include other factors that influence learning. He records observations that reveal critical thinking, creativity, persistence, self-awareness, leadership, and the emotional well-being of his students. Finally, Mr. S. knows that to be successful in this century his students are on a pathway for continuous lifetime learning. Employers want people who can learn flexibly from a variety of texts, technologies, their network of friends, and colleagues to expand their knowledge and skills. Mr. S. records in his notebook evidence that his students are developing strategies for their own personal learning.

In this classroom the students are actively, collaboratively investigating many aspects of baking cupcakes. Assessment is an ongoing component of this Integrated Arts unit. Mr. S. is also working on a personal inquiry about designing meaningful learning experiences and assessment procedures for this unit of study. He is a knowledgeable resource, a co-inquirer, and not just the final evaluator of his students' work. Together they are developing meaningful assessment principles and practices to inform themselves, parents, and other educators and stakeholders.

The references for this section are "Feedback That Fits," by S.M. Brookhart, in *Educational Leadership*, 65; *Unlocking Formative Assessment: Practical Strategies for Enhancing Pupils' Learning in the Primary Classroom* and *Formative Assessment in the Secondary Classroom*, both by S. Clark; and *Making Thinking Visible: Writing, Collaborative Planning, and Classroom Inquiry*, edited by L. Flower, D.L. Wallace, L. Norris, and R.E. Burnett.

ASSESSMENT THAT MEANS SOMETHING!

John Myers, instructor, OISE/University of Toronto

I taught three grade ten classes in a full-year high school in the inner city of Toronto. We had a culturally and linguistically diverse group of students. I like full-year courses since they give me, as they give my elementary school colleagues, a chance to see student growth. Given that history as a curriculum presents significant linguistic challenges to many students since many of its key ideas are abstract and nuanced, I had decided to concentrate on writing tasks for my classes. I gave almost weekly assignments dealing with such writing as:

- position papers arguing for or against some issue we encountered in studying Canadian history;
- newspaper-style accounts of an event in Canada's past or present;
- summaries and reactions to people, ideas, and events from Canada's past focusing on impact and significance.

With half a dozen papers graded by late January I had a sense of where students stood. Their cores, whether in A, B, C or D range, were fairly consistent. But I wanted students to improve.

An opportunity to experiment came from a workshop I had attended on "peer editing." The idea was to have students look at their classmates' papers before submitting them to their teacher. We had some sense of criteria even though this was in the days before we went full bore into rubrics.

I decided to present the idea of peer editing to my classes. I asked each of my students on a voluntary basis to get someone to read their paper before handing it in to me. "But we don't really understand what to look for," one of my students stated. Remember, this was in the days before rubrics came into fashion.

I offered the criterion of clarity. "If you read your pal's paper and know what s/he is talking about the first time, then it's probably OK. But if you read it two or three times and still don't get the message, 'Houston, we have a problem.'"

As was my custom I had students put their names on the back of their papers (to minimize my bias) and a checkmark if someone else also read the paper.

> "For teachers to be highly effective, they need to work in schools that are organized for success — schools that enable them to know and reach their students, teach to worthwhile learning goals, use productive tools and materials, and continually improve their practice."
>
> Linda Darling-Hammond, *The Flat World and Education: How America's Commitment to Equity Will Determine Our Future*

Out of ninety students about half had their papers read. The results? Every student improved. And except for a couple who were consistently in the low 90% range, the minimum grade jump was 10%. Perhaps writing for their pals made students more careful with their organization. I certainly noticed the difference in organization and clarity.

From then on this became part of my scheme. Among the changes I made:
- The name of the peer editor was included on each paper as it would promote responsibility to all.
- We used writing scales (ancestors of rubrics).

Using rubrics when the assignment is first introduced gives students a vision of quality that they can strive for. And if the writing marks all go up, I get asked, "Aren't we lowering standards?" I respond to this question with another question: "Is our job to sort talent or develop it?" This is true in sports and the arts. Should this not be the case in academics?

WHAT A REAL HIGH-PERFORMING SCHOOL LOOKS LIKE

Most studies of high performance look for teachers and schools that produce reliably high test scores and then catalog their attributes. But test scores are associated with a limited range of skills, which means we know the kinds of schools and classrooms that can knock the socks off the state test. But what if we want to know how to teach the full range and depth of skills needed for successful adulthood? By and large, the vast corpus of existing research has not much to say.

Our foray into classrooms where deeper learning takes place gives us a beginning sense of what excellence looks like. For one thing, excellence requires highly skilled teachers with finely tuned radar and improvisational ability. For another, excellence requires assessment practices worthy of the range and depth of skills taught. Our current sorry state of high-stakes testing is doing irreparable harm to a generation of rising citizens and workers. Finally, good teaching is about caring relationships, a parental affection that gives and receives, that honors the fundamentally human nature of our work as educators. In an era of big data, we would do well to remember that all our work is ultimately about a single child.

At all points of entry into the system — from the legislature to the Department of Education, from professional development to schools of education, from the classroom to the district office — we need to reimagine excellence and ask ourselves what a system looks like when it fosters excellence redefined in all schools.

James Nehring, Megin Charner-Laird, and Stacy Szczesiul,
http://www.kappanonline.org, July 2017

27. Value a range of literacies and numeracies throughout the curriculum

> We cannot know through language
> what we cannot imagine…
> Those who cannot imagine cannot read.
>
> Elliot Eisner

Adrienne Gear, in her book *Reading Power*, supports teachers in helping students to think critically and creatively while they read.

Factors affecting comprehension

Literacy teaching is about honouring each student's potential as a developing speaker, reader, and writer. In *The Courage to Teach,* Parker Palmer sums up this approach to teaching with these principles:
- a desire to help my students build a bridge between the academic text and their own lives and a strategic approach for doing so;
- a respect for my students' stories that is no more or less than my respect for the scholarly texts I assigned to them;
- an aptitude for asking good questions and listening carefully to my students' responses — not only to what they say but also to what they leave unsaid.

Focus: Literacy in the subject disciplines
David Booth

In her books *So What Do They Really Know?* and *Do I Really Have to Teach Reading?* Cris Tovani has helped us understand the need to continue teaching strategic literacy in the subject areas. Our students need to learn to read like a scientist in science, to read like a historian in social studies, to read like a mathematician in mathematics. In essence, different text expectations require different strategies, forms, and formats. For example: How do we take notes when we conduct an experiment? How will we then summarize what has happened? How can we take time to work with our students in handling a lengthy, complicated science text?

Don't know much about biology

I want students to be constantly engaged in the literacy events of every discipline — discussing, reading, writing, diagramming, researching, interpreting, representing and shaping information, and then sharing, presenting, arguing, refining, questioning, critiquing, summarizing, and responding to each other's findings and opinions, and revisiting, rewriting, revising, rethinking, reworking what we thought we knew.

"Every activity or experience in school and out is an opportunity to support the expansion of literacy. This is the key to developing literacy through using it. Words have no meaning except in the contexts in which they are experienced and to make sense of language all systems have to be present. The time to learn to make sense of and learn through new genres, new functions, is as they are encountered in using them."
Ken Goodman, Peter H. Fries and Steven L. Strauss, *Reading -The Grand Illusion: How and Why People Make Sense of Print.*

I remember visiting a school where the principal had organized a large science room for the fourth, fifth and sixth grade students. He told me that he felt his school-wide literacy program was weak, yet he had this amazing science teacher. Each class visited the science room for an hour three times a week, and I saw more literacy activity in that room than I have seen in many language arts rooms. The program was planned with exceeding care: meeting a new theme each week, the children signed up for and worked in small groups at established centres, well supplied with all types of resources. They had to follow assignment cards at each work station, and present their findings at the end of the third period. The room was always buzzing, and everyone was working. The teacher monitored and assisted where necessary, the group roles were assigned. The expectations were high, and I witnessed collaborative behaviours everywhere. There are times when planning and organization encourage and increase literacy growth; this was one such program.

ADDING AND SUBTRACTING OUR WAY TO LITERACY

My high school math teacher would try to solve the math puzzle in the morning newspaper each morning before our class began. He loved his discipline, and told stories of its use in his fighter pilot training during World War Two. I remember him fifty years later.

David Booth

Learning with and through mathematics will mean that youngsters will be engaging in thinking processes using the codes of mathematics to test hypotheses and carry out inquiries, as well as traditional language codes that will enable them to consider, structure and share the connections they are making. Students are thinking "multimodally," using two or more meaning-making systems (and they may be charting and diagramming their constructs along the way in a visual representation pattern). Becoming literate in mathematics, then, involves new ways of learning and knowing that will give the child access to the technology and structure of mathematics so that they can analyze and interpret its problems and productions — what we call meaning making with and through mathematics.

TEACHER VOICES

When working with difficult texts:
- Find ways to approach the text from students' lived experiences.
- Begin exploring content with an overview, an introduction or a summary.
- Enrich the text book with other resources, such as websites and other media.
- Let students ask questions to clarify misunderstandings.
- Try breaking the text into manageable sections. Writing a five-page report could mean one page every five days.
- Some students may need to hear the text as well as read it.
- Let students revise, rework, and rethink their responses. It takes time for comprehension to grow stronger.
- Organize feedback times, for individuals and groups, where both you and your students share questions, editing concerns, and ideas.

EVERY CHILD MATTERS

Genie Kim, PhD, elementary school mathematics teacher

> Upon entering graduate school, I cultivated a lofty goal: to become an agent of change within education. Yet, whilst conducting research for my dissertation, I found I instead had discovered a powerful change agent within a teacher I was investigating — her name is Laura Kunka. While observing this exemplary teacher in action, I was fundamentally transformed and inspired. How? To explain, Laura showed me magic in many unfathomable ways.
>
> Laura concretely demonstrated for me that teachers hold the power to enable students to become excited about all matters related to learning; incomprehensibly, she even allows her students to discover beauty in a subject that most consider to be an anathema — mathematics! Laura has a way of making teaching fresh and dynamic…even after having been in the profession for twenty-five plus years!
>
> After much analysis, I think I unlocked her magic. It is in Laura's dedication and devotion. She is devoted to her students, and it is palpably manifested through her actions. Laura dedicates her time to customizing her lessons and activities so she can achieve the greatest reach possible — from scaffolding for her most desperately struggling student, to challenging her

academically gifted child, and nurturing every unique need in between. Laura ensures each child becomes paramount. Clearly, all of Laura's students matter to her, and it shows in how she walks the proverbial talk...she literally never sits down!

Educators desiring to make a transformative impact in their classrooms must heed what Laura has masterfully put into tangible effect: "They [students] may forget what you said, but they will never forget how you made them feel." This compelling quote has been attributed to a variety of people; nonetheless, I will ascribe it to the late poet, activist, and author Maya Angelou, as she herself was, and still is, an admirable change agent worthy of emulating. Laura embodies the essence of Maya Angelou's profound words, and her students are testimony to this fact.

Laura's former students come to visit her years after leaving her classroom, to express their gratitude. Why do they come back? Laura Kunka makes her students "feel" equipped and capable of achieving their potential, confident in their abilities, excited about learning, and safe to make mistakes. In a nutshell, Laura makes teaching about each individual child.

It is insufficient to say you love/care about children. Actions speak louder than words. Laura's investment of time and energy and her tenacity in not allowing her students to remain where they are, both academically and socially, make her stand head and shoulders above many of the exemplary teachers I have come to know and respect.

All teachers, those newly minted and veterans alike, who seek to make a powerful impact within the lives of their students, would do well to ask themselves this question: How can I offer my distinctive idiosyncrasies, passions, and gifts, on behalf of my students, so they will, even years later, "feel" genuine gratitude in their hearts because I was their teacher?

Sadly, I personally don't remember ever having had such a magical teacher who made me "feel" a sense of gratefulness during my educational career. Yet — as good fortune would have it — just like Laura's students, past and present, I find myself fervently saying, "Thank you, Ms. Kunka, for teaching me!"

> For principals and school leaders, David Booth's and Jennifer Rowsell's book *The Literacy Principal* presents the foundational steps for supporting a school literacy culture.

28. Recognize the significance of the arts in education

Focus: Why the arts matter in school
David Booth

We used to write poems

During Education Week, I was asked to read to a group of students from one school district, and when I arrived at the school gymnasium, I found 600 students, kindergarten through twelfth grade, waiting for me. After a first-grade student introduced me, I shared stories and poems that I had collected over the years, all of them written by young students. At the end of my reading, I was thanked by a secondary senior, who I noticed had been standing at the rear of the room with his peers, who were all trying to physically disassociate themselves from the younger crowd. He ambled up to the stage and began his comments. "I thought today was going to be a waste of time, but as the speaker read all the stuff from the young kids, I began to remember what I had written all those years ago

> "Socially and economically disadvantaged children and teenagers who have high levels of arts engagement or arts learning show more positive outcomes in a variety of areas than their Low-arts-engaged peers."
>
> National Endowment for the Arts #55, March 2012

in elementary school. I was a writer then, with haiku, and stories, and projects. What happened for the last four years? Why did I quit writing? Doesn't high school believe in writing anymore? Mr. Booth, thanks for the memories."

Contrast this experience in my teaching life with one I had while teaching a course in Rochester, New York, in the early 1990s. As I was working with the teachers in a high school, the bell rang, and dozens of students ran down the halls clutching letters which turned out to be from American soldiers who had been sent to fight in the Gulf War. The senior class had been assigned a project in which each of them was to write to a soldier to support their efforts away from home. Those soldiers had written back, and for many students these were the first letters of significance they had ever received. Their excitement was evidence of the power that lies in learning events that go beyond skill practice into reasons for acquiring those skills. There are many stories of soldiers who kept their war letters forever, tied with a string and placed in a dresser drawer. It seems that men who would never otherwise put pen to paper will pour their hearts out when faced with the loneliness of separation. Why can't we who teach in schools find situations that call for real communication between people, so that the need to write works in favour of those who need to learn?

History

Recently, I watched a group of university students in Jamaica present a play they had improvised from documents and letters chronicling the tragic story of a young woman who was captured into slavery and taken by ship to the Americas. The students role-played different genders, different characters — from slaves to British judges — and through their dialogue, their dancing, and their ensemble choral work, they brought to life the complexities of the time, the injustice, the sadness, the history of their nation. I was deeply moved by their production, I learned so much about their stories, and I witnessed the power of action-based literacy education. If only all young people could use difficult text resources as material for literacy exploration, where through discussion and role-playing they could dig into the ideas and struggle to understand the context and the times represented in the resources, as they work and rework their attempts to construct a drama form for their interpretations of the text! Could we sing and dance our way into learning?

The writers in the book The Arts Go to School, edited by David Booth and Masayuki Hachiya, represent the various arts in education that can add creativity and imagination to the curriculum for all students.

"Yes", I explain, "usually the children take their work home."
   That which is left is by children for whom process counts more than product — the ones who pour their whole small beings, focus all of their dreams, onto a tiny piece of tattered paper showing a hero's purple cabin, a winding trail along a stone studded beach beside a wildly scribbled deep blue sea leading to a defiant red x that shows where the buried treasure is.
   They push it urgently into your hand and murmur, "This is for you."
   Michael Seary, art teacher, Art Gallery of Nova Scotia

DEVELOPING SELF-ESTEEM AND UNDERSTANDING EACH OTHER THROUGH ART
Masayuki Hachiya, professor, Graduate School of Education, Hiroshima University

One of my colleagues, whom I met at my previous work place, was formerly a junior high-school science teacher. We both worked at the teacher training program at a university. I taught art education, whereas he specialized in class activities and moral education. One day, he told me about his experiences at schools where he had experienced difficult times, but later became interested in teaching and studying in those areas.

He worked at a troubled school where teachers faced difficult situations almost daily. The teachers had challenging duties because of students' cruel behaviour against teachers, or problems of bullying among students. The challenge for him and the other teachers was to find a solution for dealing with these problems as well as to communicate with the students in daily school life. He was asked to take charge of student guidance. While he was struggling with this task, he believed that he could possibly improve students' behaviour through class activities for building human relationships, thereby leading them to better learning. He also understood that it was important to build rapport with both students and parents alongside his teaching practice. To build or foster mutual understanding, he tried various teaching materials in the classroom, and used readings and writings, films, role-plays, and questionnaires. In so doing, he began to realize that teaching had to be changed to a more fundamental way, and that art could also play an important role in building humanity through students understanding themselves and others.

At present, bullying has become one of the most critical issues in schools. If bullying becomes tangible, trouble can spread out not only to the students concerned, but also to classmates, teachers, the school and community. Moreover, there might be a risk of endangering someone's life. It is now common knowledge that preventing bullying has become a significant theme in schooling.

One day, my colleague asked me to plan an activity using art for the prevention of bullying in a high school. We planned this activity for teachers and students alike. It was a simple activity because we knew that teachers would not try it if they thought the lesson plan too difficult; we knew that there was no magic medicine for combating bullying. We made a lesson plan called "Let's Draw a Friend's Face," and implemented it in the classroom.

In art classes, drawing a human face is a standard activity that almost everyone experiences in their school years. In fact, books used for art classes include self-portraits and portraits by a number of artists. In art classes, students draw, paint, view, and appreciate the theme of human faces. Regardless of what periods and where from, it is well known that many painters have been interested in and created works of art focused on faces. A human face plays an important part in recognizing and identifying the person, and that is why it shows "very becoming of you" to be the best.

In the activity we arranged, a pair drew each other's faces, but that was not all. They talked and asked about each other's goals and dreams for the future. Moreover, the idea was to question, answer, and take note of things that most likely no one would know. Then, after drawing, each artist introduced their partner to the whole class. We did not evaluate students for being good at drawing. That was not the point. Knowing about a friend and talking about oneself, and finally introducing one's partner to the class was the objective. It was not just about revealing details from the notes taken, but introducing the reporter and the model visually through art by questioning or cross-examining what the positive aspects of "very becoming of you," or one's good and positive points are.

As professional practitioners, teachers may wish to continue to make an effort, sometimes with a struggle, while admitting each other's good and positive aspects through an art activity like this to build human relationships between teachers and students, and between students and each other, thus promoting students' growth in self-esteem and understanding of others. Art may help in this process as a way of knowing our teaching practices and ourselves.

The arts in the community

As teachers, we must remember to recognize the learning activities that happen outside school, from dance teams, the Kids' Lit International Quiz, music and drama excursions, volunteering in arts organizations, to participating in arts camps and civic events. The three examples that follow allow us as teachers to celebrate with our student communities at all levels — elementary with literature, secondary with visual arts, and young adults creating films that represent their neighbourhood.

A COMMUNITY READS A NOVEL

Tara-Lynn Scheffel, professor, Nipissing University

A few years ago, families in a Northern Ontario community were invited to participate in North Bay Reads Together, a community literacy project involving the weekly reading of a shared novel. For a span of seven weeks, a portion of the selected novel was reprinted each week in the local newspaper. As the final chapters were printed, all the students who had read the book, along with their families, were then invited to a celebration at the local public library to meet the author. The project involved partnerships with the university, the local newspaper, a well-known Canadian author, and the publisher of the novel. A blog was also created for sharing thoughts and ideas with the author, as well as to provide audio links to hear the story online.

The notion of collaborative reading of a shared book is not new. Over the past years, similar programs in other cities have been successful in promoting an appreciation of reading, bringing families together, and most important, building a sense of community by reading together. As such, North Bay Reads Together was premised on the understanding that family literacy is important to students' literacy journeys. For those considering a similar undertaking, our general process involved the following steps.

1. *Select a focus text and approach the author/publisher.* Initial contact with the author and publisher was made. *Three on Three,* a novel by Eric Walters about junior basketball, had been selected by the committee members as a book that fit the target age range of nine-to-twelve-year-olds and involved a topic we felt that junior students in North Bay might relate to: competition.
2. *Consider diverse ways to share the book publicly.* The committee brainstormed several ways to share the book, including newspaper and online sources, such as a blog and audio version that could be used by parents on iPhones or other digital devices. The *North Bay Nugget* was very helpful in getting this initiative under way, donating one page in the Saturday paper for the duration of the initiative. The page donated was already geared towards family and students and fit with the newspaper's goals of changing what was currently included on this page. The chapters were published in both print and online versions of the paper.
3. *Advertise.* Since we did not have a predetermined audience but instead a goal to reach families throughout North Bay, we advertised the initiative in the newspaper at our own cost. Our efforts included an initial advertisement to introduce North Bay Reads Together as well as a culminating advertisement to announce the celebration with the author. On the day of the culminating celebration, we also handed out

postcards around town as a way of involving anyone who had not seen the newspaper pages but were interested due to this event.
4. *Promote the goals of the collaborative reading.* In addition to advertising, the newspaper also interviewed the selection committee, writing an article titled "Open the paper, read a book." The article emphasized the goal of getting families together for the purpose of reading, building towards a sense of community revolving around literature.
5. *Using Edublogs,* a free online blogging site, we sought to create an avenue for families within the community to speak with the author. The blog was organized to include an author biography, book synopsis, and room for each week's chapter readings.

Eric Walters responded to each comment, answering questions about whether he had played basketball himself, whether he is tall, and what to do when confronted with a bully. He provided further insight into the characters of the story and connections to his own life as an author.

While it is difficult for us to determine how wide the readership of *Three on Three* was, we learned much from this community initiative, recognizing the value of such collaborative reading programs for promoting shared reading experiences at home and in the community.

THE REGENT PARK PROJECT ~ A COMMUNITY ARTS INITIATIVE FROM KICK START ARTS

Abubaker Albach, Amanda Pillegi, participants in Kick Start Arts, and Sheena D. Robertson, artistic director

There is much that schools can borrow from community arts projects. Teaching at its best should be about collaboration, creativity, and fun. It should be about knowing the young people you work with deeply, and exploring *with* them — coming from a growth mindset that values the lived experiences of the youth in front of you, and scaffolding projects that empower them to work from themselves outwards to connect with the world in meaningful and engaging ways. Kick Start Arts' *The Regent Park Project* is a free filmmaking initiative grounded in this belief.

Under artistic director Sheena D. Robertson, a former TDSB teacher and instructor at OISE, this initiative has been running for over two years. Over time, participants meet once a week and engage in the following: free acting training, industry workshops, set visits, and special events. Once capacity is built, we use a collaborative story circle creation process. Using prompts from the Artistic Director, participants tell stories that illustrate their 'lived experience'. After considerable time gathering stories the group selects the ones they are the most engaged by (and which we can imagine connecting to one another), and we work with a director to use improvisation to draft and hone the scenes. Once they are in a state we feel confident with, we video them and then scribe the videos into scripts which are constantly adapted and honed until we have a polished finished product we all feel proud of. One season of a web series based on these scripts has been filmed, and a second season is in the works.

What follows is the content of a speech given by two of its participants the night of their film premiere — it articulates so clearly the sense of empowerment and engagement felt by all the participants.

Amanda:

The beauty of this group, much like the community we are in today, is a diverse group of people coming together with different experiences and backgrounds, all with something to share. When we get together and share stories, it is healing.

When you watch our films, reflect on all of our lived experiences. When we began two years ago, we started with story circles, telling our most vulnerable and important moments to each other. This demands trust, respect, and understanding. I'm so proud to call each and every person in this project a friend, fellow artist, and filmmaker. We took these stories and developed characters and scenes, we improvised, we developed scripts and over much time, put together what you will see on screen. The content of these stories deals with racism, discrimination, culture clashes, family, and just growing up as a teenager in Regent Park and Toronto.

We had COUNTLESS conversations as a group about the decisions each character would make. It was evident that each of us held a different perspective, and we continued to learn from each other throughout this process, shifting our understanding of the world around us. Right now, there is a hunger for representation in media, and this project absolutely fills that gap. We are now a group of young talented artists whose stories deserve to be heard by large audiences.

Baker:

It's been an amazing two years, we've been able to visit TV show sets such as *Boat Rocker's, Orphan Black* and *Killjoys*, meet with agents and learn about the business, do mock auditions for casting agents, collaborate with actors from the Actor's Conservatory at the Canadian Film Centre and meet many more people working in the industry, all with a wealth of knowledge to share. Thanks to Sheena's and other artists' mentoring us during and outside of the weekly meetings, we were able to thrive much more than we could have imagined in terms of our artistic careers. We were able to get auditions, interviews, and meet many people within the film industry in order to really get a feel of what it's actually like "behind the scenes."

All this helps us develop professionally, and learn about what it takes to be an actor, writer, producer or crew member — and we even got to fill these roles during the shoot! The ability to just step into these roles is truly invaluable, this real-world experience in the industry will only help us in the future, and I know everyone who worked on this project is just so grateful.

I know that I speak for everyone in the group — meeting every Monday in a safe space where we can share stories, and grow as filmmakers, actors, and writers, it feels like a second home. It's like a family, and watching everyone grow not only as artists, but as people, is an amazing experience.

CREATING POSSIBILITIES AND BREAKING THE SILENCE

Vanessa Barnett and Elena Soní, retired TDSB arts instructional leaders and teachers at the School of Early Childhood Studies, Ryerson University

Finding Home: Personal Journeys and Visual Narratives was a three-and-a-half-month group sculpture project funded by the Ontario Arts Council. Vanessa Barnett and Elena Soní, the artist-educators and curators of the project and installation, are both immigrant women who have experienced the reality of loss, separation, longing, and memories of family left behind, having immigrated to Canada from South Africa and Venezuela respectively, escaping the climate of oppression and racism in their home countries. They worked with 250 students and 5 teachers and administrators from Marc Garneau Collegiate Institute and Greenwood Secondary School. Both schools have large ESL/ELD populations, with many newly arrived refugee students from Syria, Sudan, Colombia, Iraq, Congo, Nigeria, and Eritrea. Our participants were between the ages of 15 and 20.

Vanessa and Elena's inspiration was the Canadian government's invitation to 25,000 Syrians and new immigrants to Canada in 2015/16. The artwork created explored individual identity and the dislocation of emigrating from one's home and relocating to a new country. Participants creatively explored what the concept of "Home" meant to each young artist. Their goal was to create a safe and stimulating environment for young people to invest in the risky business of expressing their dreams, fears, conflicts, and hopes through a process of collaborative creation.

The rationale for choosing the Aga Khan Museum as their cultural partner for this project was the museum's culturally relevant collection from regions of the world where Muslim societies predominate. When the whole student body visited the Aga Khan Museum for a guided tour and a feedback session they were all able to find personal resonance in the rich cultural influence from the Muslim world. The interconnected structures the students made were each curated in conversation with one another, to form a new community of voices through the universal language of art.

The evolution of the creative process

Before any studio work could begin it was essential to acknowledge who our learners were. We were as curious to know about them as as they were to know about us. What is your name? Where were you born? Tell us something special about yourself. Vanessa and Elena shared their personal stories, communicating their initial sense of dislocation which slowly transformed into a feeling of belonging. In so doing they humanized their own identity and shared experience, creating a safety zone where emergent conversations began slowly, and with growing familiarity trust developed. The participants became more verbal sharing their personal stories. They began to bring in family photographs and significant objects and discuss the process of building and storytelling. The students started to formulate ideas of what the essence of "Finding Home" meant to them. The structures became metaphors for their ideas and emotions about the concept of "home."

Participants were stimulated by the sometimes visceral subject matter they were thinking about. As text and story became integral to the project, students drew in their journals and wrote in their first language.

Attractive wooden boards were provided as the basic modules for the individual sculptural pieces. A wonderful array of materials had been gathered as a springboard for the project. These materials had been carefully collected and creatively arranged as invitations and enticements for the students. There was a range of choice from fabrics, lace, embroidery threads, wire mesh, corrugated cardboard, Plexiglas, wood, found objects, and much more.

As artists, Vanessa and Elena demonstrated the structural possibilities and techniques needed, and then opened the conversation so that students became self-generating and imaginative in finding their own unique creative solutions. Participants were stimulated by the responsibility and ownership for their self-expression.

"I didn't know art could be about me and my family, about the things I think about and care about."

Vanessa and Elena became intentional listeners, attuned to the significance of silence, and careful observers of student behaviour. How the students presented themselves and interacted offered important social cues for breaking down barriers and often resistance. Both Vanessa and Elena allowed for and anticipated shared vulnerability and the breaking down of hierarchy, replacing it with mutual respect by demonstrating empathy and encouragement in suggesting materials and techniques and being available to help. What follows are examples of teacher engagement, breakthroughs and significant human connections:

Mihal, a young Slovakian Roma student, had attended class for three sessions and had not progressed in his work. During one of our visits Vanessa and Elena observed him talking on his mobile in a very agitated manner. When he finished they asked him what was troubling him. He told them that the promotor of his "gig" on the weekend was not going to pay him the negotiated fee. That is when they discovered he was a saxophonist in a gypsy band playing in Scarborough — an entry point to connect with Mihal! On their next visit, they brought a wire saxophone for him to work with and an immediate connection was made and he created a very personal piece.

Khoshbo, an Afghani student, had meticulously reproduced her living room in Kabul, with a window overlooking the snow-covered peaks of the Koh-i-Baba mountain range in the distance. She had recreated the textures and colours of the mud walls very carefully and accurately but kept coming to us dissatisfied that she could not replicate the traditional red Baluch carpet found in every Afghani home. In triumph, she returned the following week with her piece — complete with the Baluch carpet — and proudly told us that she had cut a piece of carpet from under the divan in her home.

Dominika, another Slovakian Roma student, arrived the same day the project began. Her English was scant, her mood forlorn, her attitude defiant. She sat looking at her mobile phone and sporadically speaking on Facetime with her friends in Slovakia. We needed a breakthrough and found it in her French manicure. "Your hands are beautiful, and your nails seem important to you." The following week Vanessa and Elena brought a wooden hand maquette and gave it to her together with a fine line pen. They suggested that she write her memories on it. When they returned, she had written the names of the friends she most sorely missed and went on to create an elaborate niche in which to honour her friendships.

Siam, a young man from Chittagong, Bangladesh, began the project with the intention of recreating the material existence he had known in his former life — red carpet, chandeliers, and the trappings of affluence he was leaving behind "for a better life and education in Canada."

As the weeks progressed he began to pare down his work to its ultimate simplicity and called it Emptiness: "My project shows my empty room before I left Chittagong, with a suitcase beside the empty bed."

Alaa, a young woman from Homs, Syria, produced a piece that is a metaphor for the different stages of destruction of her house and her family's efforts to protect themselves and stay in it for as long as possible. She wrapped wire around her structure to represent the barbed wire they scavenged to insulate themselves from marauders. She decorated it with care because she explained that even though the rain was coming through the roof and it was cold all her family was together. "We were all alive, Miss." It was only when her father was killed that the family was scattered to Turkey, Germany, and eventually Canada.

Being part of a challenging conversation was new to many, but being part of a collaborative discussion made them realize the immigrant journey is universal. When students are encouraged to draw on their cultural backgrounds and the languages they speak they understand how much richness they contribute to the fabric of our society.

When Vanessa and Elena shared their personal journeys a bond of the universality of the immigrant's duality, the romanticizing of place, loss, and longing, was created. Students were surprised and delighted to learn that what they say and feel matters to the community, and that art is well-suited to explore and express big ideas that are worth sharing. In order for trust, familiarity, and confidence to manifest themselves, time is essential. Human relations and the creative process cannot be rushed.

Relevant links:

https://www.youtube.com/watch?v=PmDDJPTCS7Q

https://www.agakhanmuseum.org/exhibitions/event/finding-home

https://www.thestar.com/life/2016/12/14/immigrant-teens-and-the-meaning-of-home-timson.html

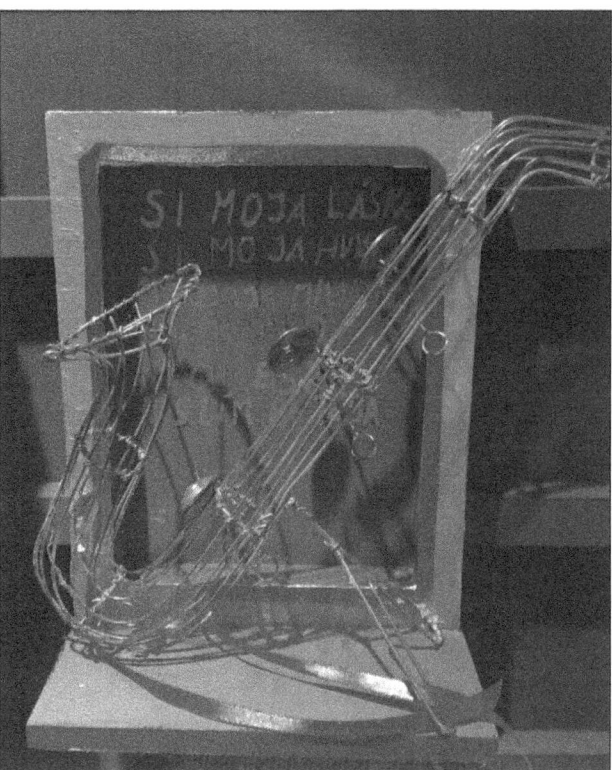

29. Include the community in your frame for teaching and learning

VOLUNTARY COMMUNITY SUPPORT FOR LITERACY

ReadUP Reading Clubs is a Toronto organization that was founded in 2005 by former Reading Recovery teacher and children's author Sheilah Currie. She started the first club at a local community centre after hearing that the newcomer Canadian families in that area were eager to find support for their children's reading acquisition. The weekly club was popular with families and, as the years passed, Sheilah opened more clubs at local schools and family shelters. There are currently seven ReadUP clubs in downtown Toronto, and it has become a registered charity. The clubs are free to families and entirely volunteer-driven.

When a child attends a ReadUP club for the first time, Sheilah does an assessment and lends a bag of 3 books at that child's optimal skill level—not too easy, not too hard. The child then reads the books to a volunteer, who helps with any tricky words, and the books are taken home for the child to read and reread over the course of the week. As the children's reading skills improve, they move up the reading levels. Sheilah also gives parents useful tips on how to support their children's reading at home.

By providing books at their individual skill levels, the club ensures that each child experiences success in reading—and that success not only motivates the child to read more, but to enjoy the experience. The children love coming to ReadUP each week. They like the casual "club" atmosphere, and the one-on-one attention from volunteers. By steadily moving up the reading levels, as they all do, the children also gain confidence and become aware of their own capacity to learn. Sheilah has worked with so many kids over the years, and she says they all want the same thing, the Holy Grail—to be able to read chapter books. ReadUP gives them that opportunity.

Focus: See parents as partners
David Booth

We as teachers need to create lines of communication between us and our students' parents. Successful communication there can lead to an increased likelihood for student success. When I began teaching, my principal told me to cover the window in the classroom door with some paper so that the parents couldn't see in. Today, we welcome their participation, even if sometimes it seems too intense.

Often parents present their own needs and fears during the parent-teacher interview, and they may value this particular forum for venting their frustration and unhappiness. Children move to and fro every weekday — from home to classroom to home and homework. How we integrate these dual worlds is one of the central complexities of raising children, and the teetertotter of childhood quickly becomes unbalanced if one party feels the other is somehow neglecting the requisite assistance that children need, especially children at risk.

Schools want to develop realistic collaborative goals for working alongside parents.

- By listening to parents, we can discover a great deal about the family literacy in their homes and incorporate that knowledge into the programs we develop for their children.
- We can increase communication during interviews or phone calls, or by a classroom newsletter, so that they are aware of how our program functions and can give appropriate support.
- We can discuss how to assist a troubled learner, why a child needs to read a book silently before sharing it aloud, how to chat with their child about their work, how to find a quiet time for reading, how to extend the range of literacy events in the family setting with TV guides or by writing weekly menus, how to use the classroom and public libraries to locate books to be read aloud (perhaps by a babysitter or older sibling).
- We need to involve parents wherever possible, without adding guilt or stress to their lives, in all aspects of their children's learning progress, while remembering that they are not teachers, and that the studying experiences at home should be natural and positive so that these children can be helped to work through their difficulties, not punished.
- Homework is often troubling for students; we need to be aware of the demands we place on children, and offer parents specific and clear suggestions for understanding what is necessary to be achieved each night, and how those tasks will support the child's growth in learning. We need to value parents as partners in the education of their children. Learning how to accomplish school tasks at home is useful, if the task can be accomplished without the teacher.
- For conferences with parents, some teachers prepare in advance demonstrations of each student's growth, using writing folders, reading logs, and videotapes of classroom activities. Sometimes, they include the student in the conference. Can you use the questions that arise during these conferences

as the starting point for further communication through personal letters, newsletters, copies of articles or self-assessment reports from the student?
- We now conduct assessments across the whole school, even using standardized tests. Can you use what you learn through such school-wide assessments as the basis for discussion about the students' competencies and potential? Can you establish benchmarks for anticipated growth through further interpretation of this material?

TEACHER VOICES

- Many studies question the value of assigning hours of homework each night.
- Homework should not be the same as schoolwork. After all, there is no teacher available. Homework requires planning with the students.
- Give homework that is achievable by the students on their own, and the work should matter to the students, and not be just repetitive drill. For example, preparing for a debate the next day can have value.
- Creative assignments often add motivation.
- Students engage in many different activities after school-music lessons, sports, babysitting, working. Keep homework time to a minimum.

Focus: Support rituals and ceremonies

David Booth

Schools need rituals: Each building is a meeting place for hundreds of children. Rituals can help students and teachers and parents to hang on to ways of behaving so that the group feels that it knows how to function in the one space, and to function for good reason. Rules are different from rituals; they are seldom imbued with pride and ceremony. The past isn't felt, at least not as deeply. I like to visit schools where I see rituals and ceremonies. The students know how to belong, what membership entails, and why we all need to accept and value them. It is often difficult in a new building to begin the careful construction of what the past will now look like in the new surroundings, but begin it must, or there will be no sense of membership. Private schools have always known this, but I am seeing some great strides in the organization of meaningful customs in public schools throughout North America. How we greet guests; the entrance foyer; the auditorium meetings, the field day; the library; the awards day; leave-takings; speeches by officials; music night; and so on.

Good-byes matter. If a child has been with a teacher for a year or more, that relationship has life-long impact. If a child has been in a school for eight or nine years, that place is locked inside memory. When a teacher or principal leaves, there is disruption in that school community; when the years is ending, the teacher and class need a means of closure; when children graduate, there are ceremonies that help move all of us forward. We teachers are part of that fabric that has surrounded that child, and how we structure removing the life-cloth at the leave-taking matters.

At my son's graduation from grade eight, each of the graduates was honoured by a grade seven student who was a friend, and as each speaker recounted the time in the school of the honouree, he or she presented the graduate with a rose. All the grade eight students were teary-eyed, as were teachers and parents. This ceremony marked the turn into adolescence for these youngsters, into high school, away from childhood. The biographical speeches, drawn from interviews and observations, were such a far cry from public speaking events; this was an authentic occasion for sharing carefully crafted reflections concerning those who now would leave the circle of that school. A significant literacy — and life — event.

My son came home from summer camp at fourteen, filled with all kinds of teenage anecdotes about living in the wilds with 200 adolescents, but the one that stood out concerned the ritual of the last day. He told how the counsellors paddled the canoes to the middle of the lake and lit torches, while those on land chose a stone from the beach that would be their memory rock of their time together. Then they sang the leave-taking song, and I could see in his young eyes that the cooperative ritual mattered. Imagine 200 young people focused on one emotional moment: does it sound like school? It could.

LEARNING THROUGH PORTAGE

Deena Kara Shaffer, PhD, learning strategist, Ryerson University

"If I can make it through this portage, I can survive any exam!"

One young man's three-day odyssey from a white-knuckle grip on his iPhone and sitting at the back of the van on the drive up to Algonquin Park, to the laser focus of constructing a fishing rod and his joyful howl on day three, "I caught a fish!"

And the subtle moments in between—quiet conversations, students teaching each other how to scramble up rocks or build a fire or register for courses or survive long-distance relationships. These are at the heart of what I've spent the last several years trying to make sense of. I am a learning specialist or strategist at Ryerson University in Toronto.

In this role, I support students with complex ways of learning due to disability. The most common concerns students articulate and for which they seek strategy support are studying, note-taking, concentration, memory, motivation, group work, reading comprehension, procrastination, and essay-writing.

A key part of my job is to offer summer transition programming, including the experiential, nature-based *Portage*. Up until last year, we took students on canoe trips in August to Algonquin Park for three days and two nights, and now, to increase accessibility and recreatability, we canoe to the Toronto Island where we camp for one evening with Outward Bound.

Early the first morning of the 2014 trip, as we set out, there was minimal and perfunctory small talk; most students had their headphones in, blocking everyone else out; all were, again, continually checking their cellphones; and there was a palpable worry about what was to come. Once at Rock Lake, our entry point, after gearing up and loading the canoes, it felt like with the first paddle stroke, *something* was happening. I watched students bond rapidly and deeply, saw them teach each other and work together to solve problems (like putting up awkwardly big tents, and backcountry campfire cooking), and alongside them, shore up bravery to jump off ever-higher cliffs, surfacing in the water moments later with the beaming-est of smiles.

These moments not only broadened but exploded wide open my view and practice of learning strategy work, so much so that I was spurred to try and make sense of it. I seldom experience traditional learning strategies, as they're currently offered, as being rich, enduring or transformative. They don't do *much* to restore focus, keep students' hope or motivation afloat, equip them to bounce back, help intervene in the face of YouTube/Netflix/Instagram/Twitter/Snapchat/Facebook/iPad/iPod/iPhone screen-saturation, or support them in engaging in *actually* collaborative group work (instead of just divvying up a group task, completing it individually, and making it *look* like it was done together).

I interviewed Jason, Hanna, Miriam, and Melissa—Melissa was the student staff—who participated in the 2016 *Portage* trip, who without vision sterned the canoe across the very busy Toronto Harbour, and who regularly seeks learning strategy sessions. From all four, I heard the central place of technological gadgetry, its impact on attention, and how time in nature can restore our focus. I heard a profound identification with cellphones in particular, and an unambiguous appreciation for disconnecting and unplugging.

Melissa: "I don't notice how it is in my day-to-day life but when I turn [my cellphone off], I notice the stress from technology…It was great to walk away from that. It's like taking a break from your life. Put[itng] everything on hold and sleep[ing] under the stars…"

Jason: "…attention is number one. If you're not attentive in the moment of learning, then all is lost…There is no better setting conducive to learning than being out in nature. Going to the woods to clear your head, pushing through that physical challenge," he suggested, "there is maybe nothing better than going on a hike for loosening up the pressures of school."

Miriam: "Students can think back on that trip or hike when they are in their urban, indoor school settings; when students are 'having a tough time,' they can go back to that nature experience."

Melissa: "…everyone just lends a hand…becomes a team. More so than… anywhere else." Everyone pulls their weight and…makes sure everyone else is okay too…you can't ignore that there's someone…struggling.

Jason: "[E]xperiences outdoors together facilitate friendships and… student success in some fairly significant ways has something to do with being able to make at least one connection with another human being on campus."

Miriam: Being outdoors "enables reflection…tak[ing] [the] brain down different paths and creat[ing] opportunities to let the mind wander, allow[ing] students to find solutions to what they're wrestling with."

Hanna: "the number one aim of a learning strategist is to instill hope…a student should leave a session feeling more hopeful…their time management skills aren't going to improve for long without hope."

And so, during this quest for meaning in *Portage*, as storied by Jason, Hanna, Miriam, and Melissa, it turns out that, as Jason noted, "[i]n the office meeting with a strategist, we're trying to get students to the same understanding as on *Portage*". And Miriam reminded, " there is [also] a permanence to these trips, two years, five years down the line" that *Portage*, in holding students as whole people, refuses to see "them as just consuming knowledge…and instead helps to inform students' how *out-of-classroom* experiences "remind us of the wider world".

LESSONS FROM THE LAND

Sandra Styres, professor, OISE/University of Toronto

As part of my dissertation requirements, I was to design and co-teach a course as part of the BEd Primary/Junior (Aboriginal) program offered by Brock University in the Northern Nishnawbe Aski Territory. For a three-week intensive model, the students, who were teaching in their communities with a Native Teaching Certificate, drive or fly in from their respective communities in the Sioux Lookout district.

On the final morning before our last sharing circle we played a slide show we had put together for the students based on all the experiences over our three weeks together. The students were asked not to talk to one another but in deep and intimate self-reflection were instructed to go out onto the Land and reflect on their individual and collective experiences and what they had seen in the slide show, and to (re)member the ways *Iethi'nihstenha Ohwentsia'kékha* (Land) forms that deeply intimate and spiritual primary relationship—the one that comes before all else—and to come back with a symbolic representation of why each of them chose the difficult and challenging path of being away from their communities and families to engage in this work here, at this time. With very little communication so as not to disrupt the reflexivity and sacred profoundness of the experience, we met in the sharing lodge once again for a final time and sat across from one another around that sacred fire. To acknowledge and respect the sacredness of that moment I chose to pass the sacred eagle feather and this, in very general terms, is what they shared.

The first student who shared chose a dead leaf and a twig with buds. The dead leaf symbolized the loss of traditional values and ways of being in the world. The buds represented the work and sacrifices that all the students were doing in that moment to make things better for their communities. The twig itself was a representation of the process of life-long learning. The tree that the twig came from grows and is nurtured by Mother Earth, which provides sunlight, water, and nutrients—very much the ways a teacher nourishes students. Every fall the leaves return to the earth—they go back to the ground and represent Land. The seeds also go back to Land, learning and giving back, being faithful, and being given the gift of life.

Another student chose the formation of the land to represent his journey through two courses. He stated that at one time his people used to have to remember the various nuances and formations of the Land to be able to find their way home—in this way Land has always been and continues to be our first teacher—it is how we find our way home.

The next student chose the sharing lodge as her symbolic representation because it was the place where we shared our thoughts, ideas, and dreams—it was a place of joy, smiles, and tears. It connected us as parents; teachers; and students. It was a representation of all of us.

The fourth student in the sharing circle chose a seed as her symbolic representation. She indicated that a seed represents the birth of a child. To flourish, plants need sun, water, nutrients, and love. Similarly, children need love, guidance, teachings, loving physical contact, and smiles to flourish.

The next student stated that the water was the symbol of her journey because in life we all go through some rough patches, like the turbulence in rough waters, such as rapids. At times our lives can be similar to the lake, which may be calm in the morning and yet unexpected things can happen. However, when we journey through the treacherous and uncertain rapids there is always.an end and a return to calm and safe waters.

Finally, we journeyed through the circle with the last student returning us to the notion of trees. This student brought forward the concept of the roots of trees, which, for her, represented who they were and where they came from as Orikwehonwe people and that the purpose in their experiences is one way of coming back to traditions and understanding some of the ways to incorporate those teachings in their own practices. She then went on to say that they are each responsible for guiding their own journeying and being grounded in their own understandings of Land.

Daily joint journaling sessions opened up spaces and opportunities for us, as instructors, to debrief, to (re)member, to reflect on student responses to Land-centred activities, and to share our experiences with each other through simultaneous recording on our laptops.

My experiences the second year differed from the first year in unexpected and critical ways. The first year was guided by Coyote the Trickster and characterized by journeying, struggle, transformation, and journeying again. In this way it was intense, immersive, and purposeful. The greatest challenge was remaining open to all the various life lessons and experiences of *Iethi'nihstenha Ohwentsia'kékha* through Coyote the Trickster. The second year I was deeper along in my understandings and experiences of *Iethi'nihstenha Ohwentsia'kékha* and felt I was more centred and grounded. When I began to notice that the concept of bringing Land into the learning environment was not being experienced by the students or in the learning environment as I had expected I felt concerned. I worried that perhaps we had somehow lost some of our initial vision; that perhaps I was not as far along in my understandings of *Iethi'nihstenha Ohwentsia'kékha* as I had thought. It was only during an early evening walk along the lake that it became clear that we were both feeling the same way. Our discussion revealed that what we were experiencing was the move from explicitly bringing Land into the learning environment to one where it was implicitly embedded in everything we, as instructors, together with the students did. We had both worked so diligently and purposefully in that first year to ensure that *Iethi'nihstenha Ohwentsia'kékha* was welcome and incorporated in the classroom that Land, in the second year, had become an inseparable part of our everyday learning experiences. The students had told us in a sharing circle that during the year between our courses, while they were working in their respective communities, they had been diligently incorporating Iethi'nihstenha Ohwentsia'kékha into their own personal and professional practices. The work that the students had done over the year was reflected in the ways each of them approached and completed their assignments and presentations, which were immersed in their (re)membered, (re)cognized, and (re)generated understandings of the connections between the course content and Land.

Prompts for reflecting

- Can you work with other colleagues to determine the issues that are most challenging (playground supervision, attendance, school breakfasts, cultural inequities) and then begin with an action plan for change?

Our colleague Sandra Styres's book Pathways for Remembering and Recognizing Indigenous Thought in Education *is a scholarly and comprehensive contribution to our understanding of and goals for Indigenous education. Indigenous education models have existed for thousands of years, yet receive very little attention. This book brings those models into focus and offers ways to integrate them into our current curriculum.*

- How does your school encourage and support growth and development in teaching?
- Do you feel like a member of the teaching team?
- How do you negotiate with administration?
- How could administrators assist you on your journey towards excellence?
- Does your school have a dedicated time for professional development sessions, and ongoing planning times for grade or subject groups of teachers?
- Do you participate actively in school-community events, building relationships with your school, parents, and the other people and agencies that support children's lives?
- How do your personal long-term goals connect to those of your school?
- How could your school build common-shared goals for the students, and encourage a collegial faculty?
- How can your school present its curriculum for learning growth so that parents will understand the program and support the teachers? For example: Are there articles and books on the subject that could be made available to parents?
- What can your school do to include parents in a significant way in initiatives?
- How can the school honour each family's way of life, while still developing a sense of school community? What changes might be necessary to promote multicultural awareness and respect for learning development in all children?
- How can you include volunteers in the classroom to assist with various activities? In what ways might parents, student teachers, high school students, older student buddies, and invited guests contribute?
- What will be the benefits of volunteering for the volunteers, the teachers, the students, and your own work as an administrator?
- How can the staff at your school take ownership of in-school or district-wide workshops to make sure the events satisfy their needs?
- How can you attend educational conferences that are coming up to support a new technique?
- Is there a framework in place for teachers to share ideas about curriculum and classroom organization?
- How might your school begin to examine its policies and articulate a plan for assessing the progress of children in various grades and divisions?
- In what ways could you share in the assessment strategies, checklists, guides, etc., that staff have collected and find helpful for assessing various concepts, skills, and attitudes?
- How can you use ideas such as concrete demonstrations of children's growth (e.g., writing folders) for preparing for teacher-parent conferences?
- How can you use the questions that arise during teacher-parent conferences as a starting point for further communications, such as personal letters, newsletters, copies of articles, or student self-assessment reports?
- How can you use standardized test results as information rather than as grades, so that comparisons among individual teachers and individual students are not made?

Addressing the problem of teaching in a vacuum, *Collaborate, Communicate, Differentiate!* by Wendy W. Murawski and Sally Spencer, offers strategies for co-teaching, connecting with students of diverse backgrounds, and communicating with their parents.

30. Develop a personal reflective action plan

It may help you to develop a personal action plan for moving along your professional journey. If you begin reflecting from a place of self-worth, of confidence in yourself that you are a good teacher, you can choose ways of continuing your own growth, of continuing to become the best teacher you can be at each phase of your life. You mustn't see these explorations as negative failure points, but as data you can use to make your own interpretations about teaching progress. One school places each teacher's personal teaching vision on the classroom doors for students to view on the first day of school. You are a member of an adult learning community that requires trust, cooperation, and collegiality in order to involve everyone in a truthful and welcoming manner. These are the same conditions you hope your students will work toward in their developing lives. Becoming better as a teacher is hard work, a lifetime series of goals, and it is absolutely worth the effort for a professional life, well-lived.

Your school district may have teacher evaluative practices predetermined using wide scale test results of your school, grade or class, and these may be used for decision-making about hiring, funding, leadership or even teaching philosophies or programs to be implemented. But for your students and perhaps your colleagues, how you respond and adapt to these conditions may include creating ways of working with administrators on committees, involving parents, finding supportive research or changing your position. But for a personal action plan, you can begin by thinking about where you are at this time in your career.

When you speak to teachers who are near retirement, you will discover which ones have had a fulfilling career, always learning about teaching and students, and we hope they are passionate about their remaining years of new adventures, supporting schools with parents and politicians, advocating for younger people considering teaching as a career, volunteering occasionally, and even writing about schools, then and now.

Prompts for a personal reflective action plan

- Look at the challenges that were outlined in this book, and choose those over which you can have some control, some effect, especially with your own relationships with your students.
- Determine the teaching characteristics and strategies that you want to alter or strengthen, your teacher capacities, using those identified from the research in this book. Start small, and keep a record of the strategies you are exploring. Perhaps share these with a colleague. If you are unsure how to begin, find an article or a useful blog that about similar issues.
- Decide on the resources that would assist you in developing a stronger hidden curriculum, the one that may determine students' well-being as members of your classroom community.
- What works well in your teaching? Where would you like to make changes? What areas cause you tension or even fear? What could you do to find support for changing these concerns?
- Use feedback approaches (surveys, interviews, tests, parents, visits to and from other teachers, videos of your and other classroom interactions using partners, student work, peer observations) to assess your teaching and instructional programs. You could discuss new classroom approaches with your incoming students, as they make or refine their community goals.
- Ask yourself why you became a teacher. Why have you remained a teacher?
- What characteristics do you think students want in an excellent teacher?
- How are you different now from during your first few years as a teacher?
- How autonomous are you in your present position?

Mindfulness for Teachers: Simple Skills for Peace and Productivity in the Classroom, by Patricia A. Jennings, is an extremely helpful resource for implementing mindfulness practice in your classroom.

- What are you still excited about learning, in your profession and in your life??
- Are you able to find ways of stepping away from school concerns or difficulties when you go home, to disengage, to distance self from job? Do you have time for family and friends? Do you practice mindfulness as a means of being a holistic person?
- Do you create opportunities for moving critical learning experiences into greater engagement with the outside community, as in interacting with parents/guardians, working with volunteers, inviting guests into the classroom, going on field trips, interviewing authorities, using technology, and taking part in social action programs?
- Do you share with your colleagues professional books, journal articles, and reports that offer strategies and structures for helping students deepen their literacy experiences?
- How does your philosophy of learning affect the programs in your school?

Conclusion

Final thoughts on becoming a "good" teacher

"... the best teachers are not up on a guru throne, doling out shining answers. They are there in the muck beside you: stepping forward, falling down, muddling through, deepening and enlivening the questions."

Kyo Maclear, *Birds Art Life*

"Finally, being a friend means accepting contradictions both within ourselves and, especially, between ourselves and others. Learning to be a friend is a lesson in learning how we are alike as human beings and how we are different in expressing our humanity. We are often drawn to others who are similar in belief, custom, and background, yet there is also great value in offering our friendship to those who are quite different. We can celebrate our humanity by offering our friendship to whomever we choose."

David Hunt, *To Be a Friend*

We want to hear our graduate students' own life stories, of their first experiences with printed texts, their school events that remain memorable (for good or for difficult reasons), their choices of texts they want to or have to read now (the ones they appreciate, the ones that cause pain). We want them to learn from each other, to be excited by a research article we find that strengthens their understanding, to meet a teacher/author who articulates in her book a passion for teaching well, to discover a picture book that demands being shared with a class, a biography that awakens children to the power of writing, online images and graphics that speak volumes — all this in a summer course. But like all teachers, we dream large, and that is the joy of working with students of all ages. And we hope their culminating papers will represent their own interests, not ours, and that we will find their sense-making about learning behaviours and events honest, referenced by the work of others in the field, and well-crafted with professionalism but also marked by their own unfolding journeys.

All of us have to follow the trail of breadcrumbs back through the forest to childhood, where students truly live, so that we can remember who we were, once upon a time, entering school, letting go of our parents' hands, and joining the world of education. For those of us involved in teaching, life in school can be a rich yet perilous quest for ways to guide and lead young people into deeper understanding of themselves and their place in the world. At times, as we work with our students inside the ever-evolving frame of teacher research, we continue to grow and change alongside the youngsters, sometimes voluntarily, but often carried into new realms of meaning-making by their energy and spirit, and their naïve and defiant refusal to accept our initial ideas as their truths.

Our hidden assumptions and biases are fodder for their explorations, and their very self-focused attitudes and behaviours cause us to twist and turn with the anxiety born in the sudden realization of where we have to journey with them next in order for something good to happen. And the most complex part of this process is that they must choose the path while we are so clear about the destination.

Like Coyote, we need to remember that we are "shape-shifters," that we can adapt not only our tricks of the trade but our own personas in order to participate in some way in the experience of learning. For the teachers we know and respect continue to enter the learning in their lives and in their work as active agents in their own professional development, living their lives, as James Britton mentioned all those years ago, as "spectators and participants," both at once, in our classrooms.

We must find opportunities — it is an imperative for us who teach — to continue to sing or play the violin; to role-play, read a script or dance; to write and design on paper and computer; and sometimes this can occur within the learning experiences of our students. But we educators teach all the while, observing with every inch of our beings, redirecting, encouraging, supporting, offering assistance, finding resources, sharing what we have found out, and marveling at what we have not yet discovered. We are both inside and outside the experience, benefiting from both spheres — risk-taking novices and astute professionals — enmeshed in the topsy-turvy endeavours of the psyche-stretching world of the complex and life-enabling place called school.

"What about us, though? Would you at least say good-bye to us?" Mindy Winkler asks.

Ms. Bixby leans against her desk and smiles. "Not good-bye, but maybe au revoir."

"Isn't that pretty much the same thing?" I'm not exactly fluent in French or anything. I'm just guessing.

"Actually, good-bye is good-bye. Au revoir is 'till we see each other again.' But believe me, even when I'm gone, you're still going to remember me. You will all be talking about me when you are grown and have kids of your own. 'Remember Ms. Bixby,' you'll say, 'with the pink hair and the thing about the chalk, who was always spouting quotes at us and making us write in our journals all the time? She was the best.'"

The class groans, some kids shake their heads, but they are just giving her a hard time because they know she's probably right. No doubt I'll remember her when I grow up, though I plan to put that off as long as humanly possible. I figure we'll all remember her in our own way.

After all—you never forget the good ones.

John David Anderson, *Ms. Bixby's Last Day*

References

Allen, K. P. (2010). "Classroom Management, Bullying, and Teacher Practices. *The Professional Educator,* 34(1), 1–15.

Anderson, J. D. (2016). *Ms. Bixby's Last Day.* New York: HarperCollins.

Ang, R. P. (2005). "Development and Validation of the Teacher-Student Relationship Inventory Using Exploratory and Confirmatory Factor Analysis." *Journal of Experimental Education,* 71(1), 55–74.

Applegate, K. (2008). *Home of the Brave.* New York: Square Fish Press.

Ball, D. L., Thames, M. H., and Phelps, G. (2008). "Content Knowledge for Teaching: What Makes It Special?" *Journal of Teacher Education,* 59, 389–407.

Bandura, A. (1991). "Self-efficacy Mechanism in Physiological Activation and Health-promoting Behavior." In J. Madden IV (Ed.), *Neurobiology of Learning, Emotion and Affect,* 229–270. New York: Raven.

Beach, R., Anson, C.M., Breuch, L.K., and Reynolds, T. (2014). *Understanding and Creating Digital Texts: An Activity-Based Approach.* Lanham, MD: Roman and Littlefield.

Bedard, C., and Fuhrken, C. (2013). *When Writing with Technology Matters.* Portland, ME: Stenhouse Publishers.

Beghetto, R.A., and Plucker, J.A. (2006). "The Relationship among Schooling, Learning and Creativity: 'All Roads Lead to Creativity' or 'You Can't Get There from Here'?" In J.C. Kaufman and J. Baer (Eds.), *Creativity and Reason in Cognitive Development,* 316–332. New York: Cambridge University Press.

Beghetto, R.A., and Kaufman, J. C. (2014). "Classroom Contexts for Creativity." *High Ability Studies,* 25(1), 53–69.

Bell, M., and Wolfe, C. (2004). "Emotion and Cognition: An Intricately Bound Developmental Process." *Child Development*, Vol. 75, No. 2, 366–70.

Berk, R.A. (2002). *Humor as an Instructional Defibrillator: Evidence-based Techniques in Teaching and Assessment.* Sterling, VA: Stylus Publishing.

Booth, D. (1994). *Classroom Voices: Language-based Learning in the Elementary School.* Toronto: Harcourt Brace and Company Canada.

Booth, D. (2002). *Even Hockey Players Read.* Markham: Pembroke Publishers.

Booth, D. (2004). *The Arts Go to School.* Markham: Pembroke Publishers.

Booth, D. (2008). *It's Critical.* Markham: Pembroke Publishers.

Booth, D. (2011). *Caught in the Middle.* Markham: Pembroke Publishers.

Booth, D. (2014). *I've Got Something to Say.* Markham: Pembroke Publishers.

Booth, D., and Rowsell, J. (2007). The Literacy Principal: Leading, Supporting, and Assessing Reading and Writing Initiatives (2nd Ed.). Markham: Pembroke Publishers.

Bouchard, D. (2017). *Proud to Be Métis.* Oakville, ON: Rubicon Publishers.

Bowman, W. (2004). "Cognition and the Body: Perspectives from Music Education." In Liora Bresler (Ed.), *Knowing Bodies, Moving Minds: Towards Embodied Teaching and Learning*. Boston, MA: Kluwer Academic Publishers.

Bronfenbrenner, U. (1979). *The Ecology of Human Development: Experiments by Nature and Design*. Cambridge, MA: Harvard University Press.

Bronfenbrenner, U. (1986). "Ecology of the Family as a Context for Human Development: Research Perspectives." *Developmental Psychology*, 22(6), 723–742.

Bronfenbrenner, U., and Morris, P. A. (1998). "The Ecology of Developmental Process." In W. Damon and R. M. Lerner (Eds.), *Handbook of Child Psychology, Vol. 1: Theoretical Models of Human Development* (5th edition), 992–1028. New York: Wiley.

Burant, T., Christensen, L., Salas, K. D., Walters, S. (Eds.) (2010). *The New Teacher Book: Finding Purpose, Balance, and Hope during Your First Years in the Classroom* (2nd Ed.). Milwaukee, WI: Rethinking Schools Ltd.

Bynum, S. S. (2009). *Ms. Hempel Chronicles*. New York: Mariner Books.

Campbell, C. (2017). *Canadian Journal of Education / Revue canadienne de l'éducation* 40:2, 21. www.cje-rce.ca

Cantrell, G. G., and Cantrell, G. L. (2003). *Teachers Teaching Teachers: Wit, Wisdom, and Whimsy for Troubled Times*. New York: Peter Lang Publishing.

Cho, Seehwa. (2013). *Critical Pedagogy and Social Change: Critical Analysis on the Language of Possibility*. New York and London: Routledge.

Clark, R. (2003). *The Essential 55: An Award-winning Educator's Rules for Discovering the Successful Student in Every Child* (1st Ed.). New York: Hyperion.

Cochran-Smith, M., and Lytle, S. L. (2009). *Inquiry as Stance: Practitioner Research for the Next Generation*. New York: Teachers College Press.

Cremin, T., Goouch, K., Blakemore, L., Goff, E., and Macdonald, R. (2006). "Connecting Drama and Writing: Seizing the Moment to Write." *Research in Drama Education*, 11(3), 273–291.

Cummins, Jim (1997). "Educational Attainment of Minority Students: A Framework for Intervention Based on the Constructs of Identity and Empowerment." In A. Sjogren (Ed.), *Language and Environment*, 89–101. Botkyrka, Sweden: Multicultural Centre.

Cummins, Jim, and Early, Margaret (2011). "Introduction." In Jim Cummins and Margaret Early (Eds.), *Identity Texts: The Collaborative Creation of Power in Multilingual Schools*, 3–19. London: Trentham Books Ltd.

Darling-Hammond, L. (2010). *The Flat World and Education: How America's Commitment to Equity Will Determine Our Future*. New York: Teachers College Press.

Darling-Hammond, L., Bransford, J., et al (Eds.) (2005). *Preparing Teachers for a Changing World: What Teachers Should Learn and Be Able to Do*. San Francisco: Jossey-Bass.

DeMoss, K., and Morris, T. (2002). "How Arts Integration Supports Student Learning: Students Shed Light on the Connections." Retrieved from:

Chicago Arts Partnership in Education: http://www.capeweb.org/wp-content/uploads/2011/05/support.pdf

Droz, M., and Ellis, L. (1996). *Laughing while learning: Using Humor in the Classroom.* Longmont, CO: Sopris West.

Duffy, Peter (2015). *A Reflective Practitioner's Guide to (Mis)Adventures in Drama Education — or — What Was I Thinking?* Bristol, UK: Intellect Ltd.

Dukes, C., and Smith, M. (2009). *Hands On Guide Series: Building Better Behaviour in the Early Years.* London: SAGE Publications Ltd.

Dweck, C. S. (2016). *Mindset: The New Psychology of Success.* New York: Ballantine Books.

Dyer, J., Gregersen, H., and Christensen, C.M. (2011). *The innovator's DNA: Mastering the Five Skills of Disruptive Innovators.* Boston, MA: Harvard Business Review Press.

Dyson, A. H. (2001). "Writing and Children's Symbolic Repertories: Development Unhinged." In S. B. Neuman and D. K. Dickinson (Eds.), *Handbook of early literacy research, Vol. 1,* 126–141. New York: The Guilford Press.

Education Week Teacher newsletters@edweek.org

Edwards, C., Gandini, L., and Forman, G. (Eds.) (2011). *The Hundred Languages of Children: The Reggio Emilia Experience in Transformation* (3rd Ed.). Santa Barbara, CA: Praeger.

Edwards, W. (2006). *The Extinct Files: My Science Project.* Toronto, ON: Kids Can Press Ltd.

Eggers, D., Calegari, N. C., and Moulthrop, D. (2005). *Teachers Have It Easy: The Big Sacrifices and Small Salaries of America's Teachers.* New York: The New Press.

Engel, S. (2011). "Children's Need to Know: Curiosity in Schools." *Harvard Educational Review*, 81(4), 625–645.

Fennema, E., and Franke, M. L. (1992). "Teachers' Knowledge and Its Impact." In D. A. Grouws (Ed.), *Handbook of research on mathematics teaching and learning,* 147-164. New York: Macmillan.

Finchler, J. (2003). *Testing Miss Malarkey.* London: Walker Children.

Finkel, D.L. (2000). *Teaching with Your Mouth Shut.* Portmouth, NH: Boynton/Cook Publishers, Inc.

Fiore, M., and Lebar, M. L. (2016). *The Four Roles of the Numerate Learner.* Markham: Pembroke Publishers.

Florida, R. (2012). *The Rise of the Creative Class: Revisited* (2nd Ed.). New York: Basic Books.

Fowler, J. (2000). *Faithful Change: The Personal and Public Challenges of Postmodern Life.* Nashville, TN: Abingdon Press.

Freebody, P. (2003). *Qualitative Research in Education: Interaction and Practice.* London: Sage.

Freire, Paulo, and Macedo, Donaldo (1987). *Literacy: Reading the Word and the World.* South Hadley, MA: Bergin and Garvey Publishers.

Friedman, T.L. (2016). *Thank You for Being Late: An Optimist's Guide to Thriving in the Age of Accelerations.* New York: Farrar, Straus and Giroux.

Fullan, M. (2012). *Stratosphere: Integrating Technology, Pedagogy, and Change Knowledge.* Toronto: Pearson.

Fullan, M., and Langworth, M. (2014). *A Rich Seam: How New Pedagogies Find Deep Learning.* London: Pearson.

Gagné, A., and Soto Gordon, S. (2014). "Participatory Action Research in a High School Drama Club -- A Catalyst for Change among English Language Learners in Canada." In G. Smyth and N. Santoro (Eds.), *Methodologies for Investigating Diversity (in Education): International Perspectives.* London: Trentham Press.

Gallagher, K. (2015). *In the Best Interest Of Students: Staying True to What Works in the ELA Classroom.* Portland, ME: Stenhouse Publishers.

Gantos, Jack (2014). *Joey Pigza Swallowed the Key.* New York: Square Fish Press.

Gay, G. (2000). *Culturally Responsive Teaching: Theory, Research, and Practice.* New York: Teachers College Press.

Gear, A. (2017). *Reading Power.* Markham: Pembroke Publishers.

Gee, J. (2003). *Literacy and Education.* Abingdon, UK: Routledge.

Goldblatt, P. F., and Smith, D. (Eds.) (2005). *Cases for Teacher Development: Preparing for the Classroom.* Thousand Oaks, CA: Sage Publications.

Goleman, D. (1995). *Emotional Intelligence.* (Bantam Books).

Goodman, K., Fries, P. H., and Strauss, S. L. (2016). *Reading -The Grand Illusion: How and Why People Make Sense of Print.* New York: Routledge, Taylor and Francis Group.

Gorham, J., and Christophel, D.M. (1990). "The Relationship of Teachers' Use of Humor in the Classroom to Immediacy and Student Learning." *Communications Education,* 39 (1), 46–62.

Halverson, E.R., and Sheridan, K. (2014). "The Maker Movement in Education." *Harvard Educational Review,* 84(4), 495–504.

Hatano, G., and Osura, Y. (2003). "Commentary: Reconceptualizing School Learning Using Insight from Expert Research." *Educational Researcher,* 32, 26–29.

Hattie, J. (2012). *Visible learning for teachers: Maximizing impact on learning.* New York: Routledge.

Hawkins, J., and Blakeslee, S. (2004) *On Intelligence.* New York: Owl Books.

Hume, Karen (2007). *Start Where They Are: Differentiating for Success with the Young Adolescent.* Toronto: Pearson.

Hunt, D. E. (2010). *To Be a Friend: The Key to Friendship in Our Lives.* Toronto: Dundurn.

Inglis, Fred (1985). *The Management of Ignorance: A Political Theory of the Curriculum.* Oxford, UK: Basil Blackwell.

Jefferies, O. (2006). *The Incredible Book-Eating Boy.* London: HarperCollins.

Jennings, P.A. (2015). *Mindfulness for Teachers: Simple Skills for Peace and Productivity in the Classroom.* New York: W. W. Norton and Company.

Jones, P. (2008). "Wrestling with Reading." In Jon Scieszka (Ed.), *Guys Write for Guys Read.* New York: Viking.

Kaufman, J.C., and Beghetto, R.A. (2013). "In Praise of Clark Kent. Creative Metacogntion and the Importance of Teaching Kids When (Not) to Be Creative." *Roeper Reviews,* 35, 155–165.

Kenner, C., Kress, G., Al-Khatib, H., Kam, R., and Tsai, K. (2004). "Finding the Keys to Biliteracy: How Young Children Interpret Different Writing Systems." *Language and Education,* 18(2), 124–144.

Kilpatrick, J., Swafford, J., and Findell, B. (Eds.) (2001). *Adding It Up: Helping Children Learn Mathematics.* Washington, DC: National Academy Press.

Kinew, W. (2015). *The Reason You Walk.* Toronto: Viking.

Kittle, Penny (2012). *Book Love: Developing Depth, Stamina, and Passion in Adolescent Readers.* Portsmouth, NH: Heinemann.

Kucan, L., and Beck, I. L. (1997). "Thinking Aloud and Reading Comprehension Research." *Review of Educational Research,* 67(3), 271–299.

Ladson-Billings, G. (1995). "Toward a Theory of Culturally Relevant Pedagogy. *American Educational Research Journal,* 32(3), 465–491.

Ladson-Billings, G. (2006). "Yes, But How Do We Do It?" In J. Landsman and C. W. Lewis (Eds.), *White Teachers, Diverse Classrooms: A Guide to Building Inclusive Schools, Promoting High Expectations, and Eliminating Racism,* 29–42. Sterling, VA: Stylus Publishing.

Ladson-Billings, G. (2014). "Culturally Relevant Pedagogy 2.0: a.k.a. the Remix." *Harvard Educational Review,* 84(1), 74–84.

Land, G., and Jarman, B. (1993). *Breakpoint and Beyond: Mastering the Future Today.* Champaign, IL: HarperBusiness.

Lee, C.D. (2007). *Culture, Literacy, and Learning: Taking Bloom in the Midst of the Whirlwind.* New York: Teachers College Press.

Leslie, I. (2014). *Curious: The Desire to Know and Why Your Future Depends on it.* New York: Basic Books.

Loomis, D., and Kolberg, K. (1993). *The Laughing in the Classroom: Everyone's Guide to Teaching with Humor and Play.* Tiburon, CA: H.J. Kramer.

Lortie, D.C. (1975). *Schoolteacher: A Sociological Study.* Chicago, IL: University of Chicago Press.

Lundy, K. (2004). *What Do I Do About the Kid Who…?* Markham: Pembroke Publishers.

Lundy, K., and Swartz, L. (2011). *Creating Caring Classrooms.* Markham: Pembroke Publishers.

Maclear, Kyo. (2017) *Birds Art Life.* Toronto: Doubleday Canada.

Major, K. (2003). *Hold Fast.* Toronto: Groundwood Books.

Maley, A., and Duff, A. (2001). *Drama Techniques in Language Learning: A Resource Book for Communication Activities for Language Teachers.* Cambridge, UK: Cambridge University Press.

Marks Krpan, C. (2013). *Math Expressions: Developing Student Thinking and Problem Solving through Communication.* Toronto: Pearson Education.

Marks Krpan, C. (2017). *Teaching with Meaning: Cultivating Self-Efficacy through Learning Competencies, Grades K–8.* Toronto: Pearson Education.

Marsh, H.W., and O'Mara, A. (2008). "Reciprocal Effects between Academic Self-Concept, Self-Esteem, Achievement and Attainment over Seven Adolescent Years: Unidimensional and Multidimensional Perspectives of Self-Concept." *Personality and Social Psychology Bulletin,* 34, 542–552.

Martin, R.A. (2007). *The Psychology of Humor: An Integrated Approach.* Burlington, MA: Elsevier Academic Press.

Martin, R.A., and Kuiper, N. A. (1999). "Daily Occurrences of Laughter: Relationships with Age, Gender, and Type A Personality." *Humor: International Journal of Humor Research,* 12(4), 355–384.

Marzano, R. J. (2010). *On Excellence in Teaching.* Bloomington, IN: Solution Tree Press.

McCarty, T.L., and Lee, T.S., (2014). "Critical Culturally Sustaining/Revitalizing Pedagogy and Indigenous Education Sovereignty." *Harvard Educational Review,* 84(1), 101–124.

McCombs, B. L. (2004). "The Learner-Centered Psychological Principles: A Framework for Balancing a Focus on Academic Achievement with a Focus on Social and Emotional Learning Needs." In E. Zins, R. P. Weissberg, M. C. Wang, and H. J. Walberg (Eds.), *Building Academic Success on Social Emotional Learning: What Does the Research Say?* 23–39. New York: Teachers College Press.

McDonagh, C., Roche, M., Sullivan, B. Glenn, M. (2012). *Enhancing Practice Through Classroom Research: A teacher's guide to professional development.* New York: Routledge.

Mcleod, S. (2012). *Zone of Proximal Development.* https://www.simplypsychology.org/Zone-of-Proximal-Development.html

McTighe, J., and Wiggins, G. (2013). *Essential Questions: Opening Doors to Student Understanding.* Alexandria, VA: Association for Supervision and Curriculum Development.

Medina, J. (2008). Brain Rules: 12 Principles for Surviving and Thriving at Work, Home, and School. Seattle, WA: Pear Press.

Miller, J. P., Nigh, K. (Eds.) (2017). *Holistic Education And Embodied Learning.* Charlotte, NC: Information Age Publishing, Inc.

Murawski, W. W., Spencer, S. (2011). *Collaborate, Communicate, Differentiate!: How to increase student learning in today's diverse schools.* Thousand Oaks, CA: Corwin.

Naiman, L. (2014, June 6). Can creativity be taught? Results from research studies. Retrieved from https://www.creativityatwork.com/2012/03/23/can-creativity-be-taught.

Neebe, D., and Roberts, J. (2015). *Power Up: Making the Shift to 1:1 Teaching and Learning.* Portland, ME: Stenhouse Publishers.

Nehring, J., Megin Charner-Laird, and Stacy Szczesiul. (2017). What a real high-performing school looks like. http://www.kappanonline.org

Nieto, S. (2011). In J.K. Peters and M. Weisberg, *A Teacher's Reflection Book: Exercises, Stories, Invitations*, 145. Durham, NC: Carolina Academic Press.

Nieto, S. (1996). *Affirming Diversity: The Sociopolitical Context of Education.* White Plains, NY: Longman.

Nieto, S. (Ed.) (2014). *Why We Teach Now.* New York: Teachers College Press.

O'Neill, A. (2002). *The Recess Queen.* New York: Scholastic Press.

Ontario. Ministry of Education (2013). *Creating Pathways to Success: An Education and Career/Life Planning Program for Ontario Schools; Policy and Program Requirements, Kindergarten to Grade 12.*

Ontario. Ministry of Education (2013). *Culturally Responsive Pedagogy: Towards Equity and Inclusivity in Ontario Schools.* Capacity Building Series, # 35. Toronto: Queen's Printer for Ontario.

Ontario College of Teachers (2016). "Ethical Standards for the Teaching Profession, and the Professional Learning Framework for the Teaching Profession." *Foundations of Professional Practice.* https://www.oct.ca/-/media/PDF/Foundations%20of%20Professional%20Practice/Foundation_e.pdf

Ontario College of Teachers (2016). "Ongoing Professional Learning." *Foundations of Professional Practice.* https://www.oct.ca/-/media/PDF/Foundations%20of%20Professional%20Practice/Foundation_e.pdf

Ostroff, W.L. (2016). *Cultivating Curiosity in K–12 Classrooms.* Alexandria, VA: Association for Supervision and Curriculum Development.

Palmer, P. (1998). *The Courage to Teach.* San Francisco: Jossey-Bass.

Pappano, L. (February 9, 2014). "Learning to Think Differently." *New York Times.* Educational Life, 8–10.

Paris, D. (2012). "Culturally Sustaining Pedagogy: A Needed Change in Stance, Terminology, and Practice." *Educational Researcher,* 41(3), 93–97.

Paris, D., and Alim, H.S. (2014). "What Are We Seeking to Sustain through Culturally Sustaining Pedagogy? A Loving Critique Forward." *Harvard Educational Review,* 84(1), 85–100.

Park, S., and Oliver, S. (2008). "Revisiting the Conceptualization of Pedagogical Content Knowledge (PCK): PCK as a Conceptual Tool to Understand Teachers as Professionals." *Research in Science Education,* 38, 261–284.

Paul, M. *3 Ways to Reflect with Purpose.* Edutopia, May 6, 2016.

Peters, J. J., and Weisberg, M. (2011). *A Teacher's Reflection Book: Exercises, Stories, Invitations.* Durham, NC: Carolina Academic Press.

Phillips, M. "The Importance of a Healthy Ego." Edutopia July 17, 2015.

Pink, D.H. (2006). *A Whole New Mind: Why Right-Brainers Will Rule the Future*. New York: Riverhead.

Pino-James, N., PhD. "Golden Rules for Engaging Students in Learning Activities." Edutopia, December 11, 2015.

Quinn, R. E., Heynoski, K., Thomas, M., and Spreitzer, G. M. (2014). *The Best Teacher in You: How to Accelerate Learning and Change Lives*. San Francisco: Berrett-Koehler Publishers.

Ragoonaden, K. (Ed.) (2015). *Mindful Teaching and Learning: Developing a Pedagogy of Well-being*. Lanham, MD: Lexington Books.

Raine, A., Reynolds, C., Venables, P.H., and Mednick, S.A. (2002). "Stimulation Seeking and Intelligence: A Prospective Longitudinal Study." *Journal of Personality and Social Psychology*, 82(4), 663–674.

Reason, C. S., and Reason, C. (2011). *Mirror Images: New Reflections on Teacher Leadership*. Thousand Oaks, CA: Corwin.

Rhodes, J.E. (2002). *Stand by Me: The Risks and Rewards of Mentoring Today's Youth*. Cambridge, MA: Harvard University Press.

Rogers, D. L., and Babinski, L. M. (2002). *From Isolation to Conversation: Supporting New Teachers' Development*. Albany, NY: State University Of New York Press.

Rosenblum-Lowden, R. (2000). *You Have to Go to School — You're the Teacher! 250 Classroom Management Strategies to Make Your Job Easier and More Fun* (2nd Ed.). Thousand Oaks, CA: Corwin.

Rowsell, J. (2013). *Working with Multimodality: Rethinking Literacy in a Digital Age*. New York: Routledge.

Runco, M.A., and Jaeger, G.J. (2012). "The Standard Definition of Creativity." *Creativity Research Journal*, 24(1), 92–96.

Sachar, L. (2004). *Wayside School Is Falling Down*. New York: HarperCollins.

Salyers, F. S. "Social-Emotional Intelligence Is Missing from School. Here's Why That Matters." edweek.org, June 28, 2017.

Sawyer, K. (2010). "Learning for Creativity." In R. A. Beghetto and J.C. Kaufman (Eds.), *Nurturing Creativity in the Classroom*, 172–190. New York: Cambridge University Press.

Sawyer, K. (2013). *Zig Zag : The Surprising Path to Greater Creativity*. San Francisco, CA: Wiley.

Schwartz, S., and Pollishuke, M. (2018). *Creating the Dynamic Classroom: A Handbook for Teachers Plus Companion Website — Access Card Package* (3rd Ed.). Toronto: Pearson.

Serafini, F. (2015). "Multimodal Literacy: From Theories to Practice." *Language Arts*, 92 (6), 412–422.

Sergiovanni, T. J. (1994). *Building Community in Schools* (1st ed.). San Francisco: Jossey-Bass.

Shonkoff, J.P. (2004). *Science, Policy and the Developing Child: Closing the Gap between What We Know and What We Do.* Washington, DC: Ounce of Prevention Fund.

Shulman, L. S. (1986). "Those Who Understand: Knowledge Growth in Teaching." *Educational Researcher,* 15(2), 4–14.

Shulman, L. S. (1987). "Knowledge and Teaching: Foundations of the New Reform." *Harvard Educational Review,* 57(1), 1–22.

Stein, S.J., and Book, H.E. (2011). *The EQ Edge: Emotional Intelligence and Your Success* (3rd Ed.). Mississauga, On: John Wiley & Sons Canada Ltd.

Styres, S. (2017). *Pathways for Remembering and Recognizing Indigenous Thought in Education: Philosophies of Iethi'nihstéhnha Ohwentsia'kékha (Land).* Buffalo, NY: University of Toronto Press.

Swartz, L. (2013). *The Bully-Go-Round: Literacy and Arts Strategies for Promoting Bully Awareness in the Classroom.* Markham: Pembroke Publishers.

Tomlinson, Carol Ann (2001). *Fulfilling the Promise of the Differentiated Classroom.* Alexandria, VA: Association for Supervision and Curriculum Development.

Villegas, A.M., and Lucas, T. (2002). "Preparing Culturally Responsive Teachers: Rethinking the Curriculum. *Journal of Teacher Education,* 53(1), 20–32.

Wang, Z. (2017). *Investigating Mathematics Teachers' Knowledge for Teaching and Their Learning Trajectories.* Unpublished doctoral dissertation, University of Toronto.

Weaver, L., and Wilding, M. (2013). *The Five Dimensions of Engaged Teaching: A Practical Guide for Educators.* Bloomington, IN: Solution Tree Press.

Wiggins, G., and McTighe, J. (2006). *Understanding by Design* (2nd Ed.). Upper Saddle River, NJ: Pearson.

Wisniewski, D. (1998). *The Secret Knowledge of Grown-Ups.* New York: Lothrop, Lee and Shepard.

Wolf, M. A. "How Students See the 'Good' Teacher." Getting Smart.com March 14, 2017.

Wormelli, R. (2001). *Meet Me in the Middle.* Portland, ME: Stenhouse Publishers.

Wright, S. (2011). *Children, Meaning Making and the Arts.* Frenchs Forest, NSW: Pearson Australia.

Zager, T. J. (2017). *Becoming the Math Teacher You Wish You'd Had.* Portland, ME: Stenhouse Publishers.

Index

adaptive confidence, 37
adaptive expertise, 46
apprenticeship of observation, 46
arousal theory, 24
arts in education
    community and, 125–126
    developing self-esteem and understanding through, 123–125
    group sculpture project, 128–131
    importance of, 122–123
    Regent Park project, 126–127
assessment
    classroom-based, 116
    cupcake example, 116–118
    described, 114–115
    integrated ongoing approach, 114–116
    key to, 115
    large-scale, 116
    scenarios, 118–119
    standardized tests, 115
    types, 115–116

backward instructional design, 84
biology, 120
blogging, 125–126
bullying, 18, 40, 88, 98, 124

caring, 9, 23, 31–34
ceremonies, 133–134
challenging assumptions, 7–8
classroom community
    building, 39–42
    importance of, 42, 88
    reflecting on, 40–41
classroom dynamics, 87–91

classroom management, 98–100
classroom talk, 91–92
collaborative culture, 108–109
collaborative reading, 125–126
colleagues, 9–10
community, 32
community arts project, 126–127
community reading, 125–126
compassion, 31–34
computer and video games, 101–102
conferences, 10
confidence, 37–39
constructivist learning, 65
creative teachers, 51–52
creativity, 51–52
critical pedagogy, 49–51
critical thinking, 48–49, 51–52
cultural diversity, 64–67
culturally relevant pedagogy, 65
culturally responsive teaching, 65, 66
culturally sustaining pedagogy, 66
culture of opportunity, 82
curiosity, 96–98
curriculum
    content, 42
    goals, 82
    knowledge, 13

differentiated instruction, 77–80
discipline, 98

Edublogs, 126
educational team, 113–114
effective schools
    arts in education, 122–131

assessment procedures, 114–119
community, 131–138
literacies and numeracies, 119–122
personal reflective action plan, 139–140
planning and teaching teams, 112–114
professional community, 108–112
ego, 37–39
empathy, 34
ethical standards, 13
expectations, 55–57
expertise, 10

felt imperative, 44–45
forgiveness, 32
frameworks for examining teaching excellence
described, 12
"good" teaching characteristics, 14–15
Ontario College of Teachers, 13
reflective model, 14
students' wants, 16–18
teacher knowledge, 13

gender issues, 76–77
"good" teachers / teaching
characteristics, 14–15
colleagues, 9–10
defining, 7
dynamic intersections of learning, 90–91
final thoughts, 141–142
memories of, 15–16
models and mentors, 9
personal reflections, 55–57
teaching practices, 20–21
what students want from, 16–17
good-byes, 133
graduation, 134
group sculpture project, 128–131
group work, 69–71
guest teacher, 8

health, 39
history, 123
holistic teacher, 32–33
homelessness, 36–37
human library, 54
humility, 38–39
humour, 23–25

immediacy of the teacher, 32
incongruity theory, 23–24

Indigenous cultures
lessons learned, 136–137
schools, 45
teaching, 67–68
inherent change, 109
innovative thinking, 46–48
inquiry groups, 94–98
interactive learning, 49
iPad use, 95–96

language of possibility, 49
laughter, 23–25
learning
active process, 27–28
curiosity and, 96–98
mistakes and, 43–45
modelling, 25–26
objectives, outcomes, and standards, 82–86
students' views on, 28
learning partnership, 87
learning pathways, 68–72
life stories, 61–63
literacy
biology and, 120
comprehension and, 120
mathematics and, 121
subject disciplines, 120–122
technology and, 101
voluntary community support for, 131–132
longitudinal study, 19–21

mapping learning, 68–70
mathematics, 121
meaning making
creative, 51–52
critical, 48–49
memory, 44
mentoring, 112
mentoring webs, 25–26
mentors, 10, 25–26
mindfulness, 31–34
mirth, 24
mistakes, and learning, 43–45
modeling learning, 25–26
models, 10, 25–26

New Teacher Groups, 14
novel studies, 84–85
numeracy, 119–122
nurturing classrooms, 23

Ontario College of Teachers, 13
open-ended questions, 104–107

parents
    as partners, 132–133
    as researchers, 41
    letter to teachers, 62–63
    school community and, 19
pathways to success, 68–72
pedagogical content knowledge (PCK), 13
peer editing, 118
personal reflective action plan
    described, 139
    prompts, 139–140
photography, 35–36
planning, 112–113
planning and teaching teams, 112–114
poetry, 122–123
portage, 134–136
positive tone, 23
principal, 109–110
professional beginnings, 7–9
professional community, 108–112
professional development
    challenges affecting, 18–19
    classroom research, 43–44
    human library, 54
    reflective model of, 14
professional learning
    developing, 21
    framework, 13
professional learning community, 111–112
professional vs. personal life, 39
project-based learning, 95

questioning, 104–107

ReadUP Reading Clubs, 131–132
reflection
    feedback and, 58
    finding paths for, 58–59
    lesson plans and, 59
    mistakes and, 43
    peer observation and, 59
    prompts, 60
    self-reflection, 57
    stress and, 58–59
    student input and, 60
    teaching and, 57–58
reflective model, 14
Regent Park Project, 126–127

relationships with students, 27–31, 41–42
relevance, 52–53
rich resources, 88
"Ring of Truth" game, 47–48
rituals, 133–134
routine expertise, 46
rural schools, 45

scaffolding, 27
science, 53–54
self-efficacy, 37–39
self-esteem through art, 123–125
self-reflection, 57
sociocultural consciousness, 65
sociocultural responsiveness, 64–68
socio-emotional intelligence, 33–34
space, 87–88
stages of development, 72–77
starting out, 11–12
storying teachers, 62
strategic teaching, 82
stress, 58–59
student-generated questions, 104–105
student voice, 91–94
students
    ages and stages of, 72–77
    cultural identities, 65
    decision-making, 28
    educational reform, 28
    empowering, 88
    engaging, 52–54
    enjoying and appreciating, 23–25
    homeless, 36–37
    knowing, respecting, and advocating for, 61–63
    learning about, 66
    learning from, 17–18
    learning pathways for, 68–72
    memories and wishes of, 73–76
    modeling and mentoring for, 25–26
    prompts for supporting, 79–80
    reflection and, 60
    relationships with, 27–31, 41–42
    setting expectations for, 55–57
    sociocultural responsiveness to, 64–68
    understanding the work, 83–84
    views on learning, 28
    what they want from teachers, 16–17
subject matter knowledge (SMK), 13
superiority theory, 24

teacher-generated questions, 105–106

"teacherly" identity
    appreciating students, 23–25
    caring, compassion, and mindfulness, 31–37
    classroom community, 39–42
    critical and creative meaning making, 48–52
    ego, self-efficacy, and confidence, 37–39
    engaging with students, 52–54
    innovating and adapting, 43–48
    modeling and mentoring students, 25–26
    reflecting, 57–60
    setting expectations, 55–57
    student-teacher relationships, 27–31
"teacherly" self, 37–39
teachers
    ego, 37–39
    knowledge, 13
    meaning of, 109–110
teaching in a vacuum, 138
teaching practices, 20–21
teaching profession
    ethical standards, 13
    professional learning framework, 13
teaching strategies
    classroom dynamics, 87–91
    classroom management, 98–100
    inquiry groups, 94–98
    learning objectives, outcomes, and standards, 82–86
    questioning, 104–107
    student voice, 91–94
    technology, 100–104
technology
    effective use of, 100–104
    incorporating, 102–103
    literacy and, 101
    tips for integrating, 103–104
    video and computer games, 101–102

understanding others through art, 123–125

voluntary community support for literacy, 131–132

year-end maps, 68–69

zone of proximal development, 55, 56–57